PILLARS OF THE CHURCH

✠ ✠ ✠ ✠ ✠ ✠ ✠ ✠ ✠ ✠ ✠ ✠

PILLARS

OF THE

CHURCH

By

THEODORE MAYNARD

Essay Index Reprint Series

 BOOKS FOR LIBRARIES PRESS
FREEPORT, NEW YORK

INTERNATIONAL STANDARD BOOK NUMBER:

0-8369-1940-8

LIBRARY OF CONGRESS CATALOG CARD NUMBER:

76-136763

PRINTED IN THE UNITED STATES OF AMERICA

To

CHARLES AND KATHLEEN BRUCE

PREFACE

The title *Pillars of the Church* left me free to omit any Pope from consideration, for Peter is the Rock. That this is so is, I confess, a convenience to me, because even with this limitation it has been hard enough to confine myself to only twelve representative Catholic figures. My purpose was not merely to illustrate Catholic variety but to choose with an eye on nationality. Three of these Pillars are Englishmen — four, if one remembers that Saint Patrick was born in Britain. Saint Patrick, however, will have to serve as my Irishman, to which I imagine nobody will object. I have three Spaniards, though Saint Francis Xavier, as a Basque, would have resented being called Spanish. There are two Frenchmen, and of the three Italians one, Mother Cabrini, has to do double duty as my American selection. She did most of her work in this country and became naturalized as a citizen of the United States. As she will be the first of our citizens to be canonized I passed over in her favor Cardinal Gibbons, par excellence the American Cardinal, and Orestes Brownson, the most illustrious mind that American Catholicism has produced. In Mother Cabrini's case, too, there was the advantage of being able to include a second woman, for I did not feel that I could have both Saint Teresa and Saint Catherine of Siena ; and Saint Louis takes the place I would have liked to have given to Saint Joan of Arc.

Saint Dominic has been preferred here to Saint Francis of Assisi, mainly for the reason that Saint Francis has been more often written about. But by way of extenuating this omis-

sion, I draw attention to the fact that three Franciscan tertiaries are included — Saint Louis, Coventry Patmore, and
Mother Cabrini, who considered herself to be one even after
she had founded her own order.   The Franciscans also claim
Saint Thomas More, though it would seem that he was really
a Benedictine Oblate.

As it happens, my twelve Pillars, with only one exception,
are all canonized saints.   This circumstance causes me some
regret, as I fear it will impart a hagiographical coloring I
wished to avoid.   Had the limitations of time and space permitted I would have dealt with Dante, whom nobody is
likely to consider a saint, although Raphael, when painting
his *Disputa* for Leo X, set him among the Doctors of the
Church.   Nor is stormy old Brownson (who is also regretfully passed over) a promising candidate for the aureole ;
and had I admitted him I could hardly have left out the
greater Chesterton.   If I have allowed Patmore to appear on
a scene where Newman is not to be found, this is for the
reason that Newman has often been dealt with, whereas Patmore — whom Francis Thompson called the greatest genius
of the nineteenth century — has been neglected, most neglected of all in Catholic circles.   About him I do not feel
particularly apologetic.

But what must be apologized for are the big time-gaps.
There is no Pillar between Saint Vincent de Paul in the
seventeenth century and Patmore two hundred years later.
A still wider gap is that between the Venerable Bede and
Saint Dominic.   My rather lame excuse is that I was hard
put to it to keep my Pillars down to only twelve ; so would
you be, if you tried the same thing.

The apostolic and patristic ages have been excluded altogether, again for the sake of convenience. And if I start with Saint Benedict instead of Saint Patrick, who chronologically comes first, this is because with Saint Benedict the Middle Ages — what Newman called the Benedictine Centuries — may be regarded as beginning, and that made a good point at which to open my book. Then what, you may ask, is Saint Patrick doing here at all? To which I can only answer that he is here because I wanted to have him. Let it go at that.

This book is made up of the second series of the Heywood Broun Memorial Lectures, which are to be given annually at Assumption College, Windsor, Ontario, the first series having been given by Mr. Wyndham Lewis. Though they have been slightly revised, they are essentially unchanged.

THEODORE MAYNARD

CONTENTS

I

SAINT BENEDICT

Whenever an educated man of the western world thinks of a monk, he instinctively thinks of a Benedictine. He knows, of course, that monasticism existed before Saint Benedict, and he knows that there were many later developments and modifications of the monastic idea. But vague as he may be as to details, he is quite right in regarding the Benedictine Rule as the norm, the central thing to which all that went before and all that came after must be referred, and Saint Benedict as the man who set the pattern for the religious life. As Dom David Knowles puts it : "For almost six hundred years, over the whole of civilized Europe outside the Balkans, to be a religious, that is, to serve God according to the Gospel counsels, was to be a Benedictine monk."

In later chapters I shall have occasion to touch lightly upon the rich florescence of variety that monasticism produced from the thirteenth century on. At this stage it might be worth while to trace briefly the emergence of the Benedictine idea. However great were Benedict's innovations, they were led up to and prepared for by a long series of experiments. A life dedicated to poverty, chastity and obedience was by no means uncommon during the Apostolic age itself, though there was as yet no distinguishing name — still less any distinguishing dress — for those who already foreshadowed the monasticism that was to follow. It did not take very long to appear as such ; by the end of the third century there were in Syria and Palestine groups of men and women known as ascetics ; and these already constituted a closely organized social class, though they were not differentiated, except by their fervour, from the mass of contemporary Christians. They were recognized as standing apart from the world, yet they still had no rule or canonical position. Not until Saint Anthony, at the beginning of the fourth century, sought the solitude of the desert and drew to him many inflamed with an enthusiasm similar to his own, can it be said that any definite step was taken in the direction of true monasticism.

Even then its organization was of an exceedingly loose kind. Hermits grouped themselves in lodgings not too far from one another, and not too near either, but within range of a public church, and practised in a highly individualistic, often even in an extravagant and eccentric fashion such penances as might occur to them. Rufinus of Aquileia, as translated by Helen Waddell in *The Desert Fathers*, described how, "There is another place in the inner desert, about nine miles distant : and this place, by reason of the multitude of cells dispersed through the desert, they call Cellia, The Cells. To this place those who have had their first initiation and who desire to live a remoter life, stripped of all its trappings, withdraw themselves : for the desert is vast, and the cells are sundered from one another by so wide a space, that none is within sight of his neighbour, nor can any voice be heard. One by one they abide in their cells, a mighty silence and a great quiet among them : only on the Saturday and the Sunday do they come together to church, and there they see each other face to face as folk restored in heaven." Not until the time of Saint Pachomius can community life, as we understand it today, really said to have begun. But though individualism was somewhat curbed, it was far from being at an end. The Pachomian concept was that the monastery was a kind of novitiate for the hermitage, to which the monk would be permitted to withdraw as soon as he was judged capable of it. Egypt, and to a less extent Asia Minor, had its solitary places filled with monks and hermits of this sort.

The popular idea of these desert solitaries is that of grim, emaciated, and forbidding figures. And indeed it must be admitted that the austerities of some of them strike the modern Catholic, no less than the man of the world, as being in the nature of "stunts." One of the most notable Benedictines of our time, Abbot Butler, writes : "The favourite name to describe any of the prominent monks was 'great athlete.' And they *were* athletes, and filled with the spirit of the modern athlete. They loved to 'make a record' in austerities, and to contend with one another in mortifications ; and they would freely boast of their spiritual achievements." Yet the somewhat frantic emphasis they laid upon a merely physical discipline is understandable enough when we remember that they thought of the world as so desperately evil that the only remedy seemed to be flight, and the only means of blotting out all memory of its evil that of furious penances. Nor must we forget that these men were for the most part Orientals and had minds tinged with the pessimism of the East. It was in the lands from which they came that the devastating heresies of despair arose.

This, however, is only one side of the picture, and not its truest side. Grimness and pessimism were certainly to be found, but more often it was merely a question of fussiness. Pelagius the Deacon tells of how the Abbot Arsenius came to a place where there was a bed of reeds, and the reeds were shaken by the wind. "And the old man said to the brethren, 'What is this rustling ?' And they said, 'It is the reeds.' The old man said to them, 'Verily, if a man sits in quiet and hears the voice of a bird, he hath not the same quiet in his heart : how much more shall it be with you, that hear the sound of these reeds ? ' " Yet Pelagius also reports the Abbot Anthony as having said, "There be some that wear out their bodies with abstinence : but because they have no discretion, they be a great way from God."

As against this Miss Waddell's charming anthology is full of stories that might have come out of the *Fioretti*. Here are two of them : "There were two old men living together in one cell, and never had there arisen even the paltriest contention between them. So the one said to the other, 'Let us have one quarrel the way other men do.' But the other said, 'I do not know how one makes a quarrel.' The first said, 'Look, I set a tile between us and say, "That is mine," and do thou say, "It is not thine, it is mine." And thence arises contention and squabble.' So they set the tile between them, and the first one said, 'That is mine,' and the second made reply, 'I hope that it is mine.' And the first said, 'It is not thine, it is mine.' To which the second made answer, 'If it is thine, take it.' After which they could find no way of quarrelling."

Even more delightful is this : "They tell that once a certain brother brought a bunch of grapes to the holy Macarius : but he who for love's sake thought not on his own things but on the things of others, carried it to another brother, who seemed more feeble. And the sick man gave thanks to God for the kindness of his brother, but he too thinking more of his neighbour than of himself, brought it to another, and so that same bunch of grapes was carried round all the cells, scattered as they were far over the desert, and no one knowing who had first sent it, it was brought at last to the first giver." From these it is clear that the desert was not so sandy as one might suppose. The hermits who lived on the tops of pillars were not the only Pillars of the Church.

The trend had been away from individualistic practices and eccentric austerities for some time before Saint Benedict legislated for monks. What his Rule did was definitely to discourage monks from going in for, I will not say merely extravagant penances, but for all penances not indicated in the Rule itself. The Seventh Chapter of the *Regula* lays it down that "the monk should do nothing except what the common rule of the monastery and the example of superiors exhorts." And the Forty-ninth Chapter, on the keeping of Lent, adds that even during that season no special mortification should be performed without the approval of the Abbot. The last chapter but one even has Saint Benedict saying, "As there is a harsh and evil zeal which separateth from God and leadeth to hell, so there is a virtuous zeal which separateth from vice and leadeth to God and life everlasting." The Rule, in short, did not wish to quench zeal but to control it and, by controlling it, to make it more effectual.

During the fourth and fifth centuries the Pachomian type of monasticism — that of a community governed by law — was introduced into the Western Church by the writings of Rufinus, Cassian, Palladius and Jerome. Meanwhile in the East Saint Basil wrote his two rules — admonitions rather than rules proper — and Saint Augustine organized his diocesan clergy upon a monastic basis. These rules had as their central idea that of establishing a moderate level of austerity binding upon all monks, while strongly encouraging each monk to go beyond this minimum, in so far as he was able to do so. The spirit remained that of the Desert, even while a rein was put upon it.

This was true also of early Irish monasticism, whose origins are somewhat shrouded in obscurity, and of the monasticism promoted by Saint Martin of Tours, who died in 397. In Gaul illustrious monasteries were being founded, including those of Lérins, Marmoutier and Ligugé. But in them was a type of monasticism that was soon to be made obsolete by the Rule of Saint Benedict. Even the rule written by Saint Columban (543–615) for his Irish monks in Gaul, when it met the Rule of Saint Benedict in the monasteries of central Europe, was supplanted by it. Until then monastic practice had emulated the fasts and vigils and macerations of Egypt and Syria.

So much for early monasticism. Let us turn to Saint Benedict himself.

We know very little about the details of his life except what Saint Gregory the Great has told us in his *Dialogues* and what we can infer from the Rule itself. Saint Gregory has the point of view about biography of many men of his time and so generally omits the historical background, as a matter of little interest. And, as Abbot Herwegen remarks, "As far as our knowledge of the great Father of Monks is concerned [the *Dialogues*] are rather a delicately woven veil." What Gregory does tell us a great deal about are Saint Benedict's miracles — much to the distress of many moderns who, even when they theoretically admit the miraculous, are inclined to be somewhat embarrassed by it. I do not think we need to be embarrassed, even those of us who do not fully accept Abbot

Chapman's thesis that the Saint obtained his prestige as a monastic legislator because of his previous prestige as a wonder-worker par excellence. What we must say of Saint Gregory is that he was able to consult several men who had known Saint Benedict and that he must be allowed to be — within the limits he set himself — an accurate biographer as well as a charming writer.

If Benedict was born in 480 — the usually accepted date — then it was only four years after the Western Empire had ceased to exist as such. Society was in chaos, and Western Europe shortly afterwards was almost wholly under pagan or Arian ascendency. Only in the northwest of Gaul and in Ireland and Western Britain did completely Catholic districts exist. Benedict appeared, in other words, very much at the psychological moment.

He was of a good family of Nursia, and some say at the age of fourteen — though others (and I am one of them) think that it was more probably at the age of eighteen — he went to Rome to study. The tradition is that his studies were of the usual rhetorical sort. This may be so, though his Rule shows small traces of his having been touched by the over-elaborate literariness which was then the mode. His Latin is such exceedingly low Latin that, on the supposition of literary studies, he must have deliberately turned away from the prevailing fashion in favour of the more popular and readily comprehensible Latin then emerging. One is disposed to deduce from the terse and laconic language of the Rule that his studies in Rome must rather have been that of law — another reason for believing that he went to Rome later than early tradition has it. Be that as it may, he was appalled by the moral conditions among the students and so, actuated at the outset by the same impulse that drove the first ascetics into the desert, decided after three years to retire to seclusion and solitude.

There was a short stay — just how long we do not know — at Enfide, which is the present Affile, about thirty-five miles from Rome. The young Benedict was accompanied there by a woman named Cyrilla who is described as his nurse, and whom we may suppose to have been an old retainer of his family in Nursia deputed to look after him. At Enfide, Saint Gregory tells us, "they were detained by the charity of many good people, and abode awhile in the Church of the Apostle Saint Peter." This Dom Justin McCann thinks means either that they stayed at some annex or dependency of the church or that Benedict began there his pastoral studies. The second surmise, however, would seem to be unlikely in view of the fact that Benedict never proceeded to the priesthood.

Now occurred the first of the miracles recorded by Saint Gregory. Cyrilla had borrowed an earthenware sieve and accidentally broke it. "But Benedict, pious and loving youth that he was, when he saw his nurse weeping, had pity on her sorrow, and taking with him the two pieces of the sieve set himself to earnest prayer. When he arose from his knees the sieve beside him was whole and entire, nor was there any mark to show that it had been broken." That sieve, Gregory goes on to say, was hung up in the porch of the church and remained there until the time of the Lombards.

The immediate result was that every woman with a broken pot came pestering Saint Benedict to mend it. Seeing that he would find no peace there, he fled — this time alone — to Subiaco to begin his career.

At Subiaco he led a strictly eremitical life for three years.

There, according to Pliny, an artificial lake had been made by the Emperor Claudius which had taken the work of 30,000 men for eleven years. And by it were the ruins of one of Nero's palaces. In a grotto, halfway down a precipice, Benedict lodged in a cave, fed only by a local monk named Romanus who let down daily a small portion of bread, announcing its coming by ringing a little bell. Though he was deliberately to turn his back upon this manner of life, he had no quarrel with those who preferred it, so long as they did not carry it to the point of extravagance. Years later, when he encountered near Monte Cassino a hermit named Martin who had riveted himself to a rock by an iron chain, Benedict's only remark was, "If thou art truly the servant of Christ, do not bind yourself by a chain of iron but by the chain of Christ." Upon this Martin took off his chain but never went further from his rock than when he was bound.

During this period in the cave at Subiaco came the great temptation, to which had Benedict yielded we should never have heard of him again. The image of a woman he had once seen so assailed him that he was almost on the point of leaving his hermitage and going to find her. Instead he threw himself naked into a thorn-bush nearby — a heroic remedy which proved so efficacious that never again was he troubled by the allurements of the flesh. Concerning this incident Abbot Cabrol has written : "The question has naturally arisen : who was this woman whose memory after so many years of penance still haunted the mind of Benedict ? All that can be discovered is unworthy of mention. What does it matter, after all ? The woman is simply Woman ; she is the temptation which tormented a Saint Anthony, and after him every solitary who, each in his turn, went through the critical hour in which his virtue was proved." Centuries later, according to Luke Wadding, the Franciscan annalist, Saint Francis visited Benedict's cave. There he blessed the thorn-bush — and instantly it flowered with roses.

In this cave Benedict was discovered by some shepherds whom he converted and made his first disciples. His reputation was growing so rapidly that when the monastery at Vicovaro — about eighteen miles from Subiaco on the road to Tivoli — lost its abbot, the monks begged Benedict to take his place. He consented, though very reluctantly, because he saw from the start that the plan would not work. Plainly enough he told them that their way of life and his would not agree, but they insisted, and then, when he attempted to introduce discipline — for like most monasteries of the time, its only rule was the will of the abbot — these strange monks made an attempt to poison him. If you are amazed by that, let me remind you that a thousand years later Saint Teresa's Discalced Carmelites had to guard against being poisoned by their Calced brethren. At least some of them thought it advisable to take precautions against that happening.

One would have supposed that after this experiment Benedict would have returned permanently to his cave. He did indeed live again for a short period as a hermit, but he soon made another experiment in monasticism, for though his rule at Vicovaro had failed, his time there had served to suggest ideas to him. Now he founded twelve monasteries, each consisting of twelve monks and a prior, all governed by himself, and all following — so Abbot Tosti conjectures — the Rule of Saint Basil. It was not an absolutely new concept — that of a cluster of monasteries — and it was one that he was eventually

to abandon.   But the concept was at least a further stage on
the road to his mature and rounded plans.

The actual occasion for Benedict's leaving Subiaco was that
he incurred the hostility of a priest named Florentius.   Again
there was an attempt at poison.   Florentius sent him an
elogium, one of the loaves then blessed at the Offertory at
Mass.   But Benedict realized the malice behind this and
ordered a raven which he fed daily to take the loaf and cast it
in some place where it could never be found.

As he had not succeeded with poison, Florentius managed to
smuggle six depraved women into one of the monasteries in the
hope of seducing the young monks.   This was a bit too much.
Saint Benedict had long been thinking of another type of
monastery, and even the death of Florentius shortly afterwards
would not take him back to Subiaco.   Off he went immediately to Monte Cassino with his followers to put Benedictinism
into practice.   Saint Gregory explains the hatred of Florentius : "He himself would have liked to enjoy the same reputation, though he took the greatest care not to live the same life."
Perhaps this was the reason why Saint Benedict wrote in the
Fourth Chapter of the Rule : "Do not wish to be called a
saint before you are one, so that later it may be said with
greater truth."

The establishment at Monte Cassino was made in 529, or
near that date.   It was there that the Rule was written and a
fully developed Benedictinism given to Benedict's monks and
eventually to the world.

Monte Cassino had long been a spot famous in pagan
religion.   It had a sacred wood and temples to Jupiter and
Apollo, and perhaps the rites of Mithra had also been celebrated

there, for these had been popular among the Roman legions which had once had an acropolis on the summit of the mountain. That Benedict was able to remove the vestiges of paganism suggests that he had been given absolute possession of the place — it has been surmised through the influence of Tertullus, the father of the boy-monk Saint Placid. Official authorization was, after all, at that time still necessary for what Benedict did. However this may be, it is certainly the fact that Benedictinism reached perfect flower at Monte Cassino — not until then.

This came about through the Rule — a rule written for Benedict's own monks but with an eye to its possible adoption by other monasteries. Abbot Chapman even argues that it was produced at the direct instance of the Pope with a view to codifying the whole monastic system. But its slow diffusion and its subsequent existence side by side with other monastic rules would seem to indicate that though, in the end, standardization did result, this came about because of the merits of the Rule itself and not because it was officially imposed. It supplanted all other rules by virtue of its being so reasonable, so well fitted to the European temperament, so well fitted (one might add) to the nature of man.

Montes Benedictus amabat, says the famous distich that attributes to Bernard a preference for valleys, to Francis the towns, and to Dominic the great cities. Yet though Benedict located monasteries on mountains, the more arduous heights of asceticism were avoided by him. Before his time monasticism was still very largely oriental in tone, even when it had degenerated into a merely formal austerity. Almost every monastery was somewhat eclectic, choosing, according to the taste of its abbot, from this or that rule specific provisions, but

often enough without much consideration of their suitability
to the temperament of those asked to obey them. The result
was that a particular abbot might have a good deal of influence
during his lifetime, and that his community would fall into a
state of hopeless confusion after his death. On the one hand
there was excessive rigour, on the other there was appalling
laxity. The vagabond monk was becoming a religious and
even a social problem.

Benedict begins by saying, "We are therefore about to found
a school of the Lord's service, in which we hope to introduce
nothing harsh or burdensome." He ends by saying that what
he has written is only a "beginning" of the monastic life. He
does not profess any penitential purpose but instead assumes
that those joining him have never been guilty of malice but
only wish to purge themselves of "the sloth of disobedience."
He is not providing a place where the notorious sinner may
expiate his sins, but is rather writing for the ordinary man of
good will. Not poverty but frugality is his concept of the
monastic life, and though the life for which he legislates is,
after all, ascetic, its asceticism is very mild when compared with
the extravagance that had prevailed, and was sometimes to prevail again. The Benedictine Rule was to be interpreted in a
rigid sense by Saint Bernard, and still more so by the "Thunder-
ing Abbot" of La Trappe, Armand de Rancé, yet its keynote
is moderation or, as Saint Gregory put it, discretion.

An instance of this appears in the regulations regarding the
Opus Dei. Though nothing was to be preferred to this, the
distinctive function of monks, Saint Benedict ordered that the
Ninety-fourth Psalm at Matins was to be dragged out so as to
give time for loiterers to find their places in choir ; and again at
Lauds the Fiftieth Psalm was similarly to be said slowly. This

shows, comments Abbot Butler in his great book *Benedictine Monachism*, "that the kind of discipline Saint Benedict expected to secure and aimed at securing was not the discipline of a regiment, where everybody has to be punctual to the minute . . . but the freer discipline of a well-regulated family life." He continues, "If there should be a Benedictine monastery wherein no one ever was late for anything, no one ever broke the rule of silence or the other rules, no one ever gossiped or went to sleep when he ought to be reading or working, — well, such a monastery might be, to use Palladius' favourite word of the Egyptian monks, θαυμάσιον, wonderful ; but it would not be Benedictine." Indeed, though the primitive monastic schedule, as worked out by Abbot Butler, may strike us as exacting, he points out that when the time-table is analyzed, it is seen to allow ample time for sleep and imposed hardly more external hardship than that to which the monks had been accustomed before they entered the monastery. It is really a reaction against austerity. The Thirty-ninth Chapter, which legislates concerning food, says that a monk should not eat to excess, lest he get indigestion, and the Fortieth Chapter says that he should not drink too much. One *hemina* (a pint) of wine a day, Saint Benedict thinks, ought to be enough for any man, appending, "Although we read that wine is not at all proper for monks, yet, because monks in our times cannot be persuaded of this, let us agree to this, at least, that we do not drink to satiety but sparingly." "I wonder," comments Abbot Butler, "is there any other religious rule in which such a sentence can be found !" The whole emphasis on mortification is laid in the famous Seventh Chapter on humility.

Abbot Butler, who governed Downside so long with genial wisdom, makes much of the elasticity of the Rule. "This," he says, "is a very good term. What is elastic allows itself to be modified by the presence of external forces ; but elastic, unless it be worn out, ever tends, as the pressure of such forces wanes, to return to its original condition, and when the forces cease to operate, it does reassume its native form. It is in this property that elasticity lies, and that elastic differs from putty." From this he argues that the spacious interpretation given to the Rule at Downside, and indeed generally given to it by Black Benedictines, is in closer consonance with the Benedictine spirit than would be a literal application with all the Rule's provisions. Yet it is still open to such communities as wish to carry out the Rule with precise archaic fidelity to do so.

The moderation of the Rule — which Saint Benedict sometimes almost seems to be apologizing for — is what makes it so original. For though he had undoubtedly studied the regulations of Saint Basil and Saint Pachomius, as well as those of other monastic legislators — especially Cassian — he usually gives something very different. What he wrote is at once impersonal and revealing ; so much so, that as Abbot Cabrol puts it, "Certain chapters of his Rule are equal to so many pages of an autobiography." Benedict's own life was so sunk in his Rule that it is the mirror of his life. Saint Gregory says with truth, "This holy man could not teach otherwise than he had lived."

What cannot be stressed enough is that Benedict never thought of himself as founding a religious order. Even today the Benedictines do not constitute a religious order in the sense that the Jesuits or the Dominicans are such. At Subiaco there was what may be called a religious order, at any rate in germ. The Cluniac reform created a religious order — but only by departing, in its centralization, from Saint Benedict's own idea.

And Leo XIII, in creating an Abbot Primate, probably intended that he should be a General. But Leo's plans were not fully carried out, so that Abbot Butler is able to be thankful that, after fifty years of primacy, no signs of centralization have as yet occurred, even though he fears that, "human affairs being what they are," an ambitious primate will sooner or later arise who will try to aggrandize his position into that of a generalship. Meanwhile Benedictinism remains what it always was, a loose association of autonomous abbeys, so that Abbot Ford points out that "a Benedictine may more truly be said to enter or join a particular household than to join an order"; and Dom David Knowles concludes that the Benedictines are not an order but a way of life.

Another of Benedict's leading ideas was the vow of stability. This was of course always inherent in monasticism but had not been greatly insisted upon, with the result that there was much wandering about, and the vagabond monk appeared. Now a man entered an abbey with the express intention of living and dying there. No centralized novitiate existed, though young monks might be sent for a while to a house of study outside his own monastery. This stability was, and always will be, an essential feature of Benedictinism. The friars of the thirteenth century needed a greater mobility than the Benedictines possessed; anything like a vow of stability would have only hampered them in their work. And this was even more true of sixteenth- and seventeenth-century religious orders. But the Benedictine life would have been impossible except under stability, which has been defined by Archbishop Ullathorne as the binding of the monk "to an irrevocable life in the community that has witnessed his profession." Yet though the later orders found that they could do their best work in small units, or even through isolated men sent out as pioneers, it was a distinct advantage to them that the abbeys remained as a stabilizing and balancing force. To be able to think of the community as a family was a consolation to men who knew that they would have to pass most of their days separated from the family circle. Here as in other respects the Rule of Saint Benedict continued to be the norm of the religious life.

It is very much of a question whether early monasticism universally insisted upon formal vows, though everywhere a man who had entered the monastic state and then left it was regarded as an apostate. Even the Basilian rule only demanded the profession of celibacy. For that matter Saint Benedict's Rule does not, in so many words, call for what has come to be regarded as the marks of the religious state — the promise of poverty, chastity and obedience. What it asked instead was that the monk should vow to accept the monastic manner of life, stability, and obedience to the Rule. During the eighth century, in fact, only obedience and stability were promised, on the ground that the others were implied in them. And though all this is now sometimes made more explicit by the taking of the three ordinary vows as well, as these had always been sufficiently covered by the Rule itself, the Benedictine monk or nun from the beginning took what was the equivalent of five vows.

The Rule itself, however, exacts only the acceptance of the monastic state, *conversatio morum*, regarding this as the end, and stability and obedience as the means to that end. Abbot Tosti sums it all up by saying, "The scope of the Rule of Saint Benedict is to bring back the monk, by the labour of obedience, to God, from whom he had departed by the sloth of disobedience." Everything therefore is comprised in obedience, as the Rule makes clear just what is expected of those who take upon themselves the monastic mode of life.

Abbot Butler would appear to be asserting too much when he calls all later monastic developments a revulsion against Saint Benedict and even a reversion to the individualism of the Desert.   A Jesuit might well smile at the following passage, though none can deny that it contains a good deal of truth. "These medieval and modern orders, be they offshoots from the Benedictine trunk, or modern congregations of clerks regular, or what not, have all been characterized by the emphasis laid in varying degrees on the practice of corporal austerity in manner of life, and of self-inflicted bodily mortifications ; and by a shifting of the center of gravity of the spiritual life from the canonical office to the cultivation of private mental prayer.   And all the subjectivity of modern spirituality, with its self-introspection, its hankering after self-inflicted austerities, its analysis of motives, its methods of meditation, its marking progress in virtue, its conscious advancement in perfection, even its daily charts of defects and acts of virtue and mortification, and its preference of private over common prayer, — what is it all, but a reversion to the individualism of the earlier monachism of Egypt, from the objective concrete monastic life symbolized by Saint Benedict in calling his monastery a school, not of perfection, but of God's service ?"   Dom Justin McCann feels obliged to insert a footnote on Abbot Butler in his own *Saint Benedict*: "Abbot Butler's book is charged with all the force of his own vigorous personality, and . . . this, while adding greatly to its power and interest, detracts from its objective value and even makes it misleading for the unwary reader.   His personal convictions tend to dominate the argument and determine its course, so that his conclusions must be received with a measure of caution." It can hardly be denied, however, that with the abandonment of the choral Office on the part of recent orders there arrived the tendency to introspection that colours so much of modern spirituality. But an increase in physical austerity — no, it has not meant that ; quite conspicuously it has not meant that.

What is true is that there has been a lessening of the corporate life. Saint Benedict aimed at bringing men into a family circle in which they might seek and praise God in cooperation, under a direction that would be firm but not severe. The abbot was not to break the vessel in removing its rust. He had to remember, however, that he would be called upon to give an account to God of his stewardship, and that his sole duty was that of leading his brethren to Christ. Moreover, his authority was not dictatorial. In all important matters he had to consult the assembled community, and the Rule carefully laid it down that he was to listen to the views of even the youngest monk, "because the Lord often revealeth to the youngest what is best." The system was comprehensive, without being too minutely detailed or restrictive, and it proved to be really workable. The good sense and practicality of his Rule was Benedict's most notable achievement. The fire of the Desert soon burnt itself out, whereas the cheerful and companionable glow of the monastic hearth would last for ever. It was in this way that Saint Benedict brought what may be called a quiet revolution to Church and society.

Perhaps the most striking instance of Benedictine development lies in the fact that the early communities consisted almost wholly of brothers, whereas all the later communities consisted of priests, except for the special class of lay-brothers.

It was of course necessary that for the saying of Mass and the administration of the sacraments a priest should be available. But there is nothing in the Rule to show that Mass was said every day in the monastery, or that its chaplain was always a member of the community. The main duty of the monks was the solemn performance of the *Opus Dei*, and for this monks who were laymen, presided over by an abbot who was a layman, sufficed. Changing circumstances made it necessary — though only by degrees — that all the choir monks should be either priests or clerics being trained for the priesthood ; but these circumstances, it was discovered, called for no change in the original Rule. Even in a matter of such moment as this it proved its flexibility. Just as the Rule was only the more perfectly carried out when Benedictine monks became missionaries and teachers, so the *Opus Dei* was given a grandeur and solemnity that had not been possible under primitive conditions. Benedictines accordingly grew not less but more Benedictine as a consequence.

The social effect was enormous, extending even to that teaching of good manners to the barbarians which Abbot Cabrol and others have indicated. The Middle Ages were called by Cardinal Newman the Benedictine Centuries. A world that appeared to be on the point of dissolving into chaos with the breakdown of the old Roman order, was remodelled and blessed by Benedict's sons. Yet any specific social intention was probably not in Benedict's mind at all. Canon Hannay remarks : "The Benedictine Rule aimed at making good men and left the question of their usefulness to God. It is, perhaps, just because they denied themselves the satisfaction of aiming at usefulness that they were so greatly used."

The elasticity and adaptability of the Rule made it perfectly in keeping with almost any work, the engaging in almost any functions. As to that Abbot Butler writes : "There was a Europe to be converted, christianized, civilized anew ; law and order to be restored ; the fabric of society to be rebuilt ; the dignity of labour to be reasserted ; agriculture, commerce, edducation, the arts of peace to be revived ; civil and political life to be renewed ; in short, a Europe to be remade." In this the Benedictine order was the most powerful of all the instruments at the disposal of the Church, and this was very largely for the reason that it did not establish parishes but monasteries — because, in short, it was based upon the vow of stability. The monastery was the centre of everything, and at a time when the world was in flux such settled centres were more than ever needed. And though monks were sometimes sent out in smaller groups for special missionary efforts — as for that matter, freelance Benedictines during the past century in the United States did much valuable work, not to be done otherwise — a monastery was always set up as soon as possible. Stability is still the distinguishing feature of Benedictinism.

About the social effect of the monastic institution nobody has ever spoken better than Newman : "Saint Benedict found the world, physical and social, in ruins, and his mission was to restore it in the way, not of science, but of nature, not as if setting about to do it, not professing to do it by any set time or by any rare specific or by any series of strokes, but so quietly, patiently, gradually, that often, till the work was done, it was not known to be doing. It was a restoration, rather than a visitation, correction, or conversion. The new world which he helped to create was a growth rather than a structure. Silent men were observed about the country, or discovered in the forest, digging, clearing, and building ; and other silent men, not seen, were sitting in the cold cloister, tiring their eyes, and keeping their attention on the stretch, while they painfully deciphered and copied and re-copied the manuscripts which they had saved.   There was no one that 'contended, or cried out,' or drew attention to what was going on ; but by degrees the woody swamp became a hermitage, a religious house, a farm, an abbey, a village, a seminary, a school of learning, and a city."   And again all this reposed upon stability and could not have been brought about without it.

Corporateness, not individual efforts, however brilliant, is the mark of the Order.   But though this is obviously indispensable to the proper performance of the liturgy, it does not form part of Benedictine life solely for that reason.   Saint Benedict's abbey is a family, ruled by its father, the abbot, and the family operates as a single entity.   But it was only to be expected that Benedictines, starting with Prosper Guéranger of Solesmes, and extending through Maria Laach and other Benedictine centres, should now be the leaders in what promises to be the most fruitful of all means for the elevation of Catholic life from the mediocre spirituality which has plagued us since the Reformation to the liturgical prayer which is at the very heart of true Catholic piety.   The liturgical revival is not distinctively — still less is it exclusively — Benedictine, and no Benedictine would want it to be considered as such.   But that it was not completely lost sight of during the "age of devotions" has been due to Benedictine life, to that more than to anything else.

This, of course, must not be understood as implying that private prayer is neglected by Benedictinism.   That Saint Benedict himself was a mystic, and a mystic of a high order, comes out in the experience related of him by Saint Gregory the Great — his vision of "the whole world collected under a single sunbeam." Saint Bernard took this to mean that Benedict was momentarily raised to the manner of the knowledge of the angels, who see God face to face, contemplate His wisdom clearly in itself, and know creatures in God. And Saint Gregory, so far from thinking of contemplation as beyond the reach of all but an exceptionally endowed few, held on the contrary, "It is not the case that the grace of contemplation is given to the highest and not given to the lowest ; but often the highest, and often the most lowly . . . and sometimes also those who are married receive it. If therefore there is no state of life of the faithful from which the grace of contemplation can be excluded, anyone who keeps his heart within him may also be illuminated by this light of contemplation." It has been a great pity that some later systems have sometimes tended to create the impression that this is a thing reserved to specialists and experts. If they have not quite succeeded we have largely to thank the Benedictine insistence upon the Catholic truth that the whole body of believers make up the Mystical Body of Christ and may realize their part in it through the liturgy of the Church.

We get one indication of Saint Benedict's sanity of outlook from the fact that he loved to pray in the open air. Another is in the maxim *ora et labora*. Though the Benedictine never set out to be a "pure" contemplative, his was nevertheless a contemplative life and one that did not professedly seek that balance of activity and contemplation which Saint Thomas Aquinas, speaking for his Order, defined as the explicit Dominican aim. This was *contemplata aliis tradere*. Though Benedictine monks, as individuals, did much in the way of imparting to others the fruits of their own contemplation, this was not their professed object. If it comes to that, perhaps only a hermit can be a contemplative and nothing else, and the hermit himself can attain to undistracted contemplation only intermittently. The Abbot Silvanus of Mount Sinai once remarked to his disciple Zachary : "Martha is necessary to Mary, for because of Martha is Mary praised." Cynics have suggested that Mary was able to sit at the Master's feet because Martha was willing to do Mary's share of the housework as well as her own. The truth, however, is that well-ordered monastic life contrives to unite Mary and Martha, and though the degree to which this is brought about varies from order to order, and also in individual cases, too sharp a distinction drawn between contemplation and activity is usually misleading. It certainly has little meaning if applied to the Benedictine concept of religion. The question is merely one of proportion and degree.

The end of the Saint has the same human quality that marked it throughout. Once a year, we are told by Saint Gregory, he used to spend a day with his twin sister Saint Scholastica. At their last meeting she begged her brother not to leave her that night but to speak until morning of the joys of heaven. His answer was, "You must not ask me this, my sister, for on no account must I remain outside of the monastery at night." It was a beautiful evening, but Scholastica changed all that. Putting her hands upon the table, and her head upon her hands, she prayed ; upon which so tremendous a storm arose that Benedict and those with him could not think of leaving their shelter. Then Benedict said, "May Almighty God forgive you, my sister. What is this that you have done ?" To which Scholastica replied serenely, "I asked you to remain and you would not listen to me ; so I asked my Lord and he has answered me. Now go, if you can ; leave me and go back to your monastery."

Three days later Scholastica died and Benedict, looking from the window of his cell had a vision of her soul flying in the form of a dove to heaven. Her body was buried in his monastery in the grave he had prepared as his own.

He was not long in following her there. Six days before he died he had her grave reopened for him. Then, feeling death upon him, he had himself carried into the church and received the Body and Blood of Christ. Then standing erect, tall, white-bearded, more spare of frame than ever, and upheld only by the hands of the brethren, he breathed his last amid words of prayer. Saint Gregory continues with : "On that same day two of his monks, one in his monastery, the other far away, saw the selfsame vision. They saw a path strewn with rich coverings and flashing with innumerable lamps, stretching eastwards from his monastery to the sky. And beside it above stood a man in venerable garments who asked them whose path it was that they saw. When they confessed that they knew not : 'This,' said he, 'is the path by which Benedict, the beloved of the Lord, ascended to heaven.' " He was laid to rest by the side of Scholastica at the very spot where seventeen years before he had destroyed the altar to Apollo.

In 1581 the Lombards sacked Monte Cassino and the monks fled to Rome. Cut down, the abbey grew again, as cut down once more only recently, it will surely grow again. The first destruction helped to spread out Benedictinism from Rome as a centre, and until 717 Monte Cassino was utterly deserted. Meanwhile Saint Gregory, Benedict's biographer, unable to go to England as a missionary, owing to his election as Pope, sent Saint Augustine to evangelize the Anglo-Saxons. This is the first certain record we have of the establishment of the Order beyond the borders of Italy, though we hear of Saint Maurus, who had been one of Saint Benedict's beloved boy-monks, being sent to France not long before Benedict died.

Expeditions were sent from Benedictine houses in France in 673 to find the grave of Benedict and Scholastica. After some difficulty this was located, and the bones of the Saints were taken to France — those of Benedict to Fleury-sur-Loire (now Fleury-Saint-Benoît) and those of Scholastica to Le Mans. This pious theft — of a kind not uncommon at the time — aroused such protests that in 750 Pope Zachary wrote to the French bishops asking that the bones be returned. But there were evasions, and though some relics were given, the bones were kept. Only the ashes of Saint Benedict and Saint Scholastica are at Monte Cassino. And despite the destruction of the abbey, the gorgeous tomb that covered them is still intact.

II

SAINT PATRICK

There are at least two considerable handicaps for anyone who attempts to speak or write about Saint Patrick. One is that so many of the details are of such a character that they have to be fitted ingeniously together like a jig-saw puzzle in order to obtain anything like a plausible picture of the whole ; and then, though plausibility may be obtained, certainty is not. Another difficulty is that, even when what is related of Patrick is definite enough, it is only too apparent that fiction is freely mingled with fact ; therefore some people think it the safer course to treat everything as fiction — a much too easy evasion. Even Patrick's authorship of the few scraps of writing which purport to be his has been disputed. Well, there may be some reason for that in the case of the poem "The Blessing on Munster," but much less reason in the case of what is variously called "Saint Patrick's Breastplate" and "The Deer's Cry." But of the two prose pieces, what Archbishop Healy wrote of *The Confession Before Death* in his *Life and Writings of Saint Patrick* seems to me to apply equally to the *Letter to Coroticus* : "Like the Epistles of Saint Paul, it proves its own authorship ; so that the most sceptical critic cannot doubt its authenticity." If ever writing rang true, it is here.

But though I am not disposed to regard as a mere legend any story that appears late — and even legends often throw so much light on history that it is only a stupid historian who allows them no value — I must admit to finding some of these stories to be of a kind that it is hard to accept. I take, for example, what we are

27

told happened on that famous first visit of Patrick's to Laoghaire, the High King at Tara.   One of the druids, it seems, the
second in importance of those present, insulted Patrick and
blasphemed the Christian faith.   Now Patrick, as appears from
several things we know about him, was a somewhat hot-
tempered person.   According to the story as told in the *Tripartite Life* : "Patrick thereupon looked wrathfully upon him,
and cried out to God with a loud voice, saying, 'Lord, Who
canst do all things, and on Whose power dependeth all that
exists, and Who hast sent us hither to preach in Thy name to
the heathen, let this ungodly man, who blasphemeth Thy name,
be lifted up and let him forthwith die.'   Hardly had he said
these words, when the druid was caught up into the air and
forthwith cast down again, and his skull striking against a rock,
his brains were scattered on the stone and he was killed before
their very eyes, and the heathen folk at the sight were a-dread."
Now there I think I can find echoes of the contest between
Elias and the priests of Baal, as I think I can find in the contest
that followed between Patrick and the druid wonder-workers
an echo of what we are told in Genesis about Moses and the
Egyptian priests before Pharaoh.   Mingled with both incidents are colours of the sort that occur in so many of the tales of
the Irish heroic age.   Therefore, they bear to my mind the
marks of invention, or at least of embellishment.

As I do not believe these things ever happened, at any rate as
related, I do not feel it necessary to make any apology for Patrick.   But how does Mr. Hugh De Blacam try to explain the
killing of the druid ?   He offers us two explanations, giving us
good measure for our choice.   The first of these, given on page
54 of his *Saint Patrick*, is that the druid perished in a fit of
apoplectic fury.   (How he knows this I cannot pretend to

say.) His other explanation, as given on page 169, is that the druid's death is only a fashion of speaking, a "rhetorical exaggeration." " 'Och, he murdered me !' and 'I 'm destroyed walking,' are commonplaces of present-day speech in Ireland which might be treated as evidence of atrocity or of alleged death-and-revival, by the kind of writer who dismisses the old *Lives* of Patrick as incredible." The second explanation is worse than the first, being merely silly. Obviously the story meant just what it seems to mean ; equally obviously we cannot believe that a saint would behave in this fashion. But it does not follow that all the stories in the *Tripartite Life* have to be rejected because a few of them are incredible, any more than great value should be denied to Mr. De Blacam's book because of two or three instances of poor judgment. Elsewhere Mr. De Blacam shows very good sense, as when he calls the stories that link the Saint and the Fenian, Oisin and Patrick, a "literary coupling," and adds of one of them, "In it we discern this great truth — that in Ireland there was a reconciliation, a harmonizing, between the enthusiasm of the poets and the devotion of the religious. While the Northern sagas have been pitted against Christianity by some Germanic neo-pagans, the Irish hero-tales were given their just place as images of natural virtue, were preserved by monks, and became aids, as it were, to the higher and supernatural development of the nation. We are led by the Gaelic writers to conceive Patrick as a man who could relish a tale of the hunt or a gallant battle, as he talked with the men whom he sought to convert to the faith — and we can believe that such a man might well succeed as we know that Patrick succeeded, and as his Irish successors succeeded when they evangelized Pictland, Northumbria, and pagan Central Europe." Quite so : that is the proper use of legends. We accept them not necessarily as historical fact but as nevertheless conveying the spirit of history. The dashing of the druid to death did not scandalize its first hearers. That it could be told to them at all shows what kind of people they were, and in what kind of an age they lived.

We have a problem of a different sort when we try to find out just where Saint Patrick was born. As to that Patrick himself is very specific : he tells us that he was born at Bannaven Taberniae (sometimes it appears as Bannaventa Berniae) a small town near which his father had a villa. The only question is : where was Bannaven Taberniae ?

About this the earlier writers seem to have had no doubt : it was Dumbarton ; about this more recent writers also have had no doubt — they all rule Dumbarton out, though otherwise they violently disagree. But it is anything but clear as to why Dumbarton was ever suggested : it is not in Britain, and Saint Patrick is very positive about Britain. On the contrary, it is in a wild part of what would then have been called Pictland, far inland on the Clyde estuary, north of Glasgow, a place where there could have been none of the amenities of life Patrick describes as being enjoyed by his well-to-do Roman-British family. I suppose that Britain was formerly rejected because it was hard for a good Irishman to bring himself to believe that Patrick could possibly have been born in that country. Now the consensus of scholarly opinion is that his birthplace was in the Severn valley or the coast of Wales, though this is as far as the opinions of scholars coincide. Carwent, near the estuary of the Severn, is suggested by Mrs. Concannon. She points out that it had a forum and a basilica, along with other signs that it was a comfortable and even a luxurious town of the Roman sort. Dr. John McNeill, on the other hand, advances the claims of Abergavenny, while Dr. Oliver Gogarty argues in favour of Pembroke. On the hill above Saint David's there is a rocky spot called Saint Patrick's chair, from which on clear days the hills of Wicklow may be seen. And a Saint Patrick's well and a Saint Patrick's chapel nearby support Gogarty's contention, though we must remember that Kilpatrick, near Dumbarton, also has a Saint Patrick's well.

I might remark here that though Oliver Gogarty's *I Follow Saint Patrick* is not, strictly speaking, a biography but what might be described as a geographical history, and though it was not written by a professional scholar, it has what I should consider the advantage of having been written by a poet. Dr. Gogarty has used his eyes as well as his brains, and he supplies us with a good deal of information not easily found elsewhere. Nor do I think his humour comes amiss. He writes, "Daventry's Bannaven Taberniae will not do. And here is a reason of my own (and do not disregard it though it appear facetious) : 'What would — to use an expressive Irish construction — thousands of people be doing with only one tavern ?' I must confess that my peregrinations did not take me to Daventry."

But let us turn to what Saint Patrick himself says. He tells us in his *Confession* that his father was Calpurnius and his grandfather Potitus. His grandfather, we learn further, was a priest and his father a deacon and also a decurion, that is, a member of the town senate, clearly a man of position and some wealth. The British family name was Sochet ; but we must bear in mind that Britain by this date had been so thoroughly Romanized that the original names had been changed to Latin equivalents. As for the Saint's mother, she was Concessa and was of Gaulish origin. She may even have been a sister of Saint Martin of Tours, though on the face of it that seems a bit far-fetched.   Between Britain and Gaul there was a good deal of traffic ; both were well organized and prosperous parts of the Empire.

The Empire, however, even at the time of Saint Patrick's birth in 389, showed ominous signs of weakness.   The legions were being withdrawn from Britain during Patrick's boyhood, and though the old Roman life went on, it was already doomed. Had not this been the case, Patrick would probably never have gone to Ireland at all.

What would have happened instead is that he would have followed in the footsteps of his father and grandfather as a prosperous citizen, of the kind who live their little day and are forgotten more completely than are rogues and vagabonds. That Patrick was not, by his own confession, a good student would not have seriously handicapped him ; for if he found it hard to keep to his books, this was not because he was dull — on the contrary, a certain amount of dullness is usually required for the making of a good student — but because of the activity of his mind and body.   He regretted this afterwards — many of us have similar regrets — but as a matter of fact, he probably escaped a good deal, even though he did not escape in later life the charge that he was "rustic" and illiterate, a charge which he freely admitted to be just.

Perhaps he was also dreamy and absent minded, if the legends are to be believed.   Sent out one day to gather firewood — why he should have to do that in a house full of servants and a house that may be presumed to have had central heating, as did many of the better-class Roman houses, is not at all clear — but so sent out, he returned with a bundle of icicles under his arm. To offset this, when the other boys of the town found honey and took some of it home, and Patrick took none, he went out

again and, small boy though he was, performed his first miracle :
he filled his crock at the well, and it brimmed with pure honey !

We leave such tales for certainty. When he was fifteen or
sixteen Irish raiders descended and took back with them several
thousands of captives — Patrick among them. And for six
years he lived as a slave in Ireland.

At this point I am afraid I shall once more have to take
issue with Mr. De Blacam. He tells how Tacitus had heard his
father-in-law Agricola declare that, when he was in Britain, he
felt that with a single legion and a moderate number of auxiliaries he could have effected the conquest of Ireland. Mr. De
Blacam would have us believe that the Irish so resented Agricola's saying this — how could they have heard of it ? — that
more than three hundred years later they themselves attacked
Britain, provoked by these words. Such nonsense is quite unnecessary. Raids of this sort were of frequent occurrence
both by the Picts and the Irish on Britain, and even after the
departure of the legions the Britons were themselves sometimes able to do some raiding of their own. We do not have to
find an excuse for the harmless Irish, who, had it not been for
Agricola's unkind remark, would never have thought of retalia-
tion. This raid may have been under Niall, the father of the
High King of Ireland whom Patrick was to know later. It
may have been ; on the other hand, it may not. All that we
positively know is that Patrick was one of those carried off.

As a slave in Ireland he was apparently not badly treated.
Certain it is that, when tending the herds of his master Milchu,
a minor chieftain, on Mount Slemish in Antrim, he made lifelong friends of Milchu's children. He also came during his
servitude to love Ireland, to love it so much that he formed —
though not at this time — a plan to effect its conversion.

The English and the Irish, contrary to current belief, have always got on well together, whenever they have been given the chance. And at this time the inhabitants of both countries were purely Celtic in blood, as even now the English are mainly Celtic. Moreover their languages were the same except for the difference that the British Ps and Bs were transformed into Qs and Ks in Ireland. In Ireland therefore the name Patricius was Hibernicized into "Cothrige"; it was not difficult for him during those six years to become a perfect master of Gaelic as spoken there.

But he was lonely, and in his loneliness he turned to God. Minding his master's cattle, he had many opportunities for thought and prayer, and word came to him one night, as clearly as though he had heard a Voice speaking: "Thou dost well to fast, thou who art soon to go to thy fatherland." A few nights later he heard the Voice again, "Lo, thy ship is ready."

It proved no great undertaking to get away. He met on his journey to the sea no opposition but instead only kindness and hospitality. But the ship he found at last did not want to take him. It was one bearing Irish wolfhounds to the continent, those huge dogs being highly valued there. Patrick, it may be supposed, was allowed to go with these rough men because he showed them that he knew how to handle the animals.

When Gaul was reached, they found it devastated by war. For twenty-eight days the men and their dogs wandered, without food most of the time, until one of the men said to Patrick, "Why don't you pray to your God, Christian? We are all about to perish." Hardly had Patrick prayed, when a herd of swine came through the forest. The wolfhounds ran some of them down, and the lives of all those in the party were saved.

But why did not Patrick go at once from Gaul to Britain, as

had been his intention ?   That we do not know, though it is
quite possible that he heard at Tours from his mother's relatives
that she and his father were dead.   In any event, as the coasts
of both countries were then being overrun by raiders, a journey
to Britain was almost impossible.   Whatever the reason, Patrick was to remain at Tours several years before he was able to
get to Britain.   And he still had no definite idea of his mission.

It was in his native land, when he was getting on to thirty,
that the call at last came to him.   Again there was a dream.
A man named Victoricus came to him from Ireland bearing
letters, one of which was headed, "The Voice of the Irish."
This is how Patrick tells of it : "While I was reading aloud the
beginning of the letter, I thought that at that very moment I
heard the voice of one of them who lived beside the Wood of
Fochlut which is nigh unto the Western Sea.   And thus they
cried as with one mouth : 'We beseech thee, holy youth, to
come and walk among us once more.'   And I was exceedingly
broken in heart and could read no more.   And so I awoke."

Who was this Victoricus ?   It has been suggested that it may
have been Saint Victoricus, the Bishop of Rouen and the friend
of Saint Martin of Tours.   That is not impossible, though there
is nothing to show that Saint Patrick had ever met him.   It
seems safer to believe that it was Victor, Patrick's guardian
angel, who had already spoken to him on Mount Slemish and
whom Patrick was to see again several times.   It does not matter a great deal ; what does matter is that Patrick's summons to
Ireland was sent by a heavenly messenger.

Now the question for him was how to prepare for this mission.   He was poorly educated, and Britain had been so devastated that it was not easy for anyone there to get an education.
Accordingly Patrick returned to Gaul for this purpose.

Yet in Gaul he can hardly be said to have set himself at once to making good his deficiency, except in so far as this could be done while he was giving most of his attention to something else. This "something else" was the practice of asceticism at the famous monastery founded by Saint Honoratus on the island of Lérins, just off the present Cannes. Patrick did not seek priesthood there, though his stay seems to have been one of eight years. Instead he gave himself up to the type of monasticism followed in the place, a mode of life that the Rule of Saint Benedict was soon to make obsolete.

It could have provided little room for formal studies. For this was a monasticism that modelled itself upon that of the Desert. The monks indeed met for Mass and the Divine Office, and may have met for meals; but the community was regarded as a preparation for the hermitage. It was as a hermit that Patrick lived, at least for the latter part of his years at Lérins.

This is also to some extent true of Patrick when he went again to Ireland. His missionary activities of course must have made it impossible for him to carry out regularly all the practices he desired, but now and again he would completely withdraw, even then, from the world, as during that famous Lent on Croagh Patrick, where yearly the pilgrims go, finding even one day, and a day spent in company with others, about enough for them. Yet the lesson of the second nocturn of his feast — if second nocturns are always to be believed — records, though with a cautious "it is said": "He was wont to recite every day the whole Psalter, together with the Canticles and Hymns, and two hundred prayers; that he knelt down three hundred times to adore God; and that at each canonical hour of the day, he signed himself with the sign of the cross. He

divided the night into three parts ; first he repeated the first
hundred psalms, and genuflected two hundred times ; the second was spent in reciting the remaining fifty psalms, standing
in cold water, with his heart, eyes, and hands lifted to heaven ;
the third he gave to a little sleep, stretched upon a bare stone."
That is surely more than Egyptian in its austerity.

The third abbot of Lérins was Faustus, a Briton, and it may
have been through him that Patrick went there, though the
fame of Lérins was itself great enough to have attracted him.
Be that as it may, it was when the first abbot, Saint Honoratus,
was summoned, as so many of the monks were summoned, to
the episcopate that Patrick left, to go with him to Arles.   And
there it was that he at last became a priest.

Even so, the way for his mission opened only by degrees.
After two years at Arles, where he was probably present when
the Council of Arles was held in 428, there came the mission of
Saint Germanus to Britain.   And on this Saint Patrick himself
may have gone ; certainly he was closely associated with Saint
Germanus at this time.

Pelagius had been preaching his heresy, and finding some
followers, in Gaul and Britain.   He is usually called a Briton,
though Saint Jerome's reference to him as "this most stupid fellow, heavy with Irish porridge" points to his having been an
Irishman.   Saint Jerome, however, was not always to be trusted
in matters of this sort, for no saint ever lived with a more wasp-
ish tongue.   But Briton or Irishman, it does not much matter ;
what does matter is that Saint Germanus went with Lupus to
Britain to preach against his doctrine which was living on after
the death of the heretic in Asia Minor about 420.   At a confer-
ence with the Pelagian leaders at Veralamium — the present
Saint Albans — Saint Germanus routed them.   We hear of an

appeal being made to him about this time on behalf of some Christians living in Ireland to send them a bishop. Now Patrick's chance appeared to have come.

For the moment his chance was lost ; Saint Palladius was appointed instead. He was well-known to the Pope and had proved his worth already. But by him the Irish mission was conceived as being not so much that of converting the pagans as that of organizing the scattered Christians in Ireland, many of whom, perhaps the majority, were of British origin. As Palladius was a Briton, his qualifications in that respect were equal to Patrick's ; in all other respects his qualifications were considered much better.

Against Patrick was the fact, as he himself was to record in his *Confession*, that he was no scholar. People said, he tells us, "Why does this fellow thrust himself into danger amongst hostile people who know not God ? " He adds, with the candour which was one of his notable characteristics, "They did not say this out of malice ; but it did not seem meet in their eyes, on account of my illiteracy, as I myself witness that I have understood."

Yet in spite of everything, it was not to Palladius but to Patrick that God committed the destiny of Ireland. After a short stay in that country Palladius was on his way to Gaul, presumably to gather recruits for an undertaking he saw to be greater than he had first supposed, when he died in Britain. In 432 therefore Patrick was consecrated a bishop and set out, rather late in life — he was now in his middle forties — to Ireland.

His was a mission to the ends of the earth, *ubi nemo ultra erat*, "beyond which there is nothing" — or so he thought. He had been summoned to it by a divine call received fourteen or fifteen years earlier ; now he was commissioned by the Church and financed by the Gallic bishops.

This was something he had thought over carefully, and for which he had carefully prepared. His companions, of whom there may have been twelve clerics, were Gauls and Britons ; among the Britons being Catideus, Catus (perhaps this name was the same as Cadoc) and Mochta. But women were used as auxiliaries, and they had a special part to play in the public baptisms at Easter, Pentecost and Epiphany, when after the triple immersion of the women neophytes, they clothed them in white robes. Another feature that deserves notice is that Patrick selected his assistants with a view to their being able to instruct the Irish in the useful arts. He had three wheel-wrights, and three masons, and three embroideresses in the party. Even a brewer was provided.

More important still, Patrick perceived from the outset the need of a native clergy, and lost no time in creating one. And he made it his principle never to accept gifts from the people ; rather he was prepared to spend lavishly, giving presents to the bards and brehons in order to win their favour. Once when in later years he was told by Secundius that if he had a fault it was that he did not preach almsgiving sufficiently, Patrick got quite angry and answered : "It is for charity's sake that I do not preach charity ; for if I preached almsgiving, everything would be given to me, and those who follow me would fare poorly." He did not wish to be beholden to anyone ; he was bringing the Faith to Ireland as an entirely free gift.

From the start his mission was astonishingly successful. Upon landing at Loch Cuan, now known by its Norse name of Strangford Lough, in County Down, a little to the south of

Belfast, he at once converted the chieftain Dichu, who gave him a barn — the "Saul," which became Patrick's first church. The servants of Dichu had set the wolfhounds on Patrick, but he had a way with animals, and he chanted the verse, say the legends, "Deliver not, O Lord, to beasts the souls of those who trust in Thee."

Not only Dichu but his brother Ros was converted. As to this we have a beautiful story. Ros was very old, and at first resisted the Faith. So Patrick asked him, "Would you believe if anyone made you young again ?"

"Yes," said Ros, "I would believe then with my whole heart."

Upon this Patrick prayed, and Ros became the handsome young warrior he once had been. He was baptized and with him three of his brothers and a host of retainers. But now Ros had a different view of realities, and when the choice was offered him of a long life on earth or the immediate enjoyment of the life of heaven, he made a Christian's decision. After receiving the Eucharist, he departed to the Beatific Vision.

Ascetic though he was, Patrick was also what Mrs. Concannon calls an "open-air" saint. He had to be that in Ireland, if he was to be Ireland's apostle. The legends present him to us, to quote Mrs. Concannon, as one "with a wonderful knowledge of (amongst other things) the best places to fish (as the little boy fishers of the Drouse river knew), and a wonderful love and understanding of animals. He had a special power over soldiers and hunters and growing boys." From the beginning he showed himself an Irishman among Irishmen.

His courage, too, won the Irish heart. The account of his visit to the High King at Tara no doubt contains much that is merely legendary but surely is in the main a sufficiently accurate account of what really happened. The boldness with which

Saint Patrick made his assault took everybody's breath away.

Patrick wished to win Laoghaire over — to Christianity, if possible, or at least to toleration. But against him were the druids, the priests of that nature worship which, among Celtic peoples, seems to have been free from the horrors of a more advanced and decadent paganism. They presented no definite body of belief but hardly more than a bundle of superstitions against the impact of the Faith.

One of their beliefs was that, until the sacred fire had been lit on Tara on March 25th to mark the birthday of the year, no fire might be kindled on any hearth, and this under pain of death. That year Patrick not only lit the Paschal Candle on Holy Saturday but issued his challenge to the whole system of the druids by lighting a fire on a mountain top, so that all could see it. The druids warned the High King that if this was done, "a fire would be kindled in Eire that would not be extinguished for ever." Nevertheless Patrick proceeded, nor has that fire ever been quenched.

On the way to Tara men were posted to kill him and his eight companions. It was then that Patrick appeared chanting his famous poem, known as "The Deer's Cry," and all that those in ambush saw was a herd of deer. I quote the close of the poem as translated by Kuno Meyer :

Christ with me, Christ before me, Christ behind me,
Christ in me, Christ beneath me, Christ above me,
Christ on my right, Christ on my left,
Christ when I lie down, Christ when I sit down, Christ when I
    arise,
Christ in the heart of every man who thinks of me,
Christ in the mouth of every one who speaks of me,

Christ in every eye that sees me,
Christ in every ear that hears me.

I arise today
Through a mighty strength, the invocation of the Trinity,
Through belief in the threeness,
Through confession of the oneness
Of the Creator of Creation.

In the banqueting hall — its site has been discovered and measures 759 feet by 46 — the King sat with his Queen at his right and surrounded by his druids and harpers and poets and brehons. The order had been given that when Patrick and his company entered nobody should rise, so he saw warriors crouching with their heads over their shields. Two men, however, did stand, in spite of the King's order — two poets, one of them the chief bard of the Gael. Patrick signed them with the cross as he advanced up the long narrow hall. They were the first converts he made there.

There followed the famous contest between the Saint and the druids. The *Tripartite Life* relates what happened. The druid Lucetmael by magic brought a deep snow over the plain. But when Patrick said, "Yes, we see it ; but now take it away," the druid answered that he could not do that until the same hour on the following day. Then the Saint said, "Thou art able to do evil, but not good." Thereupon he made the sign of the cross and the snow instantly vanished. Darkness was brought down and driven away, and the contest ended with an ordeal of fire, in which Lucetmael attempted treachery, only to be defeated by another of Patrick's miracles. The effect on the beholders was stupendous. But the High King, despite the pleading of the Queen, would do no more than give Patrick grudging permission to preach. His pagan words have a noble ring : "But he would not believe, saying : 'For Niall my father bade me believe, commanding me rather to be buried on the ramparts of Tara, as men stand up in battle' ; for the gentiles are wont to be buried in their sepulchres fully armed, with weapons ready facing the foe, until the day of *Erdathe* as the druids call it, that is, the Day of the Judgment of the Lord. 'Thus must I, the son of Niall, be buried, even as the son of Dunlaing is buried at Maistin, because of the endurance of our enemy.' "

Nor was opposition to Patrick lacking elsewhere, particularly from those related to the High King. At Tailté on Easter Monday of that year 433, Prince Cairbre, Laoghaire's brother, doused Patrick's attendants in the Blackwater. At Uisneach two other brothers tried to drive Patrick away, and a nephew of theirs killed two of his Gallic companions. One of these brothers, however, subsequently accepted baptism and even dedicated his son Cormac to the service of the sanctuary. And there is the charming story of how Patrick converted the High King's daughters, Eithne the White and Fedelm the Red at Clebach well. After they had been baptized, "the Princesses besought the Saint to show them, face to face, the Royal One to Whom alone they would plight their troth. He answered them : 'You must first receive devoutly the Flesh and Blood of your Spouse. Thus being quickened with the Food of Life you may pass from the impure world into the starry bridechamber.' Thus it was done ; and with the pure Body of Christ in their breasts, and the white veil of consecrated virgins on their heads, and the waters of baptism still shining on their brows, the maidens went forth to meet their Bridegroom."

That is pure poetry. The tale of the baptism of Angus, King of Cashel, might be added as a foil of slightly grim humour. As Patrick poured the water over the King's head, he accidentally drove his spiked crozier through the King's foot. Angus never moved, or gave any sign that he was hurt. "But why did you not tell me?" Patrick asked afterwards. "I thought it was part of the ceremony," Angus answered. His reward was that Patrick promised him that none of his descendants should die of wounds.

Patrick won over many of the chieftains and had still greater success among their wives and daughters. Through that country of forests — they had not yet been cut down — and marsh and bogland, less drained than now, with its reedy lakes haunted by birds, and its blue mountains overhung with low clouds, Patrick wandered, but mostly in the North, everywhere winning converts. He even dared to strike the chief idol of Ireland, Cenn Cruach, in the face with his staff.

About this staff of his a word should be said. It was supposed to have once been carried by Our Lord Himself, and therefore was a relic of the utmost sanctity. Patrick carried it with him everywhere, and it was preserved at Ballyboghil, the Town of the Staff, until in the time of Henry VIII it was burnt in the street.

Another relic, however, escaped. We still have Saint Patrick's bell, a crude thing of iron and with no clapper, but now enshrined in a rich case. Twelve years ago it was rung again. This was when a million men, women and children gathered in Phoenix Park for Mass at the Eucharistic Congress. It told that the spirit of Patrick still lives in Ireland.

Some time — probably in 440, just after he had been temporarily replaced as head of the Irish mission — Patrick made his celebrated Lent on the top of Croagh Patrick. Here he returned, as he did every now and then, to the solitude of the hermit. Here too, according to legend, he made his famous petition to the angel who came to him. "That on the day when the twelve thrones shall be on Mount Sion, that is on the Day of Judgment, I myself shall be the judge over the men of Eire on that day." The angel of course told him, "That is something that cannot be had from God." Yet Patrick persisted ; he would not leave the mountain until his petition was granted. While the angel went to heaven, to carry this message, Patrick said Mass. At the hour of None the angel returned. "All heaven's powers have interceded for thee," he said, "and thy petition is granted. You are the most excellent man that has appeared since the Apostles, save for your obduracy ; but you have prayed and you have obtained. Strike thy bell now and fall on thy knees, and a blessing will come to thee from heaven. All the men of Eire, living and dead, shall be blessed and consecrated to God through thee."

Just before this Lent on Croagh Patrick three bishops were sent to Ireland from Gaul, ostensibly as assistants to Patrick but actually, Mrs. Concannon argues, to replace him. It would seem that certain charges had been brought against the Saint, one of which probably had to do with his refusal of all gifts. There was some natural objection to this policy, for it was feared that unless financial support was accepted from the converts, the Irish mission could not maintain itself. Another charge was the one frequently brought — and always admitted — of Patrick's illiteracy. But Father John Ryan in his *Irish Monasticism* gets indignant at the suggestion that Patrick's authority was ever curtailed, though as to that we see from the *Confession* that Patrick certainly considered that he had been for a time in what he considered to be disgrace. However, he was a very sensitive man, made all the more so by the loneliness in which he had spent most of his life ; and he was short of temper : therefore he may have felt that an attack was being made on him when none was attempted. But what is clear enough is that he went in 441 to see the new Pope, Leo the Great ; and though this may have been merely a routine visit, its occurring just then points to Patrick's believing that he needed to explain Irish matters to the Pope in person. He returned to Ireland fully cleared of whatever accusations had been brought against him, and with Ireland made an ecclesiastical province over which he was to rule as first primate. Until then he had been under the general jurisdiction of Arles and Auxerre ; after this time the centre of government was set up at Armagh.

As to how he obtained from the chieftain Dáire the gift of the hill he wanted for the site of his cathedral there are several curious stories. Patrick got it in the end only because of his persistence. Then he and Dáire went there together. "On the summit they found a doe with her fawn lying on the spot where now stands the left-hand chapel in Armagh ; and Patrick's people wished to seize the doe and her fawn." The Saint would not permit this. Instead, "He himself took the fawn and carried it on his shoulders, and the doe followed him tamely and confidently, just as a ewe follows the shepherd when he carries her lamb, until he loosed the fawn in a brake to the north of Armagh, where even up to our time there are not wanting marvellous signs." But Saint Patrick's cathedral no longer stands. Its site is now occupied by the Protestant cathedral, the successors of Saint Patrick having been driven elsewhere in Armagh.

The establishment of Armagh took place in 444, when Patrick was fifty-five. He still had seventeen years of work

before him, but his own missionary activity probably now less-
ened and was more and more reduced to his pastoral visits as
metropolitan.   All parts of Ireland saw him, but most of all he
was in the North, in Ulster.   What has come down to us is his
blessing on Munster, and though there is reason to doubt
whether the poem is really Patrick's, there can be no doubt that
this is how he felt towards Munster — towards all Ireland.   I
give Kuno Meyer's translation :

> *God's blessing upon Munster,*
> *Men, women, children !*
> *A blessing on the land*
> *Which gives them fruit.*
>
> *A blessing on every wealth*
> *Which is brought forth on their marches !*
> *No one to be in want of help :*
> *God's blessing upon Munster !*
>
> *A blessing on their peaks,*
> *On their bare flagstones,*
> *A blessing on their glens,*
> *A blessing on their ridges !*
>
> *Like sand of sea under ships*
> *Be the number of their hearths :*
> *On slopes, on plains,*
> *On mountain-sides, on peaks.*

This Briton had made himself an Irishman, though without
ever losing his love for his native land.   For this reason he was
all the more wounded when Coroticus, a British raider, who

may have been the Caredig who gave his name to the county of
Cardigan, took away newly-made Christians while they were
still in their white baptismal robes. *The Epistle to Coroticus*
opens : "I, Patrick, the sinner, unlearned as everybody knows
— I confess that I have been appointed as a bishop in Ireland."
That this injury to his flock should have been perpetrated by a
man of his own race, and one also with whom it has been
surmised that Patrick may have had some ties of kinship,
aroused his indignation.   Moreover the man was, at least professedly, a Christian.   "Therefore I grieve for you, I grieve, O
ye most dear ones to me ; yet within myself I rejoice.   I have
not laboured for nothing, and my journey to a strange land was
not in vain.   And yet, there has come to pass this crime so hor-
rid and unspeakable.   Thanks be to God, it was as baptized believers that you departed from the world to Paradise.   I can behold you.   You have set forth to that place where there shall
be no night, nor sorrow, nor death any more, and you shall
tread down the wicked and they shall be ashes under your feet.
Therefore you shall reign with apostles and prophets and martyrs.   You shall take everlasting kingdoms."   But for Coroticus himself Patrick has only wrath.   The letter is to be carried to Britain and read in the presence of the wicked man, in
the hope that it will inspire him to repent and make amends,
"That they may liberate the baptized captive women whom
they have taken, so that they may deserve to live to God and to
be made whole here and in eternity."

Whether Patrick's letter had that effect — or any effect —
on Coroticus we do not know.   But it reveals his own indignant and tender heart.

The *Confession before Death* opens with almost the same
phrase as the Epistle : "I, Patrick the sinner, am the most rustic

and the least of all the faithful." Yet for an "illiterate" man Patrick writes with extraordinary force. His language may not have the somewhat artificial adornments of the decadent style of the time which passed for "literature," but if literature is something more than that, then Patrick has what a great writer should have : the ability to convey his moving sincerity. It is from the *Confession* that we get most of our certain knowledge about him. "And this is my confession before I die !" Could any words ring more nobly than those ? "Behold, again and again I repeat my confession. I testify in truth and in exultation of heart before God and His holy angels that I had no purpose save the Gospel and its promise in returning to that people from whom aforetime with difficulty I escaped. But I pray those who believe and fear God, whosoever among them shall deign to look upon or receive this writing which Patrick the sinner and the ignorant wrote in Ireland, that never shall it be said that any little thing that I have done or demonstrated by God's pleasure was done out of my poor merit ; but judge ye, and let it be believed, that it was God's own gift."

Patrick proved himself one of the greatest of all missionaries not merely because he was a saint but because he understood the Irish. He learned their language so thoroughly as almost to forget his British tongue and Latin, though of course he had to use Latin for official purposes. He conformed to Irish social usages, except in those rare cases where they could not be made to conform with the faith he had introduced. The result was that, while Rome the ancient empire was breaking up, he founded a new empire for Christ on the edge of the world. Though he did not live to see all the Irish converted, most of them were Christians before his death ; all became Christians before long, and their loyalty to the Faith has been such that they may well claim to be the most Catholic nation of the modern world. All this directly stems from "Patrick the sinner," Patrick the British slave who was inspired by God to return to save those whom he had served as a slave.

And here I quote a passage which is to be found towards the end of Oliver Gogarty's book : "Inherent in the religion which he taught were ideas which, when translated into the secular world, were of inestimable advantage to the nation. These were the ideas which were to release the country from a system of tribal sub-divisions, and in the end to emancipate the country's mind from a petty parochial outlook and to unite it to the civilization of Europe. While the Imperium Romanum was going down in chaos, those who were to become the Irish nation and the saviours of what was left of Christian civilization were being brought into one fold in Ireland by the Saint. Relapses to political narrowness there have been now and then, but generally the far-flung Irish race is inseparably identified with Roman Christianity the world over. The personality of the Irishman has gained amplitude from it, and there is a certain friendliness in the idea of a Paddy. He is a person whose general characteristics are well known. He is not despised as a prig or avoided as a bigot : there is something wide and uninsular about him. This he got from the universality of that Empire which the Saint represented spiritually when it disappeared secularly before the wild tribes who resented its peace."

Patrick's death came in 461, and about the same time died Laoghaire, the High King, obdurate to the last. He was buried as he wished to be at Tara, standing erect in his armour and facing his ancient enemy, the King of Leinster. Patrick, feeling death upon him, wished to go to Armagh, and there are some who say that he did die there. But according to the *Tripartite*

Life, his domestic angel Victor met him on the way there and told him : "It is not in Armagh that your resurrection is to be. Go back to the townland you have left ; for it is there you shall die and not in Armagh." To which Patrick is said to have answered, "It seems that I still have no command of my freedom ; it is bondage for me to the end." And the angel answered, "It has been granted to you by God that your dignity and authority, your devotion and your doctrine, shall be in Armagh as though you were alive there." So he went back to his barn, the "Saul," his first church, where he had been living in a monastery with that old warrior Dichu, his first convert ; and it was there that Patrick died.

III

THE VENERABLE BEDE

Though the title now has a precise significance in ecclesiastical terminology, we still delight to give it to Saint Bede, feeling that it belongs to him in a special sense. This is not because he lived to be very old, for as a matter of fact he died at the relatively early age of sixty-two, but because it conveys our sense of veneration for this gentle, pious and learned man, the only Englishman who is a Doctor of the Church. Saint Anselm cannot properly be counted in this connection, for he was an Italian, long associated with the Abbey of Bec in Normandy, and is English only by virtue of having been Archbishop of Canterbury. As a speculative intellect he is, of course, superior to Bede, who was not a theologian so much as a scripture commentator. But though that is the ground upon which Bede received his title from the Church, his chief claim to fame is that charming book, *The Ecclesiastical History of the English Nation.* It is under that aspect that he will be treated here.

Several explanations have been offered of the "venerable." Here, for what it is worth, is one : a monk was trying to compose his epitaph in verse, but could get no further than the *Hic sunt in fossa*, with the next line incomplete except for the answering rhyme *ossa.* Giving it up, he went to bed, and in the morning found that angelic hands had finished the line for him. There it still stands over his tomb at Durham :

Hic sunt in fossa
Venerabilis ossa.

52

It was not a very hard job for an angelic intellect, and unfortunately for our purposes much the same story is told about other people.

Almost all that we know about Bede's life — there is an account of his death, written by one present, and this I shall quote later — is what Bede tells us at the end of his *History*. There, after a sentence about his historical method — he drew first upon the writings of the ancients, then upon the tradition of our ancestors, and finally upon his own knowledge — he proceeds to brief biographical details. He was born about 673, near the abbeys of Wearmouth and Jarrow, and entered the community of Jarrow when he was seven years old. At nineteen he was made a deacon and at thirty a priest. From then he was engaged in the varied literary works — commentaries, biographies, translations, poems, pieces of editing, of which he supplies a bibliography — to the end of his life. But though this information is meagre, he unconsciously reveals himself to us in almost every page he wrote. We know the man, even though we do not have many precise facts about him.

He may almost have been said to have been born a monk. Who his father was we do not know ; perhaps he was a pagan. Yet one gets the impression that this mellow and gentle scholar could have come only at the end of a long line of scholars, though actually he appears only about a hundred years after the coming of Saint Augustine to Kent.

If at this point I quote three passages from G. K. Chesterton's *Short History of England*, I feel that, though I must ask your indulgence, I can offer you nothing that bears better on my subject generally. "There is," he writes, "something common to all the Britons, which not even acts of union have torn asunder. The nearest name for it is insecurity, something fitting in

men walking on cliffs and the verge of things.   Adventure, a
lonely taste in liberty, a humour without wit, perplex their critics and perplex themselves.   Their souls are fretted like their
coasts.   They have an embarrassment, noted by all foreigners :
it is expressed, perhaps, in the Irish by a confusion of speech
and in the English by a confusion of thought.   For the Irish
bull is a license with the symbol of language.   But Bull's own
bull, the English bull, is a 'dumb ox of thought,' a standing mys-
tification in the mind.   There is something double in the
thoughts as of the soul mirrored in many waters.   Of all peoples they are the least attached to the purely classical ; the im-
perial plainness which the French do finely, and the Germans
coarsely, but the Britons not at all.   They are constantly colo-
nists and emigrants ; they have the name of being at home in
every country.   But they are in exile in their own country.
They are torn between love of home and love of something
else ; of which the sea may be the explanation or may be only
the symbol.   It is also found in a nameless nursery rhyme
which is the finest line in English literature and the dumb refrain of all English poems — 'Over the hills and far away.' "

I offer that without comment, except to say that, if you do
not immediately see what it has to do with the subject of this
sketch, I am counting upon you to make the discovery before I
have done.   So I proceed to the next passage : "Every now
and then there is discovered in modern England some fragment
such as a Roman pavement.   Such Roman antiquities rather
diminish than increase the Roman reality.   They make something seem distant which is still very near, and something seem
dead that is still alive. . . The important thing about France
and England is not that they have Roman remains.   They are
Roman remains."

Finally take this, also without comment but in trust that you will see its bearing on what I shall say. "Our Anglo-Saxon blood is supposed to be the practical part of us ; but as a fact the Anglo-Saxons were more hopelessly unpractical than any Celt. Their racial influence is supposed to be healthy, or, what many think the same thing, heathen. But as a fact these 'Teutons' were the mystics. The Anglo-Saxons did one thing, and one thing only, thoroughly well, as they were fitted to do it thoroughly well. They Christianised England. Indeed they Christianised it before it was born. The one thing the Angles obviously and certainly could not manage to do was to become English. But they did become Christians, and indeed showed a particular disposition to become monks. Moderns who talk vaguely of them as our hardy ancestors never do justice to the real good they did us, by thus opening our history, as it were, with the fable of an age of innocence, the beginning all our chronicles, as so many chronicles began, with the golden initial of a saint. By becoming monks they served us in many very valuable and special capacities, but not notably, perhaps, in the capacity of ancestors."

But I have not yet finished with my quotations, though I have finished with Chesterton. Let me now turn from the brilliant amateur to a professional historian — the Abbé Duchesne. "England," he writes, "is of all nations in the world that one whose ecclesiastical origins are linked most evidently with the apostolic see of Rome." And I interpolate that this is not merely because Saint Augustine was sent directly by Pope Gregory the Great. You will recall how Gregory himself had been consumed with the ambition to go as a missionary to England. There is the famous story, so beautiful and apposite that I venture to tell again of how he saw fair-haired, blue-eyed children being sold as slaves in Rome. They were from Deira. "Rather from *De ira,* from the wrath of God to be delivered !" he exclaimed. "Angles ? No, rather angels !" As Gregory, by having been elected Pope, was unable to go to them, he sent Saint Augustine instead.

I return to the Abbé Duchesne. "I shall be told that if Anglo-Saxon Christianity is not linked to Celtic origins by the British it is at least so through the Irish. No one is less disposed than I am to diminish the importance of the part played by those holy apostles of the Irish race in Northumbria and other of the Anglo-Saxon kingdoms. I feel the deepest respect and (as a Breton myself) almost patriotic pride for the venerated figures of Aidan, and Finan, and Colman, and Cuthbert. I recognize what these have done for the evangelization of England after the disappearance of Augustine and Paulinus. But is it possible to deny that their efforts were absorbed in the general movement starting from Rome and Kent ?" And again he writes : "The English Church is clearly a colony of the Roman Church. This relation is evident even in the material disposition of the buildings and their names . . . Canterbury was a little Rome ; the English Church was a daughter of the great Roman Church — a daughter born a little late, but perhaps more loved for that, and, above all, more like it than the elder daughter." And it was the Protestant historian, T. H. Green, who adds weighty testimony by pointing out how the civil organization of the State in Anglo-Saxon England consciously took that of the Church as its model.

After that string of introductory quotations perhaps we can turn to the history of England as seen by Bede, starting where he starts, with the coming of Julius Caesar.

The first thing to remember is that the Roman connection

with Britain lasted from 55 B.C. to 410 A.D. — four hundred and sixty-five years. And though it must be granted that Britain was not immediately fully Romanized, its Roman period was nevertheless very long, longer than the white man has been on the continent of North America, longer than the schism of Protestantism, very much longer than the industrial age. It was not a passing thing ; it was thorough and complete.

The second thing to remember is that Britain was a relatively thickly settled country. Diodorus Siculus and Strabo and Julius Caesar, all writing about the middle of the first century B.C., are definite about that. It should be borne in mind, in view of what follows.

Third : even during the Roman occupation there were many pirate raids in the South and West. The pirates were dealt with severely, but evidently some settled down peaceably in Britain, for we hear of a "Saxon shore." And to the North the Picts were so troublesome that Hadrian's Wall was built in 122–126 to keep them out. There was no way of keeping out the Irish marauders — the Scots as they were called then. But these matters only amounted to a nuisance ; they were raids, not an attempt at conquest.

Fourth : after the departure of the Roman legions the land was left open. It continued to regard itself as part of the Empire, but civil government functioned less and less well. As for the army, in departing it had taken with it many of the young men trained to bear arms, though of course the majority of those capable of warfare were left. The capital point, however, is that there was after that no organized military force — which in this case meant no effective police force. Hadrian's Wall — which has never been designed as anything but a connecting series of blockhouses — could not be manned. The

Picts therefore had no difficulty in raiding the North at will. The Irish raided the West from the sea. But still it was only a question of raiding ; the object was loot.

Fifth : Frantic appeals on the part of the Britons did bring back a Roman legion for a short while. When it departed, telling the inhabitants that they would henceforth have to look after themselves, the raiders knew that they would have no organized military force to deal with again. They came in considerable numbers after that — but still only for loot.

Sixth : in 449 a desperate expedient was thought of. Hengist and Horsa were hired. They came with only a small number of men, and it was merely to protect the southeastern corner of Britain ; but they soon realized that their pickings would be greater if, instead of protecting those who had employed them, they did some looting on their own account. In the *Anglo-Saxon Chronicle*, as in Bede, we hear of three "keels" coming at first — which cannot have meant more than three hundred men. Other entries in the *Chronicle* are of the same sort ; three keels arrive, or four — hardly ever more at one time. Now compare this with the later Danish raids. From 833 on we hear of these pirates arriving on several occasions with over thirty ships, and in 851 the record is of three hundred and fifty ships. All this was on a much greater scale than anything the Anglo-Saxons had ever done. Yet the Danes did not conquer England, close though they came to doing so and though the time was to come when in Canute England had a Danish king. I submit that what is spoken of as the Anglo-Saxon conquest was an event that never happened, that was, in fact, physically impossible. There was, as in the later case of the Danes, a certain amount of settling on the eastern and southeastern coasts, but more often it was merely a question of collecting what booty was available and then getting out quickly.

Seventh : if Julius Caesar found the people living in Kent more civilized than those elsewhere in Britain, this was because their contact with the continent had a softening effect. The same was true of Kent at the time of the arrival of Saint Augustine in 596, and for much the same reason. He found in King Ethelbert a man well-disposed, married to a Christian wife who worshipped in an old church dedicated to Saint Martin in Canterbury, and with no less a person than a bishop as her private chaplain. This helps to explain Augustine's easy success.

Eighth : during Roman times Christianity had been introduced. We need not suppose that this meant that all the inhabitants of Britain were Christians. Even in Italy during the fifth century paganism continued to exist, and it must have been still more widespread among the Britons. But there was a strong British church.

Ninth : the Britons had tended to withdraw to the West, but not so much out of fear of being exterminated as because of their hearty hatred of the newcomers. No effort was made on the part of the British clergy to Christianize the Anglo-Saxons. On the contrary, they remained frigidly aloof and refused even to give any help to the Roman missionaries. When the controversy arose over the date at which Easter should be kept, and the style of the tonsure, what was at the bottom of the trouble was the British dislike for teutonic foreigners. It was this dislike that kept the controversy going so long.

At this point I had better turn to what documents we have. Bede freely drew upon Gildas, who wrote in the middle of the sixth century, not questioning his statements but calling him "their own historian," as he looked upon himself as the historian of the "English." I pause merely to remark that there were as yet no English ; that name has long been used to cover a whole nation, but it was slowly formed and made up of many elements. Bede himself notes that the "nations and provinces of Britain are divided into four languages — to wit, those of the Britons, the Picts, the Scots, and the English." In this connection we must remember that the Irish were originally called Scots and yet gave their name to Scotland.

Gildas has a very lurid account of the coming of "the fierce and impious Saxons, a race hateful both to God and men," and what he says is quoted almost verbatim by Bede, though without acknowledgments. But while Gildas has much to say about the depredations of "these most cruel robbers" he also says that under Ambrosius Aurelianus (who has been conjectured to be Arthur) a great victory was won at the siege of Bath Hill, "when took place also the last almost, though not the least slaughter of our cruel foes, which was (as I am sure) forty-four years and one month after the landing of the Saxons, and also the time of my own nativity." That battle therefore was in 493, and writing fifty years after it had taken place Gildas declares it to have been decisive : by the middle of the sixth century the Anglo-Saxon "conquest" had been checked. The question I should like to ask is this : if the Anglo-Saxons had not exterminated the Britons by the time Gildas wrote — which was about 550 — when did they exterminate them ?

I turn to Bede. He is writing of a battle in 633, forty years before he was born. A Christian British chieftain or "king," in alliance with Penda of the Mercians, who was a pagan, fights an "English" king, Edwin, and defeats and kills him in battle.

Rather bitterly for so gentle a man, Bede speaks of a conflict still going on between the British and the English, and certainly not in such terms as to lead us to suppose that the English were doing much more than hold their own. More friendly is his attitude to the settlements of the Picts and the Scots ; for the British he has few kind words. My point is that the evidence of this hostile but obviously honest witness all runs against the supposititious conquest.

But how did it happen then that, if the British, the original Celtic inhabitants of the island, did not disappear, their language did ? Well, this question of language is a curious one and not quite what we might suppose it to be. I mean that, with the growth of the concept of the nation, language has come to be looked upon as the national soul. That, however, was far from always being the case. The idea of such an entity as a "nation" was hardly conceivable to a man of the seventh century, and though the word itself existed, it meant a people or a race, not a political organism. Men's minds were still full of the Empire, and that could include any number of "nations" in what was at least a theoretical equality, just as the Church regards them all as equal.

Within the Empire Latin became the universal language, or at least existed side by side with the local vernacular. There was no disposition to hang on desperately to a national language as to a national flag. The determining factor everywhere in this matter of language was the factor of convenience.

Perhaps I may be allowed to take, by way of illustration, the more recent instance of Ireland and its Gaelic language. If Gaelic virtually disappeared in Ireland, it was not because the wicked English forcibly suppressed it — though heaven knows they were willing enough to see it disappear ; Gaelic tended

to die out for the simple reason that English was a more convenient language for the Irish to use.   Gaelic studies have for
some time been promoted among them, and very properly so ;
but it is hardly possible for even the greatest enthusiast for
Gaelic so much as to imagine its ever supplanting English.   At
best it can be merely a secondary tongue.

Yet Gaelic, it must be remembered, has a rich literature,
especially in poetry.   But if, even with that advantage, it declined, how could the native tongue be kept alive in Britain ?
If it survived among the Welsh, this was because the Welsh
were isolated ; even they did not develop a literature until
later.   The Celtic Cornish, not having such a literature, lost
their language altogether, though it survived in some districts
as a spoken vernacular until the eighteenth century.

With these cases in mind, let us see what happened in Britain
generally.

Those in the West and the centre of the island were cut off
from the rest of the world.   They were cut off by their
geographical position, since the southeastern corner — Kent,
where Saint Augustine settled — was the gateway to Europe
and European culture.   But the Britons also cut themselves off
deliberately, having scorn as well as hatred for the Anglo-
Saxons.   Bede notes Gildas's acknowledgment that the British
neglected their missionary opportunities.   It was part of their
exclusiveness.   They considered themselves, as inheritors of
the Roman order — though this had been allowed to fall into
decay among them — as infinitely superior to the barbarians.
In this, of course, they were under an illusion, for whatever
cultural superiority they had once possessed hardly existed
any longer.   But as such illusions powerfully affect the minds

of men, they often have to be allowed for and treated as though they were virtual realities.

The result of all this was that when civilization returned — one might almost say when Rome returned — it was through the missionaries sent to the Anglo-Saxons by Pope Gregory. New elements came to be added, as represented by Saint Theodore, a Greek, and Saint Adrian, an African; but the missionary effort remained a Roman affair, as it was of course entirely Catholic.

Now the British Christians were not Catholic, if judged by the test of having an apostolic spirit. Because of their withering exclusiveness they allowed such cultural influence as they might have possessed, had they chosen to exercise it, to pass from their hands into those of the new missionaries. Not only that, but they themselves declined culturally as a consequence of their exclusiveness. The result was that when England, or rather Britain, was at last thoroughly evangelized, the work was done by the Roman missionaries and their Anglo-Saxon disciples. It was these newly baptized Anglo-Saxons who promoted law ; it was they, too, who promoted letters. With the triumph of the Latin language, as used for official purposes, there went also the triumph of the Anglo-Saxon language as the vernacular. The fact that everybody came to speak Anglo-Saxon, except in Cornwall and Wales, eventually mingling with it a certain amount of Danish and Icelandic and (from the start) Latin, does not mean that everybody *was* Anglo-Saxon ; the fact merely means that the Anglo-Saxons had achieved a cultural, not a political or military, triumph. The Celtic spirit lingered on, and has always been very evident in English poetry, but the Celtic language had gone. The

Celtic blood, however, remained as the predominating strain in the English race. Such at any rate is my contention, and I think it receives strong indirect support from what Bede tells us in his *Ecclesiastical History*.

Much that Bede has to relate is concerned with the controversy over the date for the keeping of Easter and the form of the tonsure of the monks. (The British shaved their heads in front instead of their crowns.) Here merely a matter of discipline was involved, doctrine not entering into the discussion. In the ecclesiastical differences involved the Irish missionaries showed themselves amenable, but the British kept sullenly aloof, with the result of suffering a serious loss of prestige when the Roman order prevailed. They also lost the cultural advantages they would have gained by cooperating with the missionaries from the continent, and because of this their own culture further declined. Doomed from the start, because of their intransigent attitude, they lost ground steadily, and at the Council of Hereford, held in 673, the year of Bede's birth, the controverted issues were settled against them. After that the Celtic influence tended to fade out of all departments of life. In the end England became completely Anglo-Saxon in culture, but only because that culture had taken over the Roman discipline and organization. But I repeat that this by no means implied any lessening of the Celtic racial strain ; to this day it remains the predominant element in the English make-up.

Now I had better come to the Venerable Bede himself. Abbot Butler says of him that he "stands out as the first Benedictine student and scholar, the type for all time." And Newman remarks, "In his person and writings [he is] as truly the pattern of a Benedictine as is Saint Thomas of a Dominican."

That he was such a distinguished scholar is very remarkable when we consider that he came of a race only recently converted. It shows with what whole-hearted enthusiasm civilization was accepted by the converts of the Roman missionaries. But that civilization must also be seen as largely inaugurated by the Benedictine Order. Nowhere did it flourish more vigorously than in England. The monastery of Saint Peter and Paul, which was established at Canterbury in 600, was the first Benedictine community outside of Italy of which definite record exists. Abbot Tosti well might say, "In England the Benedictine order got blood and nerve from the strong race of the Anglo-Saxons."

I am not so much concerned, however, with Bede as a Benedictine as I am with him as a scholar, and especially as a historian. And in this capacity he has been given these words of praise from the eminent Theodore Mommsen : "He calls himself a 'verax historicus,' and he has a right to the title ; all who have followed in his tracks will testify that few writers have treated matters of fact with such, and often with laborious, accuracy." Bede makes his own claim in his preface to his *Life and Miracles of Saint Cuthbert* : "I have not presumed without minute investigation to write any of the deeds of so great a man, nor without the most accurate examination of credible witnesses to hand over what I had written to be transcribed. . . I sometimes inserted the names of these my authors, to establish the truth of my narrative, and thus ventured to put my pen to paper and to write. But when my work was arranged, but still kept back from publication, I frequently submitted it for perusal and correction to our reverend brother Herefrid the priest, and others, who for a long time had well known the life and conversation of that man of God. Some faults were, at their suggestion, carefully amended, and thus every scruple being utterly removed, I have taken care to commit to writing what I clearly ascertained to be the truth." Could anything be more conscientious ? Bede's historical sense — and his historical methods — are truly remarkable for his time, and in fact are without parallel then for their scientific accuracy. Though the documents at his disposal must have been meagre when compared with the appliances available to a modern writer, he made every effort to test his statements and to weigh the evidence he could obtain.

In addition Bede is always the artist. A historian may be very accurate, and yet quite wooden. Michelet said that it was the business of history to bring the dead to life. Well, Bede does just that. He puts flesh upon what he has to relate. Few more charming books have been written than his *Ecclesiastical History of the English People*. And though the least charming thing about it is its title, that is accurate ; it informs us precisely what the book is about. If its style is based upon the *Dialogues* of Saint Gregory the Great, Bede has a spirit all his own. From what he tells us we can reconstruct, better than from any other source, those early centuries ; and from the way he tells it, he brings it home to us.

He was a product of the twin monasteries of Wearmouth and Jarrow. No less a person than Alcuin, who was directing the revival of letters under Charlemagne, wrote : "Blessed by God indeed is the place which has deserved to have such teachers, and blessed those who dwelling there strive to carry out their teaching ! Remember what noble fathers you have had, and be not degenerate sons of such ancestors. Look at your treasures of books. Think of the beauty of your churches, the elegance of your monastic buildings. Meditate

on the order of regular life which is there established. Happy
the man who can pass from that peaceful home into the joys of
the heavenly kingdom !" Writing to the monks of Jarrow he
said, "Let your youths be taught Holy Scripture, that in
maturer years they may be able to instruct others. He who
learns not while he is young cannot teach when he grows up.
Remember that the most illustrious master of our age, the priest
Bede, had in his youth that great love of learning for which he
is now honoured among men, and has received great glory and
regard with God. By the thought of his example, then, rouse
up your minds if you be inclined to slumber. Listen to your
masters ; open your books, study what you find therein, and
seek to penetrate into its meaning. In this way you will feed
your own souls and be able, like him, to give unto others the
food of the spiritual life."

Abbot Butler, a Benedictine scholar of our own time, has
remarked that the learned Benedictine is a myth, and that even
Saint-Maur, which specialized in scholarship, produced only a
few scholars. He points out, indeed, that no one place can
ever be expected to turn out finished scholars by the bushel.
For though it may be much easier to produce scholars than to
produce poets, scholarship nevertheless calls for an aptitude
that few men possess. But while that is no doubt true, an
equally learned predecessor of Abbot Butler's at Downside,
Cardinal Gasquet, who became the president of the Pope's
commission for the revision of the Vulgate, is able to say of
Wearmouth and Jarrow : "It was from this monastery that
has come to us the best and most correct manuscript of the
Vulgate — a scientific achievement of the highest quality.
Let us try to realize what this simple fact means. We know
in our day, with all our modern aids and processes, the time,

labour, and anxious care that are involved in investigating the
Sacred Books in order to secure the best possible text.   Only
those who have been engaged in such studies can fully understand, or indeed form any idea of, the difficulty and complexity
of the task.   Now precisely the same problem presented itself
to the monks of Wearmouth and Jarrow at the close of the
seventh and the beginning of the eighth century.   The old and
new, or Vulgate, version had been long enough in existence
together to have permitted the production of manuscripts in
which the reading of both versions was mixed in hopeless confusion.   The task which Saint Bede and his fellow-monks put
before themselves, then, was to sift and sort the one from the
other, and thus to produce as pure a text as possible of our
Authorized Version of the Sacred Scripture, which we call the
Vulgate.   This was, indeed, an undertaking proper to task the
highest scientific qualities of any age.   How the monks of
Saint Bede's school succeeded, the still extant manuscript,
known as the great Codex Amiatinus, is sufficient evidence.
As may rightly be the case with men who do good work, they
were themselves not unconscious of the value and importance
of what they had achieved for the Church.   This is evident
from the fact that when the aged Abbot Coelfrid determined
to lay aside his lifelong work and retire to Rome to die, he
caused a copy of this Bible to be prepared for him to take as the
most fitting present to offer to the successor of Saint Peter."

Bede gives an account of Coelfrid's departure which was in
716, and these are among the most tender pages of his *Lives of
the Holy Abbots*.   The last scene of all may be inserted here :
"Whilst giving them his last farewell, he admonished them to
preserve love towards one another, and to correct, according to
the Gospel rule, those who did amiss : he forgave all of them

whatever wrong they might have done him ; and entreated
them all to pray for him, and to be reconciled to him, if he had
ever reprimanded them too harshly.   They went down to the
shore, and there, amid tears and lamentations, he gave them the
kiss of peace, as they knelt upon their knees ; and when he had
offered up a prayer he went on board the vessel with his companions . . . , leaving in both his monasteries about six hundred brethren."

That passage is less famous than the one in his *History* giving
an account of how Caedmon, the unlettered farm-hand at the
double-abbey of Whitby — for nuns as well as monks — that
was ruled by the celebrated Saint Hilda became a poet when
the angel commanded him to sing.   And quite as famous as
that is Coifi's apologue to King Edwin of the sparrow flying
into a bright banquet-room from the winter night and flying
out again into the night.   These bits from Bede are so well
known that they are often accounted part of English literature
— as in a sense they are — though they were written in Latin.
Our historian knew others of the Muses besides Clio — though
even of her many historians never seem to have heard — and
not only wrote an *Ars Poetica* but composed poems, some of
which he quoted with a kind of gentle vanity in his prose pages.
In fact, when writing his *Saint Cuthbert* he let his readers know
that he had already written the Saint's life in heroic verse, and
would be pleased to supply a copy to anybody who wanted to
see it.   This Latin discipline was, after all, needed as a preparation for any literature in the vernacular.

Bede was, in fact, a scholar whose gifts ranged widely, a
humanist born long before what is usually accounted due time.
And as such he performed a service for his country and for the
Church which can hardly be sufficiently valued, especially as

it came just when it did, so early in English history. Yet scholarship, engrossing as it was, never made him forget that he was a monk and that for the monk the chief work was the *Opus Dei*, to which as Saint Benedict's Rule puts it, nothing was to be preferred. About Bede the monk Alcuin wrote to the monks at Jarrow : "Our master and your patron is reported to have said : 'I know that angels come to the canonical hours and to the assemblies of the brethren. What if they did not find me among my brothers ? Would they not have reason to say, *"Ubi est Baeda ?* Where is Bede ? Why does he not come with the brethren to the appointed services ?"' We may be sure that he was rarely if ever absent. The Office for his Feastday tells his whole story as monk and scholar in a single sentence — *Semper legit, semper scripsit, semper docuit, semper oravit* : He was always reading, always writing, always teaching, always praying."

In the pages of his *History* Bede was constantly, though quite unconsciously, revealing his own character. So he was also in his *Lives of the Holy Abbots.* What he has to say of Easterwine and Coelfrid and Benet Biscop and Sigfrid would seem to apply almost as much to himself as to them. Especially is this true of Abbot Benet Biscop as he approached death : then "to lessen the wearisomeness of the night, which from his illness he often passed without sleeping, [he] would frequently call a reader, and cause him to read aloud, as an example for himself, the history of the patience of Job, or some other extract from Scripture, by which his pains might be alleviated, and his depressed soul be raised to heavenly things. And because he could not get up to pray, nor without difficulty lift up his voice to the usual extent of daily psalmody, the prudent man, in his zeal for religion, at every hour of daily or nightly prayer would call to him some of the brethren, and making them sing psalms in two companies, would himself sing with them, and thus make up by their voices for the deficiency of his own."

His own passing was made in just the same style. We have a description of his death left by his disciple Cuthbert, and this I quote in the translation made of it by Cardinal Newman. "He was," writes Cuthbert, "exceedingly oppressed with shortness of breathing, though without pain, before Easter for about a fortnight. But he rallied and was full of joy and gladness, and gave thanks to Almighty God day and night and every hour up to Ascension Day. And he gave us, his scholars, daily lectures, and passed the rest of the day in singing Psalms, and the night, too, in joy and thanksgiving — except the scanty time which he gave to sleep. And as soon as he woke he was busy in his accustomed way, and he never ceased with uplifted hands giving thanks to God. I solemnly protest, never have I seen or heard of anyone who was so diligent in thanksgiving.

"He sang that sentence of the blessed Apostle Paul, 'It is a dreadful thing to fall into the hands of the living God' ; and many other passages of Scripture, in which he warned us to shake off the slumber of soul, by anticipating our last hour. And he sang verses of his own in English also, to the effect that no one could be too well prepared for his end — viz., in calling to mind, before he departs hence, what good or evil he has done and how his judgment will lie. And he sang, too, the antiphons, of which one is, 'O King of Glory, Lord of Angels, Who this day ascended in triumph above all the heavens, leave us not orphans, but send the promise of the Father upon us, the Spirit of Truth !' And when he came to the words, 'leave us not orphans,' he burst into tears and wept much. He said, too, 'God scourgeth every son whom He receiveth' ; and with Saint

Ambrose, 'I have not so lived as to be ashamed to have been among you ; nor do I fear to die, for we have a good Lord.'

"In those days, besides our lectures and psalmody, he was engaged in two works : he was translating into English the Gospel of Saint John, as far as the words, 'But what are these among so many ?' and some extracts from the *Notae* of Isidore. On Tuesday before Ascension Day he began to suffer more in his breathing, and his feet were slightly swollen. However, he went on through the day dictating cheerfully ; and he kept saying from time to time, 'Take down what I say quickly ; for I know not how long I am to last, or whether my Maker will not take me soon.' He seemed to us to be quite aware of the time of his going, and he passed that night in giving thanks, without sleeping. As soon as morning broke — that is, on the Wednesday — he urged me to make haste with the writing we had begun. We did so until nine o'clock, when we walked in procession with the relics of the saints, according to the usage of that day. But one of our party said to him, 'Dearest master, one chapter is still wanting ; can you bear our asking you about it ?' He answered, 'I can bear it ; take your pen and be ready to write quickly.'

"At three o'clock he said to me : 'Run fast and call the priests, that I may divide among them some little gifts that I have in my box.' When I had done this in much agitation, he spoke to each, urging and entreating them all to make a point of saying Masses and prayers for him. Thus he passed the day until evening, when the above-mentioned youth said to him : 'Dear master, there is yet one sentence not written.' He answered : 'Write it quickly.' Presently the youth said: 'Now it is finished.' He replied : 'Good ! Thou hast said the truth — *consummatum est !* Take my head into thy hands ; for it is very pleasant for me to sit facing my old praying-place, and thus to call upon my Father.' And so on the floor of the cell he sang : 'Glory be to the Father, Son and Holy Ghost !' And just as he said 'Holy Ghost,' he breathed his last and went to the realms above."

I know of no more beautiful death — the monk and scholar and poet dying as he had lived. In his death he taught, as he worked to his last breath. One can see that the disciple who has given us this account was Bede's disciple indeed — accurate, precise, anxious that the last task be finished, but tender in his solicitude, lest he be taxing the old man too much ; above all he was, like his teacher, an artist who caught and imparted to us the aroma that comes from the memory of the Venerable Bede.

IV

SAINT DOMINIC

On coming to Saint Dominic one finds hardly anything of that abundant and beautiful literature which clusters around his contemporary and friend Saint Francis of Assisi. In fact, he strikes most people, I suppose, as a figure shadowy and at the same time stiff. But while surely nobody would wish to make the least detraction from Saint Francis's unique fragrance and charm, I think it is no more than truth that his legend has sometimes bewitched the world for not quite the right reasons. He did a good deal more than pick flowers and pat animals, or the other things that sentimentalists and even sceptics find so attractive in him. The incident of the Wolf of Gubbio is, after all, much less important than his stigmata. This is not of course to suggest that Francis is not a wonderful exemplar of the poetry of Christianity, but perhaps what I am trying to say may be illustrated by that very learned French Protestant, Paul Sabatier, to whose Franciscan studies we owe so much. He was carried away by his enthusiasm to such an extent that at the end of his life he expressed privately the opinion that Francis of Assisi was a greater man than Jesus Christ. After that, one naturally wonders whether M. Sabatier could ever have had any real understanding of Francis at all.

The misunderstandings with regard to Saint Dominic are of a different sort. Even that he offered to amalgamate his order with that founded by his friend Saint Francis — if it is certain that he did — has somehow been twisted to Dominic's discredit. The suggestion is commonly made that Francis recoiled in alarm at the proposal, with the further hint that he did not wish to have too close an association with this "bloody monk," as Dominic has sometimes been called. Might we not rather suggest that the practical Dominic perceived that the Franciscan idea, beautiful as it was, would lead to just the things that we know did happen — discord and division and confusion — and that he knew that his own organizing ability would give the balance and control that were needed ? Conjectural as all this must be, it is certain that what Dominic did in a few years — only five years as actual head of a religious order — has sufficed for all the centuries that followed, whereas the Franciscan quarrels, which sometimes led the extremists very close to positive heresy, started the moment that Francis died, if they had not begun even before that date. The value of Franciscanism is that it lives as a lovely dream, a shining ideal. The value of the work initiated by Dominic is that it was a carefully thought-out plan, which contains within itself all necessary powers of adjustment to new conditions. There was no Dominican rule ; instead the Rule of Saint Augustine sufficed, with the general chapter of the Order legislating from time to time — providing the working Constitutions and so keeping everything flexible and up-to-date.

No essential difference existed between the two orders of friars regarding the end each sought to attain — not even on the subject of poverty, though poverty is supposed to be, in a special sense, the Bride of the Poverello of Assisi. But there was a considerable difference between Dominic and Francis on the means of attaining that end. Francis definitely discouraged, for example, bookishness among his followers — not merely the possession of books but a knowledge of books. And this went rather deeper than a perception of the fact that a knowledge of books would necessitate their possession — at any rate by the community — and that the possession of books, because of their costliness in those days, was inconsistent with poverty. Yet as a somewhat bookish man myself, I can see Francis's point. It is all too easy to grow dusty and musty in libraries. "If I read as many books as that man," said somebody, "I would become as stupid as he is." The poet Francis understood that danger. At the same time it must be admitted that, if the Franciscans were to do their work, they had to become learned men ; and learning soon did appear among them. Saint Bonaventure came on the scene at the same time as his friend, the Dominican Saint Thomas Aquinas, and was summoned by much the same circumstances. In this matter, therefore, Saint Francis, while he may be admired for his idealism, cannot be praised without qualifications for his discernment. He was a visionary, a poet, as contrasted with Dominic, the wonderful organizer of an enthusiasm hardly distinguishable from his own. If poets are always more attractive than organizers, nobody need grudge that advantage to them ; it is one of the very few advantages that poets have — and even this is usually accorded them only after they are dead.

But that Dominic was a great organizer, this itself is something that is not generally known. In the popular imagination the one clearly fixed notion is of Dominic as an Inquisitor — even as the founder of the Inquisition, as many people still suppose. Some of his Catholic biographers have themselves lent support to this error. Thus I find in his life as written by the famous English Dominican nun, Augusta Theodosia Drane, this sentence, "It is the constant tradition of the Order that Saint Dominic was the first Inquisitor" — though of course she goes on to point out that his activities as such were always upon the side of mercy. But her book was published in 1891, and I do not believe it would be possible to find any Dominican today who assents to her thesis. Father John B. O'Connor, for example, an American Dominican who wrote in 1916, simply points out that the Inquisition was in operation in 1198, at which time Dominic Guzman was still an unknown canon of Osma, and that he did not arrive in Languedoc until 1205. And the most learned of all authorities on Saint Dominic, Pierre Mandonnet, remarks : "Whatever may be said to the contrary, Dominic never exercised the office of a judge delegated for the prosecution of heresy, an office instituted by Gregory IX twelve years after the saint's death." The most that can be asserted is that Dominic sometimes had authority delegated to him by the Abbot of Cîteaux, for we find him writing : "To all the faithful in Christ to whom these presents may come, Brother Dominic, canon of Osma, the least of preachers, wishes health in the Lord. By the authority of the Lord Abbot of Cîteaux, who has committed to us this office, we have reconciled to the Church the bearer of these presents, Ponce Roger, converted by the grace of God from heresy to the faith." It is true that after Dominic's death the Pope insisted on the office of Inquisitor being held by a selected group of Dominicans, though this was sometimes shared with Franciscans. I need not go further in the subject except to say that the *Spanish* Inquisition — which is what most people have in mind — was a very different institution from the Roman Inquisition, and that the extirpation of heresy is, after all, the greatest work of charity that can be performed by man.

To extirpate heresy was certainly Saint Dominic's mission. But this was something to be done by preaching, and therefore to lay too great an emphasis upon the word "extirpation" may be misleading. So let me quote Père Mandonnet again : "The joint action of Saint Dominic and the papacy created a militia wholly devoted to the apostolic life, that is, to the religious development and sanctification of souls. In Dominic the medieval world realized its first great type of apostle ; in fact, no one before him had consecrated his whole strength and his whole life to the sole and permanent preaching of the gospel. This initial personal impulse communicated to the foundation of the Preachers an intensity of apostolic life which character-ized the order in the first century." In short, the whole object of Dominic was preaching and the creation of the Order of Preachers, and though he was inspired to do this by the challenge of heresy, he by no means conceived of his mission in the negative terms of refuting heresy but of propagating the truth.

Today we find it a little hard to realize how novel was the program Saint Dominic set before himself. Now most priests preach every Sunday — not always very well, to be sure, but as a matter of course. It was not so during the early middle ages. Then the office of preaching was looked upon as one of the special functions of the bishops. Saint Jerome had said, "The duty of a monk is not to teach, but to weep" ; and though many monks did magnificent work in evangelizing pagan countries, monastic preaching continued to be thought of as permissible only under special circumstances and was not en-couraged in a settled Christian society. As a pope said roundly : "Whatever a monk's knowledge, he should not presume to teach."

But by the opening of the thirteenth century a change had come. The Church came to see that preachers were urgently called for, and that the bishops were often not fulfilling the preacher's office. For that matter, the bishops were unable to preach, except in their cathedrals or when making a visitation ; and many of them were inclined to neglect their duty or had no natural qualifications for it. At the Fourth Lateran Council in 1213, which was held after Saint Dominic had begun his work, the tenth canon enacted read as follows : "It often happens that bishops, on account of their manifold duties or bodily infirmities, or because of hostile invasions or other reasons, to say nothing of lack of learning, which must be absolutely condemned in them and is not to be tolerated in the future, are themselves unable to minister the word of God to the people, especially in large and widespread dioceses. Wherefore we decree that bishops provide suitable men, powerful in word and work, to exercise with fruitful result the office of preaching. . . Wherefore we command that in cathedral churches as well as in conventual churches suitable men be appointed whom the bishops may use as coadjutors and assistants. . . If anyone neglect to comply with this, he shall be subject to severe penalties."

But before this was done officially and by the Church, something had been attempted unofficially. Preaching movements had arisen spontaneously, many of them on the part of itinerant laymen. But though these laymen were often very well intentioned, as was true of the early Waldenses, they tended to draw away from the Church, and even when they did not, they were seldom well equipped and so did perhaps more harm than good. Yet this lay preaching, even in churches, was not entirely discountenanced, and in fact went on for some time. The first Franciscans preached as laymen. And as late as the seventeenth century we find Saint Philip Neri preaching as a layman and — after he had belatedly become a priest and founded the Oratory — using laymen to instruct the Brethren, though in this case not precisely as preachers. The crying need of the Church was for preaching.

Saint Norbert, the founder of the Premonstratensian Canons, a century before Saint Dominic appeared, recognized this need and, in his efforts to meet it, foreshadowed the work of the Dominicans. That opportunity, however, was largely lost because Saint Norbert did not detach himself from the older concepts of monasticism. Though like the Dominicans who were to come, the Premonstratensians followed the Rule of Saint Augustine, they tended to conform their way of life to that of Cîteaux — and this was hardly consistent either with the poverty expected of the preacher, or the mobility demanded of him.

Saint Dominic, on the other hand, represents a radical departure from monasticism, as it had been previously understood. He was, like Saint Norbert, a canon, for he had begun his career in Spain by being attached to a group of canons whose duty it was to say the choral office in the cathedral of Osma, where they lived under a regular rule. And to this day Dominicans, though they are of course mendicant friars, delight to recall this historical link with canons regular, for whom an essential part of their work is the saying of office in choir.

How then was there a departure from the Benedictine norm? For one thing, the Office was said more rapidly and with less solemnity, as the Friar Preacher had so many other occupations that it was impossible to devote more than a minimum of time to the choir. Even so, duties proved so multifarious that a system of dispensations on a wide scale had to be introduced for the benefit of those otherwise occupied;

and to the Superior was accorded full power of dispensing himself.

Furthermore, a feature of the older monastic life was manual work. It is true that as time went on such work was not particularly onerous, and labour in the fields was commonly exchanged for the gentle occupation of the copying of books. From this the Friar Preacher had to be freed if he was to preach ; in that work he would have quite enough to do.

Merely by copying books a man does not necessarily become learned. And though there were learned Benedictines, learning was not essential to them. It was quite different with the Dominicans. To do their distinctive work it was imperative that they should study, for a preacher does not as a rule accomplish anything very solid merely on the strength of his own imagination or his own fervours. Study, therefore, while it was never regarded as the end of the Dominican life, was necessary as a means to that end. The friars therefore not only had to study but to study intensely.

There was something else : a man who knows also wants to teach, or should have that desire. Accordingly the Friars Preachers soon organized theological schools. These they could have kept exclusively for their own use, and today, under changed circumstances, a Dominican house of studies is for Dominicans just as a Jesuit house of studies is for Jesuits. But that would have been a rather selfish procedure during the Middle Ages, because of the dearth of such schools : therefore these were open to all capable of following the courses. In a city which already had a university and a department of theology, the Dominicans were incorporated into its faculty ; when a new university was founded in a place where a

Dominican house already existed and was teaching, that house was considered the department of theology.

What made all this possible was a radical departure from the massive stolidity of monasticism in its older forms. I remind you again that each Benedictine abbey was autonomous, and that the monk was attached to the abbey and that it was to the abbey that he vowed stability. There it was that he lived, and there it was that he died. This concentration of effort was of enormous benefit during the early Middle Ages, as it enabled the abbey to become the focal point, and the point of balance, for a whole district. Now new conditions prevailed. The population was rapidly shifting to the towns, and there, even when abbeys existed — and they were nearly all in country districts — they could not operate as they had done in a rural society. The friars — especially the Dominicans — tended to settle in the larger cities, as it was there that they could best accomplish their mission.

> *Bernardus valles, montes Benedictus amabat,*
> *Oppida Franciscus, celebres Dominicus urbes.*

But it was not merely necessary for the Dominicans that they should be established in the centres of population ; it was also necessary that they should be distributed in smaller groups and that the individual friar could be moved from point to point as his services were needed. Therefore instead of being attached to a particular house, he was attached to his province, and could even be transferred from one province to another. This brought about the mobility, lacking which the Premonstratensians had failed to carry out the work their founder had had in mind. It was a novel concept of the monastic life — one which we now take for granted but which seemed revolutionary when it was first introduced. Quite deliberately Saint Dominic — and this at a time when he still had only a very few disciples — sent them out, as Christ had sent out His disciples, by twos, with no money in their purses — preachers who begged their way as they went, God's light militia.

The Dominicans shared this feature of mobility, as also that of an absolute poverty, with the Franciscans and the other orders of friars. But the reason for it should be understood. There was an intimate association in the popular mind between the apostolic life and poverty. Saint Dominic discovered early in his career that the Albigenses were not favorably impressed by the Cistercians who had been sent to convert them because these kept up an abbatial state. Nor can it be denied that many of the abbeys had become, as corporations, extremely wealthy — much too wealthy for the personal good of the monks, and much too wealthy also for the exercise of spiritual influence. The monks were regarded as stockholders in large thriving concerns, even though theoretically each monk owned nothing himself. The friar perceived that he had to strip himself of all possessions if he was to accomplish anything.

Their mendicancy may strike us as rather extravagant, but was really a practical approach to the problems that confronted the preacher. Yet I am far from suggesting that Saint Dominic was merely being "practical" in this matter. He sought poverty — a real poverty — just as Saint Francis sought it. For both men it was something to be valued for its own sake, as a means of personal perfection. To follow Christ one had to be poor, and only to one recognized as a follower of Christ was the world prepared to listen.

The sons of Saint Dominic, however, had in this matter, as in others, their Father's good sense. Therefore the Constitutions of the Order amended the form of the practice of poverty and actual mendicancy ceased. I quote : "The possession of revenues in common (it is said) is not contrary to the Rule of Saint Augustine which we profess, neither does it necessarily diminish religious perfection, for poverty is not perfection, but a means to perfection. As therefore, an instrument is not used for its own sake, but because of the end it serves, it is not to be considered better in proportion as it is great, but rather in so far as the poverty it professes adapts itself either to the general end of all religious life, which is the service of God, or some special end, such as contemplation, or the instruction of our neighbour. And this seems best secured by that kind of poverty which provides frugally for the necessities of life, procured without too great solicitude, and used in common."

Saint Antoninus, the fifteenth-century Dominican Archbishop of Florence, has his explanation of the abandonment of the practice of strict mendicancy. He said that in earlier times there were not so many orders that lived solely upon alms, and that therefore it was then possible to live upon them. Moreover wars, and habits of luxury (or, as we should say, the standard of living) had mounted among the laity, so that there was less to spare for the friars. Finally, people had come to be more disposed to give for the adornment of churches than for the needs of the poor. The pressure of circumstances did no doubt necessitate the theoretical argument I have quoted from the Dominican Constitutions, though the theory did not imply a surrender of principle or permit that accumulation of wealth hardly to be avoided by an abbey supported by wide estates. Yet while admitting the force of all this, the mind travels back in a mood of nostalgia to the beauty of the primitive life. It is a youth that has gone, lovely and to some extent absurd. For all but those minds most hardened by the experiences of maturity delight to dwell upon the rainbow years.   Most of us come sooner or later to regret that practical considerations alter the shape of our dreams.   Fortunate are they who do not deny the glory of the dream !

This early Dominican poverty has a most charming legend connected with it.   There are two versions of the story, which may mean that there were two separate incidents, or that the same story has been told in slightly different ways.   It appears that the friars who had been sent out by Saint Dominic from Saint Sixtus in Rome to beg came home one day with nothing except a joyful look.   They had been able to obtain only one loaf, and feeling that this was not going to be of much use in feeding a whole community, they gave it to a poor man. When they told this to Saint Dominic, he said, "That man was an angel ; God will know how to provide for His own." Then, though he knew that there was nothing to eat, he had the brethren called to the refectory, and the blessing was given. The moment this had been done two beautiful young men came in, carrying loaves in white cloths slung over their shoulders. Before each friar they placed a loaf, and departed, without saying who they were.   Then Dominic told those whose duty it was to serve at table, "Bring us some wine."   And when they answered, "Father, there is no wine," he told them nevertheless to bring the wine the Lord had sent.   They found that of bread and wine they had enough for three days, during which nobody had to go out to beg.   There was even enough for them to be able to distribute some to the poor.

And this leads me to say that, grimly as the features of Saint Dominic have sometimes been drawn, we constantly hear in his life of extraordinary acts of corporal charity.   His spiritual works of mercy — directed to the salvation of souls — were even greater, but the physical works of mercy are the things more easily seen and estimated. Twice in his youth, out of pity for the Christian captives taken by the Moors, he tried to sell himself, so as to redeem others with the purchase price. Almost as astonishing in some respects is the way, when he was still a canon in Spain, he sold his books in order to give the proceeds to the poor. For a scholar even today to sell his beloved books would be about as big a sacrifice as he could make, but it was a heroic sacrifice in days when books were so expensive and so hard to come by. In addition, these books of Dominic's were full of his annotations that made them all the more of service to him. He is the only saint of whom such a thing is recorded, for though centuries later Saint Philip Neri also sold his books, this was because he had decided that he had no further use for them. But Saint Dominic was giving away his very heart's blood, as every scholar will understand.

Let us examine briefly the charges of sternness and even of cruelty that have frequently been brought against him. During the Albigensian crusade he was indeed present in the camp of Simon de Montfort before the battle of Muret in 1213 ; but all that he did was to pray for victory — a victory which seemed so amazing that de Montfort attributed it to Dominic's prayers. And when at the taking of Béziers a massacre followed, Saint Dominic was in no way responsible. Probably the too famous story of Arnold of Cîteaux is apocryphal, for according to this he told the soldiers, "Kill, kill, for God will know His own !" As for Dominic, even the account that represents him as going through the streets of the city, crucifix in hand, to plead for the lives of the women and children and the aged, has no foundation. It was doubtless what he would have done, had he been present ; but he happened not to be there at all. His methods with the heretics were always those of persuasion.

But before touching upon this, I think I should remind you that a lot of sympathy was at one time whipped up for the Albigenses, who used to figure as a kind of early Protestant group. The fact is that they were not Christians at all — not even Christian heretics. Lea himself, in his *History of the Inquisition,* admits that "if the Albigensians had triumphed, Europe would have returned to the horrors of barbarism." Manichean pessimists, thoroughly anti-social, and politically very powerfully entrenched, they threatened for a long while the whole fabric of civilization. From the point of view of the kings of France and England they .were such a menace that there was no means of dealing with them except that of extermination. The age being what it was, one can hardly blame de Montfort for his harshness.

But though a defence can be offered for de Montfort, if the temper of the times be remembered, it is not necessary to use such a defence for Dominic. Severity did not enter into his methods. He set himself to win the Albigenses by reason, also bringing into play his charm of manner and his kindness, qualities without which mere logic is commonly of very little use. And here I think the best words on the subject are those used by Father John-Baptist Reeves in his admirable little book, *The Dominicans* : "It was from the first the assumption of Saint Dominic that, their leaders excepted, the Albigensians were sound at heart and confused in mind. He took it for granted that to introduce them to Truth was to lead them directly to all virtue. His limitation, if such it may fairly be called, was an apparent inability to conceive malice or meanness in another.

The same characteristic is very deeply ingrained in his Order. . . . Hence the Dominican insistence on the liberty of the individual and his right to be trusted which must often appear excessive to those whose vocation is more expressly to 'rebuke the unquiet, comfort the feeble-minded and support the weak.' The same critics also find that Dominicans have an exaggerated respect for the intelligence of simple people, are too prone to see good in sinners and truth in heresy, are too impatient of easy explanations of doctrine and labour-saving refutations of error, too ready to concede points to an unscrupulous or prejudiced opponent, and too apt in their zeal for Truth to scandalize weaker brethren and offend pious ears."

I offer Father Reeves's comment at this point because it presents the whole apologetic issue. To my mind it was the main defect of that notable Catholic apologist, Orestes Brownson, that he took an exactly opposite line and thought he had accomplished his task when he had crushed his opponents in debate. He did not trust human nature sufficiently, nor would he admit that most men — however muddled they may be — are at bottom men of good will. Therefore he looked for error to confute, and seemed almost to be equally satisfied if the error was a large one or a small one. He hunted his game with as much zest when he went out after a mosquito as when he went out after a lion. The result was that while his reasoning may have done much to stimulate the intelligence of Catholics, it did hardly anything to bring about what he professed was his purpose, the winning of men to the acceptance of the truth.

Let me quote Father Reeves again, in the interesting contrast he draws between the Dominican, the Franciscan, and the Jesuit methods. "If Saint Dominic had a defect it would seem to have been inability to conceive of a man whose heart was

evil or of one whose mind was not full of questions for Christ
to answer. If Saint Francis had a defect it must have been inability to see how anything but moral fault could keep a man
from joyously accepting anything and everything that Christ
and His Church might choose to teach. Saint Dominic's mission was to fill men's minds as full of truth as they could hold ;
the mission of Saint Francis was to fill men's hearts as full of
love as they could hold. From the first it was evident that
though the emphasis was different the two were doing the same
work. . . The Jesuit emphasis, like the Franciscan, is all on the
will : its perilous power of blindly choosing evil, and of dark-
ening the mind and quenching its natural thirst for truth ; its
need of moral reform as a step to the liberation of the mind.
The Dominican mission is to men whose will is actually as good
as to be urging their minds to seek truth. The mission of
Franciscans and Jesuits is to men whose wills are potentially
good but actually enslaved by evil, which in its turn enslaves
the mind. They first of all address themselves, not like the
Dominicans to the mind with pure cold reason, but to the will :
Jesuits directly by commands, exhortations, and threats ; Franciscans, indirectly through imagination and emotion by bright
fancy and the cheerful warmth of affection. This last difference brings the Franciscan nearer to the Dominican than to the
Jesuit vocation : its method is more objective. At the same
time it brings the Jesuit vocation nearer to the Dominican than
to the Franciscan : for Jesuits and Dominicans are both more
concerned with heresy and therefore with arguments in defence of faith." I am sure, however, that Father Reeves does
not mean to assert that he has quite satisfactorily labelled and
pigeon-holed these orders, or intended more than to give gen-
eralities that might help us to get a comprehensive view.

When Dominic took *Veritas* as his motto he was not preempting truth or suggesting that other Catholic champions were indifferent to it.   All he was doing was indicating his own line of approach.   Yet even that line will not be properly understood unless it is seen to be psychological as well as logical.   There is no *one* way of leading men to truth ; truth is rather reached by many converging roads, and the mind is not completely convinced until everything contributes to its conviction.   That is why Augusta Theodosia Drane says of Saint Dominic : "Persuasion was not an art, but nature.   It was the effect of that admirable union of patience, prudence, and firmness, tempered with the charm of a sweet and tranquil gaiety."   But it was all directed by loving-kindness ; and on this Blessed Jordan, who was his successor as Master General of the Friars Preachers, was to write : "His one constant petition to God was for the gift of a true charity ; for he was convinced that he could not be truly a member of Christ unless he consecrated himself wholly to the work of gaining souls, following the example of Him Who sacrificed Himself for our redemption."

No words of this saint have come down to us, at least not in his own writing.   But we have his portrait as painted in words for us by those who knew him.   He was a slightly-built, auburn-bearded man, whose hair was never more than faintly streaked with grey.   His eyes shone luminously, full of love.   And his gentleness and affable temper were noted by all.   Yet more to the point is what we are told of his habits of prayer.   He never spoke except to God or of God.   After his long busy day he spent most of the night in the chapel, praying until he had at last to get an hour or two of sleep — which he usually took stretched out on the step of the altar.   His gift of tears was so great that the drops flowed down his face in a constant stream while he was praying. Visions often came to him, and in spite of a life of intense activity he was a contemplative. But contemplation was one of the parts of the dual Dominican contemplation, and his son Saint Thomas Aquinas has for all time fixed this in a phrase, *Contemplata aliis tradere*. Books were to be studied, and he founded a learned order — the first professedly learned order. Yet books themselves were to be used as aids to contemplation which, with Dominic, was not to be regarded merely as an end in itself but the basis of what the Friars were to preach to the world.

This made the Dominican life a very difficult one, especially in view of the austerity of the rule. For this reason there have always been Dominicans who, unable to effect a perfect union of the two lives, have mainly devoted themselves to mysticism. Among these have been Blessed Henry Suso and John Tauler and Master Eckhart. Yet it should be said that the great saints of the Order have all been extremely active — Vincent Ferrer and Hyacinth and Louis Bertrand, even Saint Thomas Aquinas, who managed to be one of the most industrious of teachers and writers and at the same time one of the loftiest of mystics, and Catherine of Siena, the ecstatic who nevertheless was immersed in political affairs. In her case the fusion of activity and mysticism was so complete that she could dictate to her secretaries while she was in trance.

The name of Saint Catherine leads me to mention that, before the Friars Preachers were founded, Saint Dominic had established at Prouille in France a convent of nuns — so that with the Dominicans the second order (one of pure contemplation) preceded the first order. But Saint Catherine was not a member of the second order but a tertiary. She was not a nun, but lived at home, as did the first canonized saint of America, the Dominican Rose of Lima.

The mention of the third order also calls for a word of comment. Augusta Theodosia Drane tells us that Saint Dominic conceived it as a military order. That, however, is not quite the case. All that can really be said is that very soon there were groups of enthusiastic laymen who gathered round the Friars, but it was not until well into the thirteenth century — in 1285 to be precise — that the third order was canonically founded, and then it received women as well as men. The military idea has just this much basis : Saint Dominic suggested to his lay followers that they should not bear arms except in defence of the Church.

The Franciscan third order long preceded the Dominican. But there was a third order which preceded both, that of the Premonstratensians, about which the world knows little ; and though the Benedictine Oblates (who are older still) are not, properly speaking, a third order — for Saint Benedict wrote only one rule — they are for practical purposes treated as such. Of all these lay bodies associated with religious orders, none has had anything like the huge enrollment of the Franciscan tertiaries, of whom there are now several millions. But this indicates that the Franciscans were always a popular order (also that Francis of Assisi is an extremely popular saint), whereas the Dominicans, though their influence among the people was hardly less than that of the Franciscans, drew from an élite and chose to concentrate on quality instead of quantity even with regard to their tertiaries.

Yet what is incomparably the most popular of Catholic devotions — always excepting, of course, that centred in the Blessed

Sacrament — is the Rosary, and the Rosary, according to Dominican tradition, was given to Saint Dominic by Our Lady herself. Concerning this there has been a good deal of controversy, into which it would be out of place to enter here. There is no use in denying, however, that there were various forms of the Rosary before Saint Dominic's time and that the Rosary, as we know it, did not come into general use until long afterwards. But there can be no doubt that it was the Dominicans who popularized this simple and effective method of meditation. Now that the dust of battle has blown over, I suppose we may take what Father Reeves says on the subject as the opinion generally accepted by the Dominicans themselves. It makes all due allowances for historical criticism while giving the Friars Preachers all due credit. He says : "It is neither reasonable nor desirable to accept [the actual giving of the Rosary to Saint Dominic by the Blessed Virgin] as a literal statement of historic fact. From very early days the Order had had zeal for the chronicling of such legends, and in 1256 it made an official collection of all bearing on its own history. Though this is avowedly incomplete, the absence of all mention of the Rosary in it and all other documents until the fifteenth century is sufficient evidence that this devotion was a late development. But that it developed within the Order in a characteristically Dominican manner, and out of elements existing there from the beginning, is beyond the possibility of a reasonable doubt." With that we may safely let the question rest. It is of no vital consequence how the Rosary originated, but there is considerable significance in the fact that it was this learned order, which produced the most luminous of Catholic minds, which also produced the most popular of Catholic devotions.

One would have expected Saint Dominic to have attracted to

him only a small number of men because of the high demands he made.   An élite was called for, and (though the terms sound contradictory) a large élite was found.   There has never been anything to compare with the rapid growth of the Dominicans except the flame of the Franciscan enthusiasm which overran the world at the same time, and that enthusiasm was really only another aspect of the same impulse which brought the Dominicans into being.   But though at first the Friars Minor made no special appeal to the highly educated — something soon to be changed — from the outset the Friars Preachers were men of high intellectual gifts and of learning.   Indeed, only men of this stamp were eligible for admission, unless in the ranks of the lay-brothers.   Yet in spite of the requirements, the order grew by leaps and bounds.   In 1216 Saint Dominic had only sixteen followers.   Five years later, when he died, the Friars Preachers had sixty houses and eight provinces.   Sixty years later again there were four hundred houses, and by 1303 nearly six hundred.   As for the numbers of the Friars, forty years after the foundation there were five thousand of them, with perhaps another couple of thousand studying to become priests.   By 1337 the Order had twelve thousand members.   The fact is clear that the need for preachers after the long period of dearth sufficed to call them forth.   Periods of decline occurred — as with every religious order — but the chief thing to note is that Dominic perceived what it was that his age most urgently required and set himself to supply it.   So well had he laid the foundations that his work went on without interruption though he himself died at forty-one, only five years after his order had received papal approbation.

A notion used to be prevalent, even among some Dominicans,

that Innocent III was reluctant to sanction a new order. The basis of this idea of there having been any hesitation on the part of the Pope is the fact that Dominic was required to select one of the already existing religious rules. But Père Mandonnet comments that it would be much nearer the truth to say that when Saint Dominic proposed his plans, "the Holy See uttered a sigh of relief and cried 'At last!'" Elsewhere in his book *Saint Dominic and his Work* he says again : "In confiding to an order the work of preaching, which had been guarded by the bishops from the first centuries as their personal office, and in making the preachers dependent on the papacy alone, the popes were truly playing their last card. Never would they have been equal to the move had they not been convinced that the good of the Church required it, and that the spirit and organization of the Order of Preachers corresponded fully to the need."

With another quotation from Mandonnet I conclude. The whole secret of the matter is contained in the following two sentences : "The personal sanctification of the Preacher was not conceived in an absolute sense or for itself, but relative to the special aim of an apostolic order. Since for every Christian sanctity consists in the exact accomplishment of the duties of his vocation, the Preacher had to sanctify himself by fulfilling the obligations of his state." In other words, with the Dominicans there arrived what was almost a new concept of sanctity, a sanctity not thought of as a merely personal affair — though of course the personal element in the matter necessarily remained — but as a sanctity achieved through work, and specifically through apostolic work. It would be an exaggeration to say that for the Friar his own holiness was secondary to his preaching, in the sense that his learning was secondary to his preaching.   Rather it was that, while preaching was the formal object of his order, it presupposed learning and holiness.   The Dominican was to preach "by word and works," and in saving others, he saved himself.

V

SAINT LOUIS

Though Saint Louis was exceptional as a king — especially as a French king — the ideal he stood for was not regarded as exceptional at all. It was merely something not lived up to, but in Louis IX it was for once completely embodied. That is why I have chosen him in preference to Joan of Arc, with whom I would have liked to have dealt, both because she was a woman and a Frenchwoman. But she was an apparition wild and romantic, something that we would declare to be impossible did we not also know that it was real. The figure of Joan has filled the imagination of the world, and particularly the imagination of the English whom she drove out of her country. Saint Louis, however, though a more sober, perhaps even a more sombre figure, should for that reason itself mean more to us. His place in history may be smaller and less brilliant than the Maid's ; yet his is the part that one expects a king to play. He represents normality — though a normality rarely found. For that reason I have put him among my Pillars.

But there is another reason. Most regretfully, and with a rather bad conscience, I have been unable to bring any Franciscan into this series. And in dealing with Saint Dominic, perhaps some of the contrasts I draw between him and Saint Francis appear to be at Saint Francis's expense. Well, as a Franciscan tertiary, Louis may, to some extent, make good this defect. He became a member of the Franciscan third order when he was twenty, and though in later life he had ideas of joining the Friars Preachers — ideas laid aside only because his duty as a king was clear, to say nothing of his duty to his wife and children — he did in fact remain a Franciscan. He used to say that he wished he could divide himself between the two orders ; actually only the Franciscans have a right to claim him.

In this connection we have a charming account of the visit he made to Brother Giles, one of Francis's first companions, a man who died in 1252. Before the old friar knelt the young king ; and Brother Giles knelt too. Thus they stayed with their arms around one another — and they parted, dear friends after that meeting, though neither had said a word to the other.

We are fortunate in having the story of Saint Louis told us by the Sieur de Joinville, a man nine years younger than Louis, but one who lived to be nearly ninety and to see his friend canonized. He wrote in 1309, twelve years after the canonization had taken place, and thirty-nine years after Louis's death. But though Joinville was very old, he kept the heart of a boy to the end, and his memory of events is remarkably clear. He is at pains to speak only out of his personal knowledge and even warns us when he is not doing so, which is not often. The story he has to tell is so vivid that in no other book — not even in Chaucer — do we get closer to the life of the Middle Ages. For example, sixty years after it happened, we find Joinville relating with gusto how his friend the young Count of Eu set up a kind of catapult in his tent, which adjoined Joinville's, and with this engine shot stones along Joinville's dining table, breaking the glasses — apparently much to Joinville's enjoyment, at any rate to his enjoyment in retrospect. That youthful prank is very much after the Seneschal's own blithe boyish heart.

I have said that Joinville "wrote" his chronicle. Actually he dictated his book during a single month, that of October, 1309 — something not very difficult to do, as the whole thing runs to hardly more than sixty-five thousand words. This was all the easier for him, because he did not take the trouble to plan his book very carefully but spoke it out of a full mind. He starts off with some account of the virtues of Saint Louis, this being the approved method of hagiography, and every now and then comes back to such matters. At the same time it is his ostensible purpose to tell the history of the crusade upon which he accompanied the king. And he also gives us what is a kind of history of France for the middle of the thirteenth century. But muddled as the design is, and though, biographically speaking, we get little more than a number of stories about Saint Louis, what emerges is after all a wonderful biography, if the test is (as it should be) its success in making us know the man about whom the author is speaking. Somehow the old knight with the young heart managed to catch Louis perfectly, so that we feel we would recognize him instantly if he came into the room. Literary art cannot go further than that.

I think this must be the only life of a saint written during the Middle Ages which records no miracles. It is true that Joinville does say that miracles have occurred, but he is not dealing in such matters. "I have no wish to put into my book anything of which I am not certain." The nearest thing we have to a miracle is a dream in which Joinville says he saw Saint Louis after his death and told him, "Sire, when you leave here, I will lodge you in my house at Chevillon." To which the Saint answered — "laughing," says Joinville — "I have no wish to leave here so soon." This set Joinville to thinking. He came to the conclusion that it would be pleasing both to God and the Saint if he erected an altar to him in the chapel of his castle.

And this he did. But except for that and one or two similar touches, the aged Seneschal writes about the sainted King as the friend of his youth.

Joinville was obviously a man as good as he was honest, and he detested blasphemy almost as much as Louis did. But he makes no pretence to special virtue. When Louis asked him, "Which would you prefer, to be a leper or to have committed a mortal sin ?" Joinville said without hesitation that he would rather have committed thirty mortal sins than be a leper. The next day Louis asked the question again, and got the same blunt answer. Then he explained to Joinville that a soul in mortal sin has a hideousness worse than that of leprosy. Further, a man cannot know for a certainty, during his lifetime, whether he has so repented of his mortal sins as to be forgiven of God ; "wherefore he must stand in great fear lest that leprosy of sin should last as long as God is in paradise." In the same way, when Louis asked Joinville whether he washed the feet of the poor on Holy Thursday, Joinville answered, "Sire, it would make me sick ! The feet of those villains will I not wash."

He records these incidents without comment ; we do not even know whether he changed his mind after what Saint Louis said. All we know is that he expressed it with absolute forthrightness, and we can imagine that it was this forthrightness that endeared him to the King. Here was a man who would always say just what he thought — no courtier, no flatterer. Indeed, though he writes so that "men will be able to see clearly that no layman of our time lived so holily all his days," Joinville was by no means dazzled by him. He used to tell the King when he disapproved of his actions, and even when singing his *Nunc dimittis* over the saint he has seen canonized, he makes it clear that there were things about him he could not praise.

Louis's attitude to the Queen was one of these ; Joinville thought he neglected her. "I had been in his company five years, and yet never had he spoken a word to me about the Queen, or about his children — nor to anyone else, so far as I ever heard. And it seems to me that there was some want of good manners in being thus a stranger to one's wife and children." Everybody would agree with Joinville on this point ; the explanation is not that Louis was indifferent to them but that his personal preference was for the cloister. Domesticity was accepted as part of his kingly duty, and at least he fulfilled it to the extent of begetting nine children. All the same it must have been hard for Margaret of Provence to be married to a husband who was half a monk.

There were other matters in which Joinville disapproved of Louis's conduct. Thus when the Abbot of Cluny gave the king a present of two costly palfreys and came back the next day to discuss some business, Joinville asked after the Abbot had gone, "Did you listen to him with more favour because of those palfreys he gave you yesterday ?" When the King, after thinking a long time, answered "Why yes, I believe I did," Joinville said, "Then I advise you to forbid all your councillors to refuse to accept anything from those who have suits to bring before you, for you may rest assured that, if they do accept aught, they will listen more willingly . . . as you have done to the Abbot of Cluny." The King not only accepted the rebuke but called his council together and told them what Joinville had said, and they all agreed that the advice was good. Louis was one of those perfectly honest — and very rare — men who realize that the plain-spoken friend is the friend to cherish. And Louis emerges all the more radiant from Joinville's pages because of the occasional frank criticism we find there.

Louis, who became king at the age of twelve under his mother's regency, had a difficult situation to handle. Blanche of Castille was a good woman and a brave woman, but she was not popular. Joinville himself did not like her over much, though he admitted that she brought her son up well and ruled firmly during his minority. Having only the Queen-dowager and an adolescent to deal with, the barons soon gave trouble. Led by Pierre de Mauclerc, Count of Brittany, who was a natural son of Philip Augustus, Louis's grandfather, they broke into open rebellion, not wishing to be under the regency of a foreign woman. But Paris rose to the King's aid, and Blanche managed affairs so skilfully that when Louis took over the reins of government his opponents had been placated or broken. It was all the more remarkable because Blanche's chief adviser was the Papal Legate, Romano Beneventura, Bishop of Porto, another foreigner. But Louis's marriage to Margaret, a daughter of the powerful Raymond Berenger, Count of Provence, helped to consolidate his position ; and the adhesion of Thibaut IV, Count of Champagne, also meant a great deal. By 1242, when Louis was twenty-eight, the last rising of the rebels was defeated, and so also was Henry III of England, who had come to their aid. Mauclerc's punishment was that he had to go on crusade with Louis, and there he expiated his crimes by a gallant death on the field.

There can seldom have been a king less concerned than was Louis about maintaining his position for his own sake. He used to tell his eldest son, "I pray thee make thyself beloved by the people of thy kingdom ; for truly I would rather that a Scot should come out of Scotland to govern the people well and equitably than thou shouldst govern it ill in the sight of all men." His own success with kingship reposed upon his care

for the public good and his sense of justice ; but almost as much
it reposed upon his tact and good sense. Thus when Robert of
Sorbon and Joinville got into an unseemly wrangle one day,
each accusing the other of wearing finer clothes than his sta-
tion warranted and going more finely clad than the king himself, Louis reprimanded Joinville and his own son Philip, and
his son-in-law, young King Thibaut, who had got into the argument. But after Master Robert had gone, he made all the
young men sit at his feet and explained that he really agreed
with them and had taken Robert's part only because he saw him
discountenanced. Regarding the question at issue, he told
them : "As the Seneschal says, you ought to clothe yourselves
well and suitably, so that your wives may love you the better,
and your people hold you in the greater honour. For, as the
sage tells us, our garments should be of such fashion as neither
to cause the aged and worthy to say that too much has been
spent on them, nor the young to say that too little has been
spent." His reproofs were usually of this quiet sort, and were
all the more effectual for that very reason.

Though he enjoyed sports, especially hunting, he was afraid
to spend too much time on them, lest it be a waste of time. His
hours and days he felt not to be his own but to belong to the
people of France. Yet there may have been about his con-
scientiousness a tinge of puritanism, for on one occasion, when
his brother the Duke of Anjou was playing dice on the ship in
which they were travelling back from the crusade, the king
went to the players and "stammering with anger" flung all their
money into the sea. In general, however, we get the impression of a reasonable and moderate man. Well might Joinville
write : "Saint Louis was considered by far the wisest of his
advisers, and whatever aught demanded immediate attention he

never waited for the opinion of his Council, but gave a speedy and decided answer."

The justice of Saint Louis became proverbial. Not only was it perfectly even-handed but it was often administered in the most informal way. So it was when, after Mass, he used to go to the wood at Vincennes, and, sitting leaning against a tree, with his court around him, there received all who had any suit. There was no usher to that assembly, but the King himself would call out, "Is there anyone who has a cause in hand ?" He often did the same thing in Paris, with the difference that there he had a carpet laid down in one of the gardens. Any of his subjects was free to go to him and was sure of being heard.

Sometimes this administration of justice had a touch of humour. Thus on one occasion the bodies of three of the King's retainers were brought to him in Paris. Upon enquiry, Louis heard that these men used to go out at night and rob people. The night before they had picked the wrong victim, a cleric, who seemed easy enough game. But this man got so angry that, though he was only in his shirt, he shot one of the rascals with his crossbow, ran after another and cut off his leg with a falchion, and caught the third as he was trying to get into a house and slashed his skull down to his teeth. They brought this valiant cleric before Louis for judgment, and this was the judgment delivered : "Sir clerk, you have forfeited your priest-hood by your prowess — and for your prowess I take you into my service, and you shall go with me overseas. And this thing I do for you, because I would have my men fully to understand that I will uphold them in none of their wickedness."

That justice was part of his faith as a Christian king. And how perfect his faith was comes out in a story he used to tell of

Simon de Montfort, but which one feels would have been told of Louis himself, had he been in the same position. It seems that some Albigenses went to de Montfort to ask him to come quickly and look at the host a priest had just consecrated and which had turned visibly to flesh and blood in his hands. De Montfort merely replied, "Go and look at it yourselves, you who do not believe in it. As for me, I believe it firmly, holding as Holy Church does of the Sacrament of the altar." Louis had another story of how a doctor of divinity had gone to the bishop, William of Paris, saying that he was tormented by temptations against faith. The Bishop then asked him, "When you get these temptations, do they give you any pleasure?" "Far from it," was the answer. The Bishop then asked, "Would you for gold or silver utter anything against the Sacrament of the altar?" "Nothing," returned the doctor of divinity, "would induce me to do it." "Then," the Bishop went on, "I will ask you another question. You know that the King of France and the King of England are at war and that in the border-land between the two is the castle of la Rochelle in Poitou. Now if you had to guard that castle, and I had to guard that at Montlhéri, which is in the heart of France, to whom would be the greater credit?" "In God's name," was the answer, "to him who guarded la Rochelle without losing it." "Very well," was the Bishop's decision. "Now my heart is like Montlhéri, for I never have the slightest temptation to doubt. But to you, because of the assaults you suffer, God owes fourfold as much as He does to me. I assure you that your state is better pleasing to God than mine." The King always seemed to find the homely and telling word, and he expressed it with humour as when he said that no one, unless he was very learned, should dispute with an unbeliever ; let him instead drive at the blasphemer's midriff with his sword, as far as it would enter.

It was eminently fitting that the Crown of Thorns once worn by Our Lord should come into the keeping of this most Christian king. It was given to Louis by the Emperor of the Eastern Empire and was received by him on August 20th, 1239. First shrined at the cathedral of Notre Dame, Louis afterwards built for it the Sainte Chapelle, one of the chief marvels of medieval architecture, a kind of reliquary filigreed in stone and glorious with its jewelled glass. It was with his own hands that Louis, barefoot and in tears, placed it there.

I have already said that Louis owed much to the training he had received from his mother. She saw to it that he had the best of tutors, first, when he was seven, the Constable de Montmorency, a man "wiser and better than any in France," and, after he was fourteen, the Franciscan, Blessed Mansueto of Castiglione Aretino. who was his confessor and who instructed him in religion. Every Friday the young king knelt before him to be shriven — oftener if necessary — and he insisted that the friar should give him the discipline and lay the blows on hard. Yet Louis was not as a rule permitted to receive Holy Communion more than once a month, which was regarded as very frequently in those days. When he did receive the Eucharist, it was always with deep sighs and many tears, though he used to reproach himself for his spiritual coldness.

But Blanche was too stern a mother to make us like her much. She had strong feelings, and when her husband died, she cried, "Would that I were dead too !" This devotion, when fastened exclusively on her son, led her to be officious in strange ways. Joinville was torn between amusement and indignation when

he tells us how she tried to control Louis after his marriage in
even the most intimate part of his life.   Never, if she could help
it, were the King and Queen allowed to be alone together except at night.   They had to have recourse to a stratagem and
meet on a winding staircase that led from his room above and
her room below ; and ushers were posted to give warning of the
Queen-dowager's coming, so that they could run back quickly
to the rooms where they were supposed to be.   When, years
later, news came to Margaret of Provence, while she and Louis
were on crusade, that Blanche was dead, Joinville found her
weeping and said in his forthright style, "After this nobody will
put any faith in a woman !   Here you are crying because the
woman you most hated is dead."   "No," Margaret answered,
"that is not why I am weeping, but because of the King's sorrow."

Indeed, poor Queen Margaret had reason to harbour a grudge
against her mother-in-law.   For once, after a difficult child-
birth, when Louis was by his wife's bedside, Blanche came in
and told Louis, "Go away ; this is no place for you."   And
Margaret had wildly exclaimed, "Whether I am dead or alive
you will not suffer me to see my lord !"   In spite of this, Margaret learned little enough ; for after the death of her eldest son
Louis, the heir to the throne, she made her second son Philip, the
future Philip III, sign a paper promising that until he was thirty
he would always act according to her advice.   As this apparently had the binding force of a vow, Saint Louis asked the
Pope to dispense his son from so preposterous an obligation.
Margaret, one can see, was trying to get a bit of her own back
by dominating Philip as Louis had been dominated by his
mother.   Yet Blanche was a good woman, and both Louis and
France owe her a good deal.   If some of her characteristics are

not very appealing, we might remember that when a young German of eighteen, who was the son of Saint Elizabeth of Hungary, appeared at the French court, Queen Blanche called him to her and kissed him on the forehead, "as an act of devotion, because she thought that his mother must ofttimes have kissed him there."

The crusades are an important part of the story of Saint Louis, and an account of the first of these (on which he went in 1244, remaining away from France for ten years) takes up the larger part of Joinville's book. Yet Louis was among the least successful of crusaders, if "results" alone are considered, and his crusades have been called "expensive ideals." Ideals they certainly were, and of a kind not easily understood by most modern people, but they were not particularly expensive. For Louis, though a generous man, was also a good manager, dealing thriftily in all affairs. In those days a king was expected normally to pay his own way upon the revenues of the royal estates, and taxation was thought of as something quite exceptional, to be resorted to only in an emergency. A war of course was just such an emergency, and a crusade was the kind of war for which it was a pious act to pay and of which it was bad form as well as irreligious to complain. Sometimes such emergencies were even used as pretexts by monarchs who wanted a means for raising money. Louis, however, though he would have been amply justified in demanding special grants for his crusades, did not do so. By careful administration and seeing to it that he received his feudal dues promptly, he increased the royal revenues fifty percent, and they sufficed for his purposes.

The crusade that he began in 1244 — the second had hardly got under way when he died, and so hardly counts, except

that Louis had the honour of dying while bearing the cross —
was from the military point of view a complete failure. Louis
was in truth not a good general, for though personally immensely brave — Joinville opens his Chronicle by listing instances of the King's valour — he was also in turns too cautious
and too rash in making his tactical decisions. So while Joinville may have had some reason for looking upon him as a
martyr, we cannot look upon him as a great commander in the
field.

It is, nevertheless, worth noting that Joinville, who was free
with his criticisms, did not bring any very specific criticisms
against Louis in this respect. We may therefore take his opinion, as that of a leading officer present at all the operations, that
he believed the King to have done all that was possible and not
to have bungled the campaign, even if he did not bring it to success. The fact is, of course, that Louis did not have adequate
means for performing what he had undertaken. He is therefore not fairly to be blamed except for this initial miscalcula-
tion. A military genius might perhaps have avoided the disaster of Mansourah, but not even a military genius could have
attained the goal of freeing the Holy Places.

The Crusade came just before a new, and as it proved, the last
rising in the reign of the refractory French barons. That
Louis chose that moment for leaving the country was extremely
risky, though, as events turned out, Blanche of Castille was able
to control the kingdom in his absence. He made his decision
during an illness when he was given up for dead. It was then
that he solemnly vowed to take the cross.

Those around him were appalled, but Louis insisted. He
sent at once for William of Auvergne, the Bishop of Paris, and
demanded the sign of the crusader. The Bishop pleaded with

him to wait until he was quite well, probably feeling that the King might be slightly delirious, or at any rate not in his calmest frame of mind. But Louis was not to be put off, and a red silken cord was made into a cross, and this Louis pressed to his heart, his eyes, and his lips, before fastening it to his shoulder. Then in a loud voice he proclaimed, "Know ye for a truth that I am now completely cured."

So indeed it seemed. But the preparations for so vast an undertaking as a crusade took three years, and during that time the King's advisers pondered the matter and were almost unanimous against his going. Though he had taken a vow, the Bishop of Paris, who had reluctantly given him the cross, delivered the judgment that a vow taken by a man so sick as Louis had been was null and void. There was accordingly a perfect excuse for abandoning the project. This, however, would not be accepted by Louis. Instead he met the situation in characteristic fashion. Very well, as he had not been in his right mind at the time he had accepted the cross, he took it from his shoulder and handed it back to the Bishop. Then he said, "But today you cannot call me sick or delirious. Today with a sound mind I take the cross again." The nobility of that fired everybody with enthusiasm.

The landing was easily made at Damietta, not far from the present Port Said, so as to avoid the Nile delta, as that would have offered too many obstacles to the invading army. Unfortunately Louis did not follow up his initial success promptly. For one thing he wished to wait until the Nile had risen ; for another, he had told his brother, the Count of Poitiers, that he would wait for his arrival, and he had no means of knowing whether the Count was even on his way. The delay gave the Sultan of Egypt, a great-nephew of the famous Saladin, ample opportunity to get ready.   He had been ill at the time Damietta was taken, and in anger for the ineffectual resistance he took the heads of fifty-four of his Emirs, so as to encourage the others.

The Grand Masters of the military orders had been for immediate attack on Cairo before the Saracens could rally.   They also argued that Jaffa be seized, as it offered an easy road to Cairo along the caravan trail, while Mauclerc, Louis's uncle and old enemy, was in favour of taking Alexandria as a second port of communication.   But there was no agreement, and Louis hesitated, which was not good for the morale of the army. Discipline grew slack, and the Count of Artois, another of Louis's brothers, showed insubordination, so much so that Longsword of Salisbury told the King that the Count was unfit for command.   Meanwhile the Templars reached the conclusion that it would be best to make an alliance with the Egyptian Sultan and then operate directly against Jerusalem.   Such shifts of political compromise were abhorrent to Louis's straightforward nature, and he rejected them.   And his policy of waiting for reinforcements seemed sound, for at last he was able to muster an army of sixty thousand men.

By that time, however, the Sultan of Egypt had strongly fortified Mansourah, midway between Damietta and Cairo, and there he waited for the crusaders to attack.   Though there were brilliant successes at the outset — or what seemed to be such — the lightly mounted horsemen of the desert lured the Christians into a trap.   This, however, was not the fault of Louis ; he had enjoined caution, and he was disobeyed by hot-headed young men.

The attempt to take Mansourah by siege was equally disastrous.   The crusaders constructed great towers of wood for storming the walls, but their enemies were able to destroy these by the use of Greek fire. In the end the Christian army, worn down by attrition and disease, was cut off and had to surrender.

Joinville had written of the Christian fleet as it left Cyprus : "It seemed as if all the sea, so far as the eye could reach, were covered with the canvas of the ships' sails ; and the number of the ships, great and small, was reckoned at eighteen hundred." And of Louis himself he said : "Never have I seen so fair a knight ! For he seemed by the head and shoulders to tower above his people ; and on his head was a gilded helm, and in his hand a sword of Allemaine." But since then dysentery and battle had taken their toll, and only a sick and pitiful remnant was left. It was all very well for "the good Count of Soissons," in the days when, in open fight, the Christians still had a chance, to say to Joinville : "Seneschal, let these curs howl ! By God's bonnet" — that was the Count's favourite oath — "we shall talk of this day yet, you and I, in ladies' chambers" ; but, in truth, few of the knights of that gallant host lived to talk about it in ladies' chambers, or anywhere else.

When they were taken prisoner torture was used on some of them, and threats were still more freely used. The Soldan himself showed some large-heartedness, for he was of the line of Saladin ; but partly for this very reason, he was murdered by a group of his own officers. That, however, gave the magnanimous Louis a chance to shine. "One of the [Saracen] knights," Joinville records, "whose name was Faress-Eddin Octay, cut [the Soldan] open with his sword, and took his heart out of his body ; and then he came to the king, his hand all reeking with blood, and said : 'What wilt thou give me ? For I have slain thine enemy, who, had he lived, would have slain thee ?' And the king answered him never a word."

They all expected to be massacred, and, as priests were not always at hand, the soldiers confessed to one another, Joinville saying that Guy of Iberlin, the Constable of Cyprus, did so to him, kneeling by his side, and Joinville answered, "I absolve you, with such power as God has given me." He noted with surprise that afterwards he did not have the slightest memory of anything the Constable had told him. But after a long quarrelsome argument which went on all day among the Saracens, it was eventually decided that, though a general slaughter of the prisoners might remove the threat of another invasion for forty years, it would be a good deal more profitable to extract a heavy ransom. Here again Louis showed his honourable nature, for when the ransom money arrived and was paid over, a mistake occurred and the Saracens received ten thousand livres less than the agreed-upon price. Gleefully Philip of Nemours told Louis of this lucky accident, only to be instantly ordered to make good the stipulated amount.

It was a miserable termination to the campaign. Even so, Louis would not abandon the hope with which he had set out. He retired to Acre with what men he had left — he had only about a hundred knights of the twenty-eight hundred he had assembled at Damietta — and was for trying again, as soon as reinforcements should reach him. As to this Joinville has a grand story to relate. He, a relatively young man, had been one of the few who had spoken in favour of remaining instead of returning to France, and he was afraid that he would be regarded as having been too rash. Then, as he stood brooding by a window, somebody came behind him and put his hands on Joinville's face. The Seneschal, thinking it was Philip of Nemours, said rather testily, "Leave me alone, my Lord Philip." But it was the King, and Louis asked in a whisper, "How was it that you were so bold as to say what you did against the advice of all these other lords ?" Blunt as usual, Joinville repeated his opinion, wondering how it would be received. Then the King said, "Be easy in your mind. I am well pleased with the counsel you have given. Only do not tell this to anybody until the week is out." Nothing gives a more vivid picture of the trust and intimate friendship that existed between the two men.

During that stay on the coast of the Holy Land, Louis was several times offered a safe escort for a visit to Jerusalem. This he refused, remembering the example of Richard the Lionheart, who, failing to take Jerusalem, had held his arm before his face and had exclaimed in tears, "Fair Lord God, I pray Thee suffer me not to see Thy Holy City since I cannot deliver it from Thine enemies." Louis felt that, should he accept the offers made him, other crusaders might be content with making a safe pilgrimage instead of fighting until they had won what they had come for. What he did do, however, was to spend the Feast of the Annunciation, 1251, at Nazareth. He entered its streets on foot, wearing a hair shirt, and in the room where, according to tradition, Our Lady had been greeted by the archangel Gabriel, Louis received Holy Communion.

At Acre Louis had an amusing encounter with the "Old Man of the Mountain," who employed assassins to extract tribute from such monarchs as the Emperor of Germany and the King of Hungary and the Soldan of Babylon. His emissaries arrived bearing the knives and the shroud they were to present if their demands for tribute were refused. But Louis was not to be intimidated ; he sent them back to the Old Man of the Mountain with a demand that suitable presents be given the King by way of apology for the insult that had been offered. The calling of the bluff worked wonderfully well. In a couple of weeks they returned carrying rich jewels and, what was still more important, the shirt of the Lord of the Assassins. This, Joinville tells us, signified that, "as the shirt is nearer to the body than any other garment, so did the Old Man hold the king to be nearer to himself in love than any other king." Louis sent suitable presents back by his envoys and a friar named Yves le Breton who was to try to convert the Old Man of the Mountain. In this he did not succeed, but at any rate a kind of alliance was effected with that mysterious personage who when he rode out had a crier call, "Turn aside from him who bears in his hands the death of kings."

The reinforcements from France did not come, or not in sufficient numbers, and, as the nobles were giving trouble in his kingdom again, since the death of Blanche of Castille, Louis saw that his duty demanded his return.

It was during 1254–1269 that he established his reputation as one of the wisest, and certainly as the most noble and holy, of the Kings of France. Yet not all his doings met with the approval of his councillors. In his desire for peace, Louis was willing to make larger concessions than were generally acceptable. This he did in the case of Henry III of England, and was satisfied with the bargain effected between them. As he was dealing with men who honoured their part of the agreement, appeasement was in this instance justified. In fact the moderation and justice of Louis became so widely recognized abroad that he was later invited to act as arbitrator between Henry III and his barons. Under the rule of Louis France prospered at home and was respected by her neighbours.

So much for Louis the crusader and Louis the king. Let us look at Louis the saint. He had always been that, but during these years of quiet his piety was more resplendent than ever.

The only criticism brought against him was that he spent too much time on his devotions. He heard at least two Masses every day ; and he assisted at the canonical hours, even rising at midnight to be present at Matins and Lauds. To these complaints Louis answered mildly : "There would be no objection if I spent twice as much time at dice or hunting. It is in serving God that I best serve the realm." But the criticisms were not very loud, for it was obvious that though Louis prayed a great deal, he made up for this by a close attention to affairs of state.

He cultivated holy and learned men. There is the well-known story, for example, of Saint Thomas Aquinas at the King's table, where he had gone in company with the Master General of the Dominicans. Suddenly the great doctor, lost in thought roared out, striking the board with his fist, "This is a decisive point against the Manicheans !" His Master General whispered to him to remember where he was, but Louis had tablets brought at once so that the argument could be put down before it was forgotten.

On the other hand Louis was not at all offended with a plain-spoken Franciscan who, when preaching at the court, said, "My Lords, I see too many religious here and in the King's company. Let me remind you that this is no place for friars, if they wish to be saved. Do not the Scriptures tell us that a monk cannot live out of his cloister any more than a fish can live out of water ?" (The answer is that Scriptures do not contain that remark. It was one made by Saint Anthony of the Desert, and has been repeated many times, among others by Chaucer commenting on the Monk of the *Canterbury Tales*. But perhaps the false attribution of its source was not the Franciscan's but Joinville's.) Louis was edified by the sermon and wished to keep this Brother Hugh with him. But the friar refused, and rather roughly, saying, "I am going where God will love me better than in the court of the King."

Louis established and endowed many religious houses, especially the Cistercian abbey of Royaumont, where a cell was always kept ready for him, and where he would often retire. Then he would take his turn serving at meals, carrying the hot dishes in the folds of his mantle or in his hat. As he was the King, the abbey of the Poor Clares at Longchamp, where his sister, Blessed Isabelle, was the abbess, was also open to him. He was indeed so pious that when the words of the litany were said, "Good Lord, we implore Thee to give us a fountain of tears," the King used to cry, "Oh Lord God, I dare not ask for a fountain of tears, but a few little drops would suffice to water the dryness of my heart." The confessor of Queen Margaret, who relates this of him, goes on, "Yet he told his confessor that our Saviour sometimes accorded to him the grace of tears while he was at prayer, and when he felt them flowing down his face, even to his lips, they seemed to him most sweet, not only to his heart, but to his taste."

In spite of all this the devout king was by no means priest-ridden. When his bishops demanded that he force excommunicated persons to make satisfaction to the Church, Louis replied that he would willingly do so providing he was given the particulars of each case. And when they answered that they would not do that, as the matters involved were spiritual, he told them that he had no intention of using the secular arm to constrain people unless he was sure that their sentence was deserved. He could, in truth, be quite sharp with the most exalted of his clergy, and even irascible, as many of the saints have been. "Sire, what will you do for me," asked the Archbishop of Rheims, "on account of the wardship of Saint Remigius, which you are taking from me? For by the relics that are here before us, I swear that I would not have upon my conscience such a sin as there is upon yours, for all the kingdom of France." To which Louis retorted, "By the relics that are here before us, I swear that for Compiègne alone you would take that sin upon your conscience, because of the covetousness that is in you. So now one of us two is forsworn!"

His love for the poor was constant and wide. Every day a hundred paupers ate at his table, though for the sake of preserving order, he made them come in by a back door. He sometimes served these men himself, before he took anything to eat or drink. Even when he was a boy and still under a tutor, he had been accustomed to go down early in the morning with a bag of money to distribute among the beggars who were waiting for him. One morning while he was doing this, a friar's head appeared at a window of the palace; it was that of Blessed Mansueto. "Sire," he called down to Louis, "I am watching your misdeeds." "Brother," the King called up to him, "I am only paying my retainers. These people fight for me by their prayers and so ward off dangers and ensure peace within my dominions." Later in life, he encouraged his daughter and her husband, King Thibaut, to help him nurse the sick in the hospitals; and Prince Louis, the heir of France, followed his father's example by washing the feet of beggars. Saint Louis, like Saint Francis before him, did not shrink even from the touch of lepers. And on one occasion we hear of a man, supposedly hungry, who had been brought in from the streets, being given a bowl of soup that the King was about to take. The unmannerly fellow put bread in the bowl and ate that, then pushed the soup aside. Instead of giving him a rebuke for his behaviour Louis sent for the bowl and ate the soup himself.

There seemed to be no end to his charities. Joinville tells of the King's maintaining houses for the blind, and for fallen women, and for workmen who had come upon evil days. That he was able to do so much was due to his good management, for just as he spared his people taxes, so he made his thrift support his charities. Though he gave personally to those in need, he employed almoners, lest his gifts should fall haphazard ; and he saw to it that his almoners sought out the poor. The warm nature of his kindness came out in the fact that if one of his destitute guests was blind, Louis cut up the meat for him, "removing the bones when it was a fish day."

It had always lain heavy on his heart that his crusade had failed. So in 1267 he decided to make another attempt to recover the Holy Places ; as he was still only fifty-three, he could reasonably hope for success. But everybody was against him this time, and even Joinville refused to take the cross, telling Louis that he had impoverished himself the time before and that now, for the good of his estates, he meant to remain in France. Yet undeterred by the advice he received, the King took the cross again in the Church of the Magdalen in Paris.

This second crusade of Louis's was not so much a failure as a fiasco. After three years of preparation, Louis got to Tunis only to die there. By one of the King's sons Joinville was given an account of the death of his father. After praying to Saint Genevieve, the King ordered that ashes be strewn on the floor and that he be laid upon them. There, looking towards heaven, and with his hands crossed on his breast, he rendered up his soul to his Creator ; "and it was the same hour that the Son of God died upon the cross for the world's salvation."

They brought his body back to France, partially embalmed, and he was buried in the vault of the kings of France at Saint

Denis. And there, says Joinville, many miracles were performed. The old Seneschal was able to give evidence at the process for the canonization, spending two whole days telling what he knew of Saint Louis's virtues. We may be sure that his utterly honest way of speaking carried a great deal of weight, and no man knew Louis better than he did. Nor can few saints have been made more alive, more human and more natural than Saint Louis is in the pages that Joinville dictated in his old age.

In conclusion let me quote the belated testimony of Voltaire, a man not much addicted to the praising of saints. In his *Essay on Morals* he wrote : "Saint Louis was the man to reform Europe, had Europe been capable of reform. The King caused France to be honoured abroad and gave her an organized government. He was in all respects a model man. His piety was that of a hermit, but this did not detract from his kingly virtues. Nor was his open-handed liberality the worse for his prudent thrift. Perhaps he is the only monarch to be praised as a wise statesman and who was yet perfectly just and fair. Prudent and firm in the council-chamber, brave but not rash on the battlefield, he was as full of compassion as though he had never known aught save misfortune. It is not given to man to practice virtue in a higher degree."

VI

SAINT THOMAS MORE

There is something fitting — though the appropriateness is rather of accident than my contriving — that the best of kings should be followed here by the man who was executed by the worst of kings. At any rate, Henry VIII almost has that reputation, though he was, as I think, not so much a bad man as a bad boy, a spoiled brat who screamed for anything he wanted. But during the gap between the thirteenth and the sixteenth century many things had happened to kingship. The idea of nationalism had emerged, so that even before the Reformation came to shatter the unity of Europe, its unity had shown signs of ending in the aggrandizement of its various parts. And of that aggrandizement the worship of the king was the symbol. It would therefore not be quite just to compare Henry with Louis. Born three centuries earlier, Henry probably would have behaved reasonably decently ; born three centuries later, Louis probably would still have been a very good man, but might never have become a saint.

These considerations, however, if followed, would lead us too far afield. They tempt me because I have just finished writing on Saint Louis ; I resist the temptation because I must restrict myself to the story of Sir Thomas More. The great Lord Chancellor of England was one of those Catholic saints to whom the world, from which he turned aside in his life, and in his writings, as much as in his death, has agreed most whole-heartedly to praise. Though there was, it is true, at one time some disposition to take seriously the accusations of persecution brought against him by John Foxe, as casting a shadow over his illustrious name, even those accusations were brought mildly, and mainly because it was supposed that an inconsistency was discovered between the tolerance preached in the *Utopia* and More's judicial practice.   Recent investigation, however, has shown these charges, such as they are, to be without real foundation.   Though some apparent inconsistencies remain, this is not one of them.   The judgment of history, and not merely the honour of canonization bestowed upon him, has covered the Lord Chancellor with a steadily growing light.

The best of More biographers has been Professor R. W. Chambers, a Protestant ; and the editor of More's English work in a magnificent edition has been Professor W. E. Campbell, another Protestant.   Perhaps this is, in part, because the first biographers, Roper and Rastell and Stapleton and Cresacre More, though all Catholics, wrote without any rancour or any attempt to use their material as religious propaganda.   The whole atmosphere surrounding More has been as sweet and sunny as the mind of the martyr himself.   There would be few people who would not concur in Cardinal Pole's decision that More was of all Englishmen the best.   Even Henry VIII who beheaded him, honoured his memory.   According to Stapleton, the news of the execution was brought to the King while he was playing dice.   Perhaps the game itself was to distract Henry's thoughts from the news he knew he was going to receive.   But when it came, it greatly upset him.   " 'Is he then dead ?' he enquired.   Hearing that it was so, he turned to Anne Boleyn, who was sitting by him, and said, 'You are the cause of that man's death !'   And rising at once he retired to another room and shed bitter tears."

Yet Stapleton's *Life,* though freely drawn upon by later

biographers, was not translated into English from Latin until Monsignor Philip Hallett published his book in 1928. Stapleton, a priest in exile, was able to use Margaret Roper's notes, along with many letters given him by the widow of the John Harris who had been More's secretary — letters that have since disappeared. He also consulted John Heywood, who was for many years a friend of More's, and Margaret Clements, who had been brought up by More as a daughter and whose husband is mentioned in the *Utopia*. And William Rastell, More's nephew, and several other people were available to give Stapleton first-hand and unimpeachable information. This richly detailed material, though of course it has been supplemented by subsequent research, has been proved to be strikingly accurate. It is therefore possible to say that there are few characters in history about whom we know as much as we do about More, or have better reason to admire. The best of Englishmen was also the most typical of Englishmen. We catch the very tone of his voice ; we savour his jests ; we can love and laugh while we praise.

Thomas More was born in London on February 7, 1478, and after his early schooling there, was placed, through the influence of his father, a lawyer who afterwards became a judge, in the household of Cardinal Morton, the Archbishop of Canterbury. The Cardinal was a scholar as well as a politician, a pluralist as well as a reformer ; not an altogether admirable person but a stimulating one. And young More's experience in his household sharpened his wits and gave him a knowledge of the world. As for Morton, he was so taken with the charming and brilliant boy as to bring him forward to show him off before distinguished guests, and prophesied freely that he would make a notable man. On one less firmly based in humour and commonsense and humility this sort of attention might easily have had a bad effect.

Then there followed two years at Oxford, where More had the famous Linacre as tutor in Greek, and probably Grocyn and Colet as well. But his father had scant sympathy with humanistic studies, so he removed him in 1494, though not before his son had acquired that passion for Greek which was to last his whole life. This, however, by no means interfered with John More's designs that Thomas should become a first-rate lawyer. At sixteen he was entered at New Inn and at Lincoln's Inn two years later, so that he qualified as a barrister at an exceptionally early age. As such, while still a very young man, he was a "reader" or lecturer on law at Furnival's Inn.

Advancement came quickly, though there emerged as quickly an independence of character which made him, as a Member of Parliament, dare to oppose the grant of an excessively large dowry when Henry VII's daughter married the Scots king. He was already showing that he had no intention of climbing in the world by the use of sycophantic arts.

He also began to show the interests that befitted the Utopian when he gave a lecture at Saint Lawrence's Church on Saint Augustine's *De Civitate Dei*. These interests befitted the martyr equally well, and from about 1499 More lived for four years near — and virtually with — the Carthusians, meditating becoming a monk, and deciding against that vocation only because he feared that his nature would be unable to bear the burden of celibacy. Later in life he admitted that his fears in this regard had been exaggerated, but that he admitted having had them is part of his charming candour. Though he married, he did not cease the austerities of his practice. He was to wear a hair shirt which few suspected to be under the scholar's gown, the jester's motley, the robes of the Lord Chancellor.

Concerning his marriage in 1505 to the elder daughter of John Colt of Essex we have a kind of family joke that many people have taken with great solemnity. Daniel Sargent commends More as gravely as does the *Encyclopedia Britannica* for not proposing to the younger daughter, lest he should hurt the feelings of the elder. Here Christopher Hollis shows good sense : "The fact . . . that More told this anecdote, as we must believe from Roper that he did, proves surely not that it was true but that it was untrue. If it was true, he certainly would not have told it. . . Roper, who had no very keen sense of humour, came later into the family, heard the story doubtless at second hand and a little stupidly missed the point of it." Family jokes are notoriously liable to be misunderstood by outsiders.

The marriage lasted until 1509, when Jane Colt died, leaving her husband with several young children. That they needed someone to look after them adequately accounts for the widower marrying Alice Middleton a few weeks later. She was of course the tilly-vally lady. Poor Jane remains a somewhat shadowy figure. It is the later family that Erasmus described and that Holbein painted. Lady Alice had no children of her own.

More's friendship with Erasmus, however, antedates either marriage. What is slightly surprising is that to the end he remained More's "darling." For where More was the most unworldly of men, Erasmus was always very wide awake to his own advantage. So far from being of the metal of the martyrs, his attitude during the storm of the early days of Protestantism was, to say the least, a bit equivocal. Though in the end he decided firmly against the so-called reformers, he had given them a good deal of aid and encouragement. Yet he remained More's closest friend.

This was probably because More understood that at bottom Erasmus was on the right side. Explicitly he said, "Had I found with Erasmus, my darling, the shrewd intent and purpose which I find in Tyndale, Erasmus, my darling, should be no more my darling. But I find in Erasmus, my darling, that he detesteth and abhorreth the errors and heresies that Tyndale plainly teachest and abideth by, and therefore Erasmus, my darling, shall be my dear darling still." Not even the brilliant and humorous conversation in which both men delighted, or their love of Greek studies, would have sufficed to hold them together, had it not been that Erasmus showed only his best side to his friend. It is by More that Erasmus should be judged.

The most famous work of More's — the only one, in fact, by which he is generally known — is his *Utopia*. A good many people even forget that More wrote it in Latin, so fully has it passed into our literature. But as More's English writings were voluminous, I might give at this point one sample of the style of this early master of our prose. It is taken from his *Life of Richard III*, a book that Hall the chronicler drew upon and, through Hall, Shakespeare for his play. Could anything be more vigorous than this ? " 'Thou servest me, I ween with 'ifs' and 'ands' ? I tell thee they have done so, and that I will make good on thy body, traitor !' And therewith, as in a great anger, he clappeth his fist upon the board a great rap. At which token given, one cried 'Treason' without the chamber. Thereupon a door clapped, and in there come there rushing

men in harness, as many as the chamber might hold. And
anon the Protector said to Lord Hastings : 'I arrest thee,
traitor.' 'What me, my lord ?' quoth he. 'Yes, thee, traitor,'
quoth the Protector. And another let fly at the Lord Stanley,
which shrank at the stroke and fell under the table, or else his
head had been cleft to the teeth : for as shortly as he shrank,
yet ran the blood about his ears. Then they were all quickly
bestowed in divers chambers, except the Lord Chamberlain,
whom the Protector bade speed and shrive himself apace, 'For
by Saint Paul,' quoth he, 'I will not to dinner till I see thy head
off' . . . Thus ended this honourable man, a good knight and
a gentle, of great authority with his prince, of living somewhat
dissolute, plain and open to his enemy, and secret to his friend ;
a loving man, and passing well beloved ; very faithful, and
trusty enough, trusting too much."

But I leave everything else for the *Utopia*, as I believe that to
have an importance even greater than is usually supposed, or at
least a significance that is sometimes missed. More's imaginary
country and its social customs have become so famous that
utopia has turned from a proper to a common noun, a generic
term. Yet the book remains something of a puzzle and to
many Catholics an embarrassment. For speaking in his own
person in the First Part of the *Utopia*, which was the second
part to be written and in which he is discussing conditions in
England and certainly giving his own views, More proclaims
himself a kind of a communist. Or if he is not quite a communist, in the sense in which we have come to think of the
word, he does at all events condemn private property as the
root social evil. As to this let us have his own words : "Thus
I do fully persuade myself, that no equal and just distribution
of things can be made, nor that perfect wealth shall ever be

among men, unless this propriety [private ownership] be exiled and banished." That is plain and specific, and it is stressed in the book in several places.

The second part of the *Utopia*, in which there is merely a description of the country, does not present such a stumbling-block. For there it must always be a question as to how far More advocated the Utopian customs. The safest thing to believe is that he was depicting those customs as interesting in themselves, and as a mode of life from which all might learn something, without advocating their adoption *in globo*. He gives us sly gibes at war, at diplomacy, at the contemporary Englishman's mania for hunting. But these are only in passing and do not touch the heart of the matter. On the other hand there are things which, if they are to be taken as representing More's own view of what life should be, are not those we should expect to hear from a Christian, much less a saint. Faced with these, many people have attempted to explain the *Utopia* away as a fanciful jest that was never intended to be taken seriously. Such is the thesis of Father Bridgett and the Abbé Bremond, for instance, and it has more plausibility than the counter-thesis, as advanced by Mr. Seebohm, that everything in the *Utopia* was meant quite literally by More. As against both of these views is the more moderate position of the Protestant biographer, Sir James Mackintosh: "The true notion of the *Utopia* is that it intimates a variety of doctrines and exhibits a multiplicity of projects, which the writer regards with every possible degree of approbation and shade of assent; from the frontiers of serious belief, through gradations of descending plausibility, where the lowest are scarcely more than exercises of ingenuity, and to which some wild paradoxes are appended, either as a vehicle or as an easy means (if·

necessary) of disavowing the serious intention of the whole of the Platonic fiction."

Now that is ingeniously put, but is a dodging of the entire problem. As a means of approaching it, I offer two observations. The first is that if we remember that More represents the Utopians as a people with only *natural* religion, we shall have no cause to be scandalized if they do not behave in all respects as Christians. He makes it clear, however sportive he may have been at times, that this natural religion did, after all, prepare them, as natural religion should, for the acceptance of the supernatural revelation.

The second observation is this : that the main point in More's description of the Utopians is their utter contempt for what most men set so much store by — that is, money.

With regard to natural religion, take this : "After they heard us speak the name of Christ, of his doctrines, laws, miracles, and of the no less wonderful constancy of so many martyrs . . . you will not believe with how glad minds, they agreed unto the same : whether it were by the secret inspiration of God, or else for that they thought it nighest unto that opinion, which among them is counted the chiefest. Howbeit I think this was no small help and furtherance in the matter, that they heard us say, that Christ instituted among his all things common : and that the same community doth yet remain amongst the rightest Christian companies." As for private property he says : "In other places they speak still of the commonwealth. But every man procureth his own private gain. Here where nothing is private, the common affairs be earnestly looked after."

Of course as the Utopians had only natural religion, they could not enforce it under penalties. But this does not mean that More held that man has an inalienable right to pick and choose among religions, once the Christian revelation has been made. He is logical here, and he represents the Utopians as logical. A prime instance is their attitude towards death, about which most Christians are highly inconsistent. These people ran to God gladly when He called, and were buried with joyful singing. But when More tells of their views about the ascetic life and the priesthood, he must not be accused of having an identical opinion — for we know that he did not. Yet even here the point of the remark, "They have priests of exceeding holiness, and therefore very few" is that all priests should be holy. Taken in the way that More meant there were, after all, very few Utopian customs which we might not ponder to our profit.

It is, however, when he comes to the end of the second part of his book that his seriousness deepens and he writes words clearly intended to apply to the England of his own times, those about the rich who by their private fraud and the common laws "do every day pluck and snatch away from the poor some part of their daily living."   Here no man could be more in earnest than was More in denouncing avarice and "the princess and mother of all mischief, Pride."

All this is sharpened by the citing of specific instances of the Utopian attitude towards what the rest of mankind considers real wealth.   There the gyves of the malefactors are made of gold ; so are chamber pots ; only to base uses is the glittering metal put, or for baubles that little children may play with. These, as soon as they are even half grown, put away such playthings of their own accord, being ashamed of them. More adds a stroke of verisimilitude by telling of a child who, seeing an ambassador and his retinue from a foreign country, ran to his mother to tell her the astonishing news of grown-ups decked out with jewels and gold chains as though they were infants. And she explains, "They must be some of the ambassador's clowns."

The argument does not depend here upon the acceptance of the evangelical counsels (of which they have never heard) but upon good sense. Of course it is only historical fact that pagan philosophers have often told men that human felicity is not increased by increasing man's needs, but by decreasing them ; that only that man is free who detaches himself from material things. And if that is true for the individual, More adds a social reason against measuring the value of men by their wealth — "a lumpish blockhead churl, and which hath no more wit than an ass, yea and as full of naughtiness and folly, shall have nevertheless many wise and good men in subjection and bondage, only for this, because he hath a great heap of gold." On top of which comes his crowning objection : man's inhumanity to man mainly springs from his lust for gain.

Now all this is pointed particularly at the England More knew. That this application was plainly intended is seen from his making Utopia an island about the same size as England, and divided, as England is divided, into forty shires. So though we have to allow some leeway to the humourist, we cannot take even the second part of the book — the description of Utopia — merely as a *jeu d'esprit*.

It seems to me that it was precisely because he did not wish the *Utopia* to appear as no more than a graceful and amusing story that he added the first part to emphasize the moral which might have been missed had he not supplied this. Even so, it is to be feared that many careless readers, by skipping this introductory section and hurrying on to the fable, have failed to catch More's purpose. This is a great pity, for More, though not a prophet of what was to come, did lay his sociological finger upon the conditions which caused the Reformation, or which enabled it to succeed in England. He puts it all in a single phrase, a very strange phrase, but a phrase which once heard is never forgotten : "Sheep are eating men." He glances in passing at many minor social ills, but the chief ill is that sheep are eating men.

Yet this appears at first sight to be subsidiary to his discussion of the severity of the English laws protecting property, laws which were to remain ferociously severe for centuries to come, and under which thousands of men, women and even children were to be hanged for petty theft. Then he goes on to ask why it is that theft had recently increased so much, and the answer comes : it is because sheep are eating men. In the form of a conversation between himself and Cardinal Morton, who died in 1500, More tells him : "My lord, your sheep that were wont to be so meek, and so small eaters, now, as I hear say, be become so great devourers and so wild, that they eat up, and swallow down the very men themselves. They consume, destroy, and devour whole fields, houses and cities. . . There noblemen, and gentlemen, yea and certain abbots themselves, holy men no doubt, not contenting themselves with the yearly revenues and profits, that were wont to grow to their fore-fathers and predecessors of their lands, nor being content that they live in rest and pleasure nothing profiting, yea much noy-ing the public weal, leave no ground for tillage, they enclose all into pasture, they throw down houses, they pluck down towns, and leave nothing standing, but only the church to be made a sheep-house." Sheep are now tigers ; sheep are eating men.

What does all this mean ? It means that long before the

Reformation began the landowners — including many of the abbots, as More points out — were enclosing the common lands. And why were they enclosing the common lands ? Because it had become more profitable to raise sheep, for the sake of the high prices fetched by English wool on the continent, than to put the lands under the plough. "Thus the unreasonable covetousness of a few hath turned that thing to the utter undoing of your island." Avarice was the main evil of the time ; the love of money was the root of all evil. So though More's solution — that of the abolition of private ownership — cannot be accepted, we must at least try to see what was the abuse he sought to remedy.

When the mass of men were being robbed by the rich — for it was not sheep but men that were eating men — what could they do to keep themselves alive but pilfer where they could ? And it was because the possessors loved their possessions inordinately that they protected them with such savage laws. Speaking as a lawyer — as the Lord Chancellor to be — More, many years in advance of his times, condemns the law as the fruit of avarice. The common good is his standard. And he dares to remind the king himself that his honour and safety are best supported by the well-being of his people as a whole, that "the commonalty chooseth their king for their own sake and not for his sake ; . . . therefore the king ought to take more care for the wealth of his people than for his own wealth."

More published his *Utopia* in 1516, and therefore before the Protestant revolt had broken out. But his book helps to explain the conditions that made the Reformation possible in England, among a people less touched by heresy than any nation in Europe. In England it would not have had the slightest chance of success had it not been that the landowners (including the ecclesiastical landowners) had already begun to reach out to seize their opportunity for vastly increasing their riches. The religious revolt was prepared for by the economic revolution that preceded it.

Let us remember another thing. If the process ended with the wholesale expropriation of church lands, it began with the expropriation of the lands of small owners. Only too often the titles of these did not rest upon formal deeds but upon custom. It was therefore not difficult for the lords of the manor, or (as in the beginning) monastic landowners to get rid of these smaller men. It could be argued with some plausibility that the regrouping of property would prove to be for the general good, that the lands would be more efficiently managed as large blocks than they had been in the hands of peasants. It was this argument that was used by Arthur Young in the eighteenth century, until he saw its fallacy.

But there had begun before the close of the fifteenth century a parallel process, which continued right into the nineteenth century, — that of the enclosure of the common lands. If you wander about England today you will still find tracts that are called "commons." What are these commons? They are merely the unfertile lands that no lord of the manor ever found it worth his while to enclose. But if they are no good to him, they are no good for the community either, except as playgrounds for children and picnic grounds for their elders. The original commons — those that were devoured — were, however, good for a great deal ; that was why they were enclosed. They and the farms of the small men and the rich abbeys all passed in the end into the hands of the rich. Without that incentive to back the Reformation, it could not possibly have succeeded in England.

We all know that under Henry's daughter Mary there was a return to Catholicism in England. But Mary perceived that she could not force the disgorging of the spoils of the Reformation. Those who had been Protestants under Edward VI, and were to be Protestants once again under Elizabeth — but who were, in many instances (including that of William Cecil) ostentatiously Catholic under Mary — were willing to be Catholic only on condition that the question of the expropriated lands was not raised. Sheep had not only eaten men ; they had already digested their meal.

This was the really decisive factor in the story of the English Reformation. Henry's breach with Rome was not decisive. His infatuation for Anne Boleyn was not decisive. Henry himself died a Catholic in his faith, except for the little matter of setting himself up as a kind of pope in England. The separation of England from communion with Rome need not have been permanent — not after Anne Boleyn's head had fallen and Jane Seymour had borne the king a son about whose legitimacy there could be no question. The permanent breach was caused by the despoiling of the Church, and the despoiling of the Church was simply a later stage of the process that started with the despoiling of thousands of small landowners and the enclosure of the commons.

More saw the beginning of the process, and he lifted his voice in sharp protest. Yet though he writes indignantly, he also writes with moderation. He does not expect everything he wishes to be brought about at a single stroke ; the most that he hopes for is that a brake be put upon greed, "for it is not possible for all things to be well, unless all men be good." Idealist as he is, he is also a practical man. In one sense, nobody is less of a Utopian than himself. He does not look for perfection, or think it possible, men being what they are. The abolition of private ownership would be (according to his way of thinking) this perfection ; as that is unattainable, "that which you cannot turn to good, [you should order so] that it be not very bad."

He was not looked upon as a revolutionary by his contemporaries. So far from the *Utopia* working against his political advancement, he seems to have been helped by it rather than otherwise. In 1518 he was made Master of Requests ; in 1521 he was knighted, appointed sub-treasurer to the King, and sent on a diplomatic mission to the Low Countries ; and in 1523 he became Speaker of the House of Commons, a more important position then than it is now, for it was his function to introduce legislation on behalf of the Crown. But he still had not reached the height of his career. In 1525 he was created Chancellor of the Duchy of Lancaster, and four years later he succeeded Cardinal Wolsey as Lord Chancellor, an office held previously only once by a layman. He had reached as high a post as any Englishman could attain. A famous man, famous as a scholar and writer as well as in public affairs, he could have had a peerage for the asking. Clearly the *Utopia* had not damaged him. What did damage him, what ruined him and made him glorious, was his adherence to principle.

But before we come to More in his last phase, we should go back a little way. In 1521 Henry VIII wrote a reply to Luther's *Babylonish Captivity of the Church*, which had appeared the previous year. In it the King showed himself a very able amateur theologian, and for his treatise obtained from Leo X the title of Defender of the Faith. Henry was, in fact, a man of considerable versatility, being a good poet, and the composer of charming music, which is still occasionally performed.

He also composed two Masses, though these have been lost. As for his theological knowledge, we must remember that, when his elder brother Arthur was alive, Henry, whom nobody expected to see king, studied with a view to taking orders and obtaining the archbishopric of Canterbury. But while Henry had some right to be proud of his accomplishments as a theologian, he sensibly recognized his limitations and so consulted people more learned than himself — notably More and Fisher. Henry in this book of his vigorously defended papal supremacy — so vigorously that More advised him not to commit himself too far. On Roper's authority — and Roper must have had his information from his father-in-law — Henry refused to alter his position, giving More a "secret" or, as we should say, a confidential reason why he should not do so. What that reason was we can only guess — for More preserved the King's confidence — but it probably had something to do with the dispensation the Pope had given him to marry Catherine of Aragon, who was, at least technically, Arthur's widow. At that time Henry would not have wanted the Pope's competence to dispense in such a case to be brought into question, as it could have been had the Pope's supremacy been questioned. We know of course that later Henry completely shifted his ground, and asserted that the dispensation was invalid because it was *ultra vires* ; when he wanted to get rid of Catherine he argued that not even the Pope could dispense from the law of God. But when he was writing against Luther, it was necessary to strengthen his thesis by advancing the Pope's power in its plenitude.

A long time afterwards, when More was being pressed to accept the King as head of the Church of England, he cleverly said, "I was myself sometime not of the mind [or the opinion] that the primacy of that See should be begun by the institution of God." . If it appear surprising that More could ever have had doubts about this, it must be borne in mind that the authority — at any rate the prestige — of the Holy See had been considerably shaken by the papal schisms, and that many good Catholics shared More's own doubts. It needed the challenge of the Protestant revolt to make More see the issue clearly and to recognize that the test of Catholicism was obedience to the Pope.

Even so, not many people in England saw the issue as More did. It is likely enough that many of the bishops who accepted the Henrican arrangement had serious misgivings ; yet only one bishop — Saint John Fisher — refused to take the oath of supremacy. This situation was reversed in the time of Elizabeth ; then only one bishop, the octogenarian Kitchen of Llandaff, refused the Elizabethan settlement. By that time the issue had become clear ; in More's day it was by no means clear. Therefore Henry was accepted by high ecclesiastical dignitaries as head of the Church, and perhaps with a reasonably good conscience — especially as the oath was administered with the proviso, "in so far as the law of God allows." This gave them a beautiful quibble : as the law of God did *not* allow it, why, the oath had no meaning. So long as they did not say that openly, Henry did not mind ; what mattered with him was that they take the oath. All except a very few did.

But though More saw his own mind plainly, he never once asserted that those who disagreed with him must be wrong ; never once did he try to persuade anyone to accept his views. On the contrary, he went as far as he could to be accommodating. He was perfectly willing to take that part of the oath bearing upon the right to the succession of such children as

Anne Boleyn might bear.   Whether or not she was Henry's true wife, it was within the competence of Parliament to legislate on the succession to the throne.

But Henry, having obtained this much from Parliament, framed the oath in such a form that the invalidity of Henry's marriage to Catherine was asserted — and therefore the validity of his marriage to Anne — along with the repudiation of any oath that had been taken "to any foreign authority, prince or potentate" — a phrase aimed directly at the Pope. This part of the oath More could not take with a good conscience ; this part of the oath he refused to take.

He resigned his office of Lord Chancellor willingly enough, and would have been content to live in quiet retirement, taking no part in controversy.   Had he not been so very prominent a person, he might have been left alone.   As it was, efforts were made to win him over to the official side.   Henry would have much preferred this to More's destruction.   He was More's friend and had delighted in his good company so much that More, in order to get some time to spend with his wife and children, had been obliged to restrain the exuberance of his wit.   For his part, he had always understood Henry.   We all know the story of how when the King dropped in one day at Chelsea uninvited, as he often did, and when Roper congratulated More upon Henry's hearty friendliness — for Roper had seen the King walking in the garden with his arm round More's neck — More smiled wrily and said, "If my neck would give the King a town in France, he would soon find a better use for it."   There More was right, but Henry's liking for him was so great that it would have been easy for More to have exploited it.   This was true even after his fall from office ; all that was asked of him was that he should be reasonable, that he should not take what seemed to everyone an eccentric position.

People tried to warn him. The Duke of Norfolk told him that the anger of the King was death, only to get the reply that the Duke, like himself, was on the way to the scaffold, and that the only difference was that "I die today and you tomorrow." (I pause to remark that had Henry lived a day longer than he did, the Duke would have been beheaded ; by then he *was* lying under sentence of death, and his son, the Earl of Surrey, the poet, was actually executed.) But where More could resist with gentle scorn the well-meant suggestions of time-serving politicians, he must have found it hard to stand out against his own family, knowing that by doing so that he was going to ruin them. It was understandable that More's wife should think her husband merely stubborn in his attitude ; "Tilly-vally, tilly-vally !" so she impatiently dismissed notions beyond her comprehension. What may have been much less easy to endure was that his dearly loved daughter, Margaret Roper, should have been out of sympathy with him. She thought, as the rest did, that he ought to take the oath.

It was therefore in complete isolation and loneliness that he had to make his decision. He did not make it without a struggle. When summoned to appear before the Council he said to Roper, "Son Roper, I thank Our Lord the field is won," which suggests that More had wavered until then in his mind. As much as any other man he feared the fate he knew was waiting him, and far more than other men he was capable of devising irrefutable arguments with which to still his conscience. He refused all subterfuges. It is his greatness that, when brought to the test, he not only laid down his life but renounced his exalted position, thus proving beyond all question that what he had said against worldliness he really meant.

For this he is admired even by those who do not agree with him. He is also admired for never striking any heroic attitude or rushing upon his doom. Instead he fought the case against him most skilfully, and would have won, had it been a case that he could win. And the King, for his part, did not press the proceedings against him precipitately ; he was willing to bargain. More was kept a year in prison, in the hope that upon reflection he would do the very little that was asked of him. Only when Henry saw that nothing else would serve, was More put upon trial for high treason. Then for what seemed a scruple he showed himself ready to go to his death. He was determined not to let the Catholic cause go by default.

How nobly he spoke at his trial ! When his judges suggested that he speed matters along by denouncing the statute, as fencing with them was of no avail, he answered, "I have not been a man of such holy living as I might be bold to offer myself to death, lest God for my presumption might suffer me to fall ; and therefore I put not myself forward but draw back. Howbeit, if God draw me to it Himself, then trust I in His great mercy that He shall not fail to give me grace and strength." In his *Dialogue of Comfort Against Tribulation,* written by him in the Tower, he deals with a scruple. Might it not be better to bow before persecution, Vincent asks Anthony, lest in the very torment of death faith be denied and the soul damned for ever ? On the other hand, by making a formal recantation for the time being, that same man might live, and do many good works, and repent before a natural death and so be saved. To that sophistry Anthony answered decisively : What is it that this man would have to repent ? What else than not having died for his faith ? "What folly is it then for fear to flee that death, which thou shalt shortly after wish thou hadst died. Yea, I ween almost every good christen man would very fain this day that he had been for Christ's faith cruelly killed yesterday, even for the desire of heaven, though there were no hell."

But to return to the trial. More was condemned largely on the perjured evidence of Richard Rich, the later Lord Chancellor. This wretched creature got Fisher condemned by much the same means. His subsequent career is interesting, if only for its contrast with More's; for he helped Thomas Cromwell, then deserted him just in time, and became one of Henry's main agents in the persecution of heretics, racking Anne Askew with his own hands. In the next reign he brought in the bill of attainder against Seymour, then helped to overthrow his patron Somerset, and, after trying to keep Mary from the throne, was conspicuous for the severities he used against Protestants. This is how More dealt with him : "If I were a man, my lords, that did not regard an oath, I need not, as·is well known, stand in this place at this time, nor in this case as an accused person. And if this oath of yours, Mr. Rich, be true, then I pray that I never see God face to face ; which I would not say, were it otherwise to win the whole world." Even as sentence was about to be passed on him, as from the beginning he had known it would be, he corrected Audley, the new Lord Chancellor, on a point of procedure : "My lord, when I was towards the law the manner in such case was to ask the prisoner before judgment why judgment should not be given against him." The correction was accepted ; everybody in that court knew that they were being judged by the prisoner before them.

After the trial More was taken back to the Tower in a barge,

and there he was put in the charge of the same Sir William
Kingston who, not long afterwards, was to act as jailor of Anne
Boleyn.   At the Tower wharf Margaret Roper ran forward,
pressing through the guards, and, throwing her arms around
his neck, kissed him ; in fact she did this several times, taking
farewell of her father and then running back to him again and
again, "the beholding whereof was to many that were present
so lamentable that it made them for very sorrow thereof to
weep."   Not many days before he had written to her, in
charcoal because pen and ink had by then been taken away,
"Written with a coal by your tender loving father who in his
poor prayers forgetteth none of you all, nor your babes, nor
your nurses, nor your husbands' good shrewd wives, nor your
father's shrewd wife neither, nor our other friends.   And thus
fare ye well for lack of paper."

Henry had commuted, as had been expected, the hanging
and drawing and quartering to a simple beheading.   But he
asked that the speech from the scaffold be brief.   More jested
with the officer in charge and with the executioner, and he
spoke only a few words.   One phrase of that speech will
always be remembered.   He said he died "the King's good and
loyal servant, but God's first."

It was More who clarified the issue.   His speech foretold
that heroic resistance to the suppression of Catholicism in
England which finds perhaps its grandest expression in the
speech of Blessed Edmund Campion.   Westminster Hall has
heard such magnificent oratory, but surely none as moving as
that of the Jesuit who, unable to raise his hands because of the
racking he had received in the Tower, said : "The only thing
we have to say now is that, if our religion do make us traitors,
then we are worthy to be condemned, but otherwise are and

have been as true subjects as ever the Queen has. In condemning us you condemn all your own ancestors, all the ancient priests, bishops and kings — all that was once the glory of England, the island of saints and the most devoted child of the See of Peter. For what have we taught, however you may qualify with the odious name of treason, that they did not uniformly teach ? To be condemned with these old lights not of England only but of the world by their degenerate descendants is both glory and gladness to us. God lives ; posterity will live ; their judgment is not so liable to corruption as that of you who are now going to torture us to death."

But it began with Saint Thomas More.

VII

SAINT FRANCIS XAVIER

Upon the discovery in 1492 of what turned out to be the New World, Pope Alexander VI divided these lands between Spain and Portugal on the strict understanding that they undertook the carrying of the Faith to the heathen of their dominions. The missionary undertakings that followed were sometimes as rough and ready as the principle of division — a line drawn from north to south — was arbitrary ; but at least an obligation was imposed upon the conquerors.   Mexico was humbled by Cortes when Francis Xavier was a little boy of five ; Peru fell to Pizarro just after Francis had taken his Master's degree in Paris and had become a professor of philosophy.   The greatest of all missionaries was therefore born at the psychological moment — the moment that drew him forth.

Most of the missionary efforts attempted were, as was natural and indeed inevitable, closely tied to the schemes of conquest and colonization.   The friars sent out to the pagan lands were usually very good men, but they were not merely apostles of the Christian faith but (at least to some extent) agents of their respective governments, from whom their support came ; and this fact hampered them.   In the case of Francis Xavier, however, there was a wholly disinterested enthusiasm.   A subject of Spain, he did not go to the New World but to the Indies ; and the Indies had been apportioned to Portugal.   This not only left him free (though his backing was derived from Portugal) but proves the perfect disinterestedness of his motives.   He thought only of Christ the King and, if of King

John at Lisbon at all, only of John as one under his command as an auxiliary.   In the last year of his life, after his mission to Japan, he wrote to the Jesuits at Coimbra asking that the Emperor Charles V be warned against making any attempt to conquer Japan which, under the terms of Alexander VI's division, might have been considered as falling within Spanish jurisdiction.   Quite bluntly he let the Emperor know that any army he sent there would meet with a very different reception from the Central and South American countries that had been conquered by a handful of men.   He was convinced that traders could best open up Japan.   Though he was himself a *conquistador*, he was certainly not one according to the Spanish model.

His letters, published first — a handful of them — in Paris but afterwards in other European countries, electrified their readers.   "How I should like to go," he wrote in one of them, "through the universities of Europe shouting like a madman about the souls that are being lost.   How many there are in such places who are thinking only of getting a high position in the Church through their reputation for learning, instead of using their acquirements for the common good.   If only they would leave their miserable ambitions and say, 'Lord, here am I.   Send me wherever Thou wilt — even to India !'   How much better their own state would be when they come to die."   Like his captain, Christ, Francis cast fire on the earth.   Though there were many phases of missionary work that he never touched, and though his successors in some ways improved upon his methods, Francis was the great blazer of the trail, the great inspirer ; rightly is he regarded as the patron of Catholic missions.

A man like Francis could not always bother himself with de-

tails — though he was far more mindful of them than is sometimes supposed. His function was that of mapping out the
plan of campaign, and this envisaged nothing less than the winning of the whole Orient — and eventually the whole world
— for Christ. He believed that this might be brought about
during his own lifetime, or that he might at least live to see
it well under way. Remember that he sailed for India when
he was thirty-five — on his thirty-fifth birthday — and that he
died ten and a half years later. It was not unreasonable of him
to count upon twenty more years of active missionary work,
and even had he been brought back to succeed Saint Ignatius as
the General of the Society of Jesus (as almost certainly would
have happened), in that position he might, with his experience,
have been all the more useful as the director of world-wide
missionary operations. What might he not have accomplished
in another twenty years ! Yet when he was on the threshold
of what could have been his greatest success — a mission to
China — he died, and at his death a tempestuous onrush seemed
to have failed.

Whether or not the plans of Francis were sound, he had plans
of a very far-reaching kind. Though he may strike the casual
observer as a man aimlessly dashing here and there, one moving
so fast that he was hardly to be seen for the dust his heels kicked
up, he did in fact act according to careful designs. Impulsive
as he was, and subject to moods of depression, his emotions were
controlled. The resilience of his nature — to say nothing of
his confidence in God — did not allow him to be depressed for
long. That is the important thing to seize about him at the
outset. Fiery ? Impassioned ? He was all that. But he
thought things out and never did anything until he *had* thought
them out. In small matters he was an ingenious improvisor,

and he was never at a loss in a new situation ; but his large schemes were never improvised on the spur of the moment.   In short : he was an exceedingly complex character, and one of enormous versatility ; but everything was directed to a single aim.   In that alone was he simple ; in that alone was he fixed.

Saint Ignatius said that of all the men he had ever encountered Francis Xavier was the hardest to mould.   The winning of him took a long time and boundless patience.   But Ignatius had always known that the trouble was worth the taking, for stubborn men like Francis, especially when they have the flame of genius, are not only going to last but are going to impart their driving force to others.   A cold, calculating man, though with his own dash of fire, Ignatius knew what he was up to. For Francis he paid the highest of prices — and got the greatest of bargains.

Francis, like Ignatius, was a Basque ; and the Basques are a very strange people, a unique people.   They are to be found on the northern side of the Pyrenees, in France, and they are to be found on the Spanish side of the mountains.   But if you want to insult a Basque, tell him that he is a Frenchman — or a Spaniard.   Just as their language has no discoverable relation to any other, so their race has no relation to any other.   They are an enigma, and are proud of it.   Though Francis Xavier left his native land, soon after it had lost its independence, and went to the University of Paris, and afterwards to India — following a few years in Italy — he remained a Basque to the end, in spite of his cosmopolitan upbringing.   He had indeed few opportunities to speak his native language ; French, Spanish, Portuguese, Italian — these were the tongues he used, and later in the Orient he picked up a smattering of several other languages, including the Tamil, a dialect of southern India ; but when he was dying at the close of 1551 he forgot all of them, and those beside his bed heard him muttering his prayers in Basque.

It was the attachment of the Xaviers to the royal house of Spanish Navarre which ruined them, for never would they be reconciled to the annexation of their country to Spain. Ignatius Loyola, a fire-eating, romantic little man — but also a shrewd one, not much given to the following of lost causes — took service as an officer under the Spanish King. But it was not so with Francis's family. When Loyola had his leg fractured by a cannon ball at the time he was in command of the defence of Pamplona, among the besiegers were two of the Xavier brothers. It is not at all impossible that one of them may have fired the cannon that changed the whole course of Loyola's life. Not until three years later, nine years after the annexation of Navarre, could they be brought to make their submission to Charles V.

In that same year of 1524 Francis Xavier went to the University of Paris. That he went there would indicate that he was seeking the best education obtainable, for though he was a man of action rather than a scholar — and perhaps too brilliant ever to have settled down contentedly with his books in a silent study — he was after all at that time seeking his advancement through learning.

He thought also of this advancement as being attainable through the Church. In it there were magnificent openings for a man of good family and good parts and good education. If Francis did not propose self-sacrificing devotion — for the Church was to serve him, if he was to serve the Church — he intended to be a good Christian and to perform his duties faithfully. But his motive was ambition, an ambition that might have led him to worldly success, and the oblivion of his name.

A very different fate was prepared for him, while he was still studying at Paris, by a man whom he had not as yet met. A Basque soldier, still limping from the wound he had received at Pamplona, had begun to study Latin among young boys, though he himself was a grown man, at about the same time that Francis Xavier was entering the College of Saint Barbara. Ignatius had already made his long retreat in the cave of Manresa and had gone on pilgrimage to the Holy Land and had sketched out his *Spiritual Exercises*. Since then he had wandered from place to place in Spain, often regarded with suspicion by the Inquisition, and in Flanders and England. When at last he limped into Paris in February, 1528, behind a donkey carrying his books and the manuscript of the *Exercises*, his great work was just about to begin. It was there that he was to gather his first permanent disciples — among them Francis Xavier.

Ignatius registered at the same college that Calvin had attended, but about the time that Calvin was leaving. He soon transferred, however, to Saint Barbara's, where he shared a room with Francis, who for a while coached the elderly and rather backward student before passing on the job to Peter Faber. By dint of sheer doggedness Ignatius did eventually obtain the bachelor's and even the master's degree, something that Francis also obtained, though far more easily.

It is amusing to record that the founder of the Jesuits got into trouble at Saint Barbara's over an infraction of discipline caused by one of his acts of charity. And as college students in those days were punished like small boys, Ignatius had to run the gauntlet after dinner. Among those waiting to give a good whack at his bare back was a young Scot, who was a professor at the college. He was to become famous as a Latin poet and infamous as one of the most unscrupulous enemies of Mary Queen of Scots. His name was George Buchanan, and there is little doubt that he was one of the forgers of the Casket Letters. But he never laid any blow on Ignatius. Just when the scourging was about to begin, the culprit walked in arm-in-arm with James Govea, the rector of the college, to whom he had explained everything satisfactorily. This Govea was later to be instrumental in obtaining Jesuits to serve in the King of Portugal's dominions in India ; he was also to be the editor of the first collection published of Francis Xavier's letters.

Francis passed his final examinations in the spring of 1530, being soon afterwards appointed to teach philosophy at the Collège Dormans-Beauvais, and Ignatius went plodding along with his studies and trying to effect Francis's conversion. The question always put to the ambitious young professor was, "What shall it profit a man if he gain the whole world and lose his own soul ?" But M. André Bellesort, the author of what is perhaps the best of the popular lives of Francis, throws out the plausible conjecture that Ignatius did not try to show his friend that he was too ambitious but that he was not ambitious enough. After all, what was it that Francis was aiming at ? Only a good ecclesiastical job, a comfortable living, what Edward Gibbon was to call "the fat slumbers of the Church." Ignatius, though not a showily brilliant man, was a profound psychologist, and he may well have indicated how one object could be replaced with another. There was of course no idea of missionary work in India as yet ; in so far as Ignatius had any definite plans it was only for taking his disciples to the Holy Land. But there was the idea of an absolute dedication to the service of God — whatever form it might take.

We know what followed.   After Francis had been won, he and Ignatius and five other men, all of them students at the university or professors there, walked to the other side of the river from the Latin Quarter to a little tumble-down church on the summit that belonged to the Benedictine nuns.   There was only one priest among them — Peter Faber — and he said Mass, after which all seven of them took a vow of chastity and poverty and pledged themselves to go to the Holy Land.   There was no vow of obedience, for there was no superior, nor was there any rule.   That August 15, 1534, the Feast of the Assumption, was the birthday of the Society of Jesus.

Not until after this did Ignatius put Francis through the *Spiritual Exercises,* though usually this preceded everything else.   Then as Père Brou, the writer of one of the two most heavily documented lives of Xavier puts it :   "Francis came out of the Exercises changed and another man.   From now on, it is the life of a saint that we write."

At first, however, his was the life of a somewhat injudicious saint.   Like Ignatius before him, in his first headlong enthusiasm he went in for extreme physical mortifications, to such an extent that he came near crippling himself.   That phase soon passed ; like Ignatius again he came to perceive that he could best serve God by keeping his health.   On this point the founder of the Jesuits was obliged, many years later, to write the Duke of Gandia, our Saint Francis Borgia, the great-grandson of Alexander VI, a long letter in which, out of his own experience, he tells him :   "We ought to love and cherish the body in so far as it is obedient and helpful to the soul, for with such obedience and assistance the soul can the better dispose itself to serve and praise our Creator and Lord. . . With regard to the castigation of the body, I would be for avoiding altogether any form of it that would cause a single drop of blood to appear. . . Instead of seeking to shed our blood, it is much better to seek directly the Lord of us all and His holy gifts, such as tears for our sins . . . an intensification of our faith, hope and charity, joy in God, and spiritual peace. . . Each of these gifts ought to be greatly preferred to all corporal actions, which are good only in so far as they tend to obtain these gifts for us." Like Francis of Assisi, Francis Xavier came to see that he had been too hard on "Brother Ass." He needed all his strength for the work ahead of him.

Ordination came for Francis in Italy and in September, 1540, the Society received papal approval of its Constitutions. By that time Francis was already in Lisbon, waiting for a boat to take him to India. It was not he who had originally been selected for the mission, for he seemed a man already broken in health. But it is rash to make such judgments of saints, or even of men of genius ; and Francis Xavier was both. Much of the world's best work has been done by hopeless invalids. Bobadilla was to have gone, but as he fell ill at the last moment, Ignatius took his chance with a man slightly less ill. He got the reply from Francis, "Well, here I am — ready." The next day he left for Lisbon.

Some of the early biographers have told how when Francis was on his journey there he passed the home of his boyhood but showed such detachment from earthly things that he would not even go to see his mother. Idiotically that has been praised ; a little less idiotically it has been condemned. The truth is that Francis's mother was at that time dead and his brothers living elsewhere. Moreover, it is even unlikely that the route by which Francis went passed anywhere near the Xavier castle, and he was travelling in the entourage of the Portuguese Ambassador, an impatient man who wished to get to Lisbon without unnecessary delay.

There the pious King John would have detained him and his companion, Simon Rodriguez. A compromise had to be made, so as not to offend the King on whom the support of the mission depended. Rodriguez was left behind and Francis, alone except for an assistant whom he had picked up in Portugal, went to India.

The friendship formed between the King and Queen of Portugal and Francis was very valuable to him. He had to rely on their backing in the difficulties encountered in the Indies, where the Portuguese officials often opposed and hampered his work. Then he had no hesitation in bullying John, even going so far as to threaten him with hell fire unless he kept his officials in order. As for the Queen, on one occasion he calmly appropriated certain revenues that were set aside for her on the Malabar pearl-fisheries and that were called her slipper-money. Having pocketed this money for the use of his missions, he wrote to tell her that by doing so he was providing her with slippers with which she might climb into heaven.

Goa, which he reached on May 6, 1542, after over a year at sea, was the administrative and ecclesiastical centre of the Portuguese possessions in the Orient. It was also a sink of appalling moral corruption and official venality. For though the succession of governors appointed by the Crown were all conscientious men, many of their underlings were brazenly rapacious. It was this that sometimes made Francis almost despair and forms the theme of half his indignant letters to Ignatius and the King.

Francis did what he could to improve conditions in that city, though he had not gone to India for the sake of the Portuguese but of the heathen. It was in Goa, however, that he initiated methods that proved so effectual that he used them everywhere for the rest of his life. This was the putting of the Catechism into verse and teaching people to singsong it. The mnemonic device might still be used to good purpose — if a good enough poet could be found to make the Catechism. Helen Parry Eden showed what might be done with it in her *String of Sapphires*, a rhymed life of Our Lord.

The missionary work did not get fully under way until October of the year of Francis's arrival. It was then that he went to the Paravas of the Malabar coast, a low caste that had a few years before accepted baptism *en masse* in order to put themselves under the protection of the Portuguese but who had been left ignorant of Christian doctrine and who were still practicing their debased superstitions.

This part of India I happen to know very well, for it was there that I spent my boyhood, travelling over much of the ground that Saint Francis traversed, with a Protestant missionary, my father. And India — that land of seven hundred thousand primitive villages — has not changed much in those places since Francis's time. Though he does not as a rule give detailed descriptions in his letters, all that he does say perfectly corresponds with my own observation. For those who want a minute account of Indian customs as they were in the eighteenth century — but as they also were in the sixteenth and as they are today — I recommend the remarkable account written by the Abbé Dubois, which was published in two volumes in Paris in 1825 and appeared in English translation in 1898.

The Brahmins Francis encountered only in passing. As André Bellesort has said, there was in all India no man who was less of a Brahmin than this Basque nobleman, the master of arts of Paris. His opinion of the sacred gentry was low, and his references to them often scathing. He addressed himself almost solely to the lower castes, as they offered the greatest opportunities.

He could hardly have done otherwise with the means at his disposal. But it should be added that he was temperamentally unfitted to use methods similar to those of the seventeenth century Robert de' Nobili and his associates. These did succeed in winning many Brahmins to Christianity, though it was charged that this was brought about only by making impermissible concessions. Though it would be unjust to de' Nobili to say that he presented the Christian religion to the Brahmins as a kind of esoteric hinduism, and still more unjust to say that he made too many accommodations, it would seem that he had no objection to the Brahmins thinking that the missionaries who had come to them were Brahmins themselves. They appeared to be initiates in mysteries of a special profundity (as of course they were), and these they expounded in the terms of Brahminical philosophy with which they had thoroughly familiarized themselves. They dressed as ascetics, and they wore the sacred cord and the caste marks. They were punctilious about observing the thousand and one details of Brahmin usage, in so far as these could be used by Christians. And they had so perfectly mastered the language of Southern India that Beschi, one of the band, wrote an epic poem on the life of Saint Joseph which is still regarded as one of the classics of Tamil literature, though native critics sometimes object that it is a trifle too florid. By these means the seventeenth century Jesuits brought in — for the first and last time — Brahmin converts by the thousand ; and to this day there are Christian communities near Madura who regard themselves socially as Brahmin and hold themselves aloof from the Christians who come from the lower castes. These are the descendants of de' Nobili's converts.

The Paravas of the Malabar coast, on the other hand, were poor and despised and ignorant, and the pearls for which they dived did not bring them much profit, most of this being filched from them by the local rajahs or the Portuguese officials. Inland on the apex of the peninsula was a bare, parched country, cultivated by primitive methods and irrigated by methods even more primitive. Coconut palms and bananas gave some fruit, the palms also supplying a juice that quickly fermented into a heady intoxicant. There were fields of rice and *cholum*, a grain cheaper than rice and therefore almost the only food eaten by these people. Their huts were built of mud and bamboo and banana tree trunks, and were thatched or covered with palm leaves. Their only fuel was dried cow dung. Their only furniture was a fibre mat for a bed. Rats and bedbugs infested everything, and the hair of the women was full of lice. You may still see them in India sitting in long rows, searching one another's coarse black locks and handing whatever they find to the owner for execution — a point of punctilious etiquette. From the magnificent temples, rising tier on tier like flattened pyramids and profusely sculptured with fantastic obscenities, the lower castes were excluded. They were even excluded by the Brahmins from an understanding of their religion, which was kept as an esoteric affair beyond the capacity of their degraded minds. All that was left to them was these wayside shrines, but these they had by the thousand ; and their worship was a compound of the cult of the devil and erotic superstition. For this they could hardly be blamed ; it was all that the priestly class wished them to have. Let them by all means guard their poor fields by providing a local deity with a stable of life-sized horses on which to ride at night, and an inverted earthenware pot, spotted with white paint, as a remedy against the evil eye. Brahminical metaphysics were not for them, though it should be added that relatively few Brahmins themselves bothered to do more than carry out a ritual and to collect their tribute.

For the priestly caste Francis had an angry contempt as for arrogant impostors. It was among the poor and the oppressed that he reaped his most abundant harvest. Up and down that coast he went, under the blazing sun, baptizing all day until his arms ached, but doing something besides baptize : he had to create a system of catechists, establishing one of these so far as possible in every village or group of villages to complete what he was obliged to leave undone. At first he had to use interpreters, as he knew no Tamil ; but he learned that beautiful language later, though he never appears to have known it very well. He is credited with the gift of tongues, but this is not borne out by his letters, in which he tells how painfully he acquired all the languages he used and how imperfectly he succeeded in making himself understood. Yet there may have been occasions when he received supernatural aid to supplement his natural powers. Everywhere he was followed by huge crowds, and six or seven thousand people were often present when he hoisted himself into a many-rooted banyan tree to preach. An entire Indian caste was for the only time in history brought into the Church.

Many of them proved to be, as was only to be expected, rather unsatisfactory Christians. Their intelligence was not great, and they had slight strength of fibre. Not only were there moral lapses but relapses into paganism. But though the quality of the converts was often disappointing, we must not forget that a very large number of the Catholics in Southern India stem directly from these men and women, and among them the name of their apostle is held in the highest esteem. For that matter, it is venerated even among the pagans, and there is some reason to believe that this Catholic saint was admitted to the Hindu pantheon, which contains so many hundreds of millions of godlets that nobody has ever been able to enumerate them all.

If the native Christians were often of poor quality, they were at least much less reprehensible than were many of the Portuguese, who had been Christians from their youth. Francis burned with indignation against the officials who should have been helping him but whose scandalous lives and inappeasable greed were stumbling-blocks to the Gospel. "Nobody can count," he wrote in January, 1545, to Simon Rodriguez, "the devices they have for theft or the number of pretexts under which they commit it ! I have never ceased wondering at the number of new inflexions they have added to the conjugation of the verb *to rob*." He therefore appealed to the King, demanding the appointment for India of an ecclesiastical official with power to punish the venality and vice of the men who were causing the trouble. But little was effected, except the establishment of the Inquisition at Goa, which was not what Francis had had in mind. In the end Francis left India for Malacca, partly in disgust, but partly because he was burning to break new ground. India, however, remained his headquarters ; however many and how long his journeys, it was always to India that he returned.

Malacca turned out to be a place quite as corrupt as Goa, and as it was farther away from the eye of the Governor, crimes could be committed with even greater immunity than at Goa. Francis was received with wild enthusiasm ; he effected a temporary improvement in morals; but he soon left to press on to what were then called the Spice Islands.

It was now that he reached many places little known until the present war, but whose names have been frequently in the news of late — Amboyna and Celebes among them. He did not intend to stay long ; it was his purpose merely to do what he could in the time at his disposal, to survey the ground, and to select spots for the establishment of permanent missions later. It is worth noting that when he left he took back with him twenty Moluccans with a view to having them educated for the priesthood. Although they proved unsuitable for that office, he did manage to obtain a few Tamil boys who were eventually ordained and who did good service. He recognized from the start the need for a native clergy, even if his attempts to create it turned out rather premature.

Back in Malacca in December, 1547, Francis encountered a young Japanese trader named Anjiro. It was he who fired Francis with the idea of going to Japan. As Paul of the Holy Faith he accompanied Francis when, after a year spent there in organizing his work, he sailed for what was the most remarkable of all his missions.

Paul was of considerable use to Francis in the beginning, though he seriously misinformed him about Japanese conditions. Moreover, Paul failed his trust, when things got too hot for him. His end is uncertain, but according to reports that came in later, he turned river-pirate in China and was killed on one of his forays. But that profession was considered respectable enough, and at least he had led Francis to Japan.

It was on the Feast of the Assumption, August 15, 1549, that Francis arrived at Kagoshima, at the southern tip of the most southernly of the four principal islands that make up the Japanese kingdom. It was the fifteenth anniversary of the vows of Montmartre, a highly auspicious day. And it must be said that, though Francis saw the faults of the Japanese clearly, he reached the conclusion that "this Japanese nation is the only one which seems to me likely to maintain unshaken the Christian faith if it once embraces it." Arrogant as he found their nobles to be, and corrupt as he considered their priests — even the children were the most malicious little devils he had ever encountered — he observed that those who became Christians were fervent and steadfast in their faith and added to their ceremonial politeness the real spirit of courtesy, an exquisite charity. He even struck up a friendship with the abbot of a Buddhist monastery, an old noble who had retired from the world, who seems to have been very frank when talking to Francis. One day he said of his monks as they sat in meditation, when Francis asked what was the subject of their thoughts : "Well, some of them are adding up how much they collected in gifts last month ; others are thinking about their food and clothes ; others again about how they are going to amuse themselves. Of this you may be sure — not one of them is thinking of anything important." But in spite of his disillusioned cynicism about Buddhist monasticism, the abbot showed no desire to become a Christian himself.

Francis, like the practical man he was, set himself to obtain the favour of the daimyos, for he saw that nothing could be done in this rigidly feudal country without their permission. He did not make converts of any of them, but he did receive permission to make converts. And though these came in slowly, a Church was built up. That the work was done thoroughly by Francis and his successors is shown by the fact that when, early in the seventeenth century, there broke out what is perhaps the most cruel and persistent persecution any Christian people has had to undergo, the Faith lived on underground in Japan for two hundred and fifty years, without priests, and without any of the sacraments except baptism.

The Mikado was sought out by Francis. But in this matter Paul of the Holy Faith had led him astray : at this time the Son of Heaven was a nominal ruler, officially divine of course, but a neglected man who lived in a dilapidated sprawling palace, surrounded by his concubines, suffered to exist merely because his nobles thought it hardly worth their while to get rid of him. Even the Shogun, the commander-in-chief of the army, was in temporary eclipse. The daimyos were everything. Fortunately some of them were induced to protect Christianity because of the prospects of trade. And here things looked so bright that Francis wrote to Pedro da Silva, the commandant of Malacca, suggesting that he act as his commercial agent in Japan, and guaranteeing a hundred percent profit. This offer was made because it was through trade that he hoped to win the goodwill of the Japanese ; and if ships came regularly to the country, they would be very useful for the transportation of missionaries. He himself had ventured there on a Chinese junk whose captain he had had reason to suspect was a pirate.

Again Francis showed his good sense. He had been received contemptuously in Kyoto, the capital, because he arrived there in rags. The palace guards had asked only one question : "Where are your presents ?" As he had brought none, he failed to get an audience with the Mikado. After this experience

Francis changed his tactics. He dressed well and he gave handsome gifts to the nobles ; we hear of musical instruments, a painting in oils, a clock, mirrors, watches and brocade. It is amusing to record that it was the Saint who introduced port into Japan ; until then there had been nothing but rice wine. By these means Francis won favour, and his knowledge of astronomy excited admiration.

But the converts still came in very slowly. There was, however, one man who, baptized under the name of Lawrence, entered the Society and proved a most valuable acquisition. This half-blind ballad-singer was wonderful with any audience, whether it was a crowd gathered in the streets or with the nobles and priests. Thousands were converted by his preaching. He did more perhaps than any other man to spread the Faith in Japan. Those who later complained that he was never ordained forget that no bishop arrived in the country until 1592 ; they also forget that Lawrence's increasing blindness made him ineligible for the priesthood. In any event it was better to leave him as he was, uneducated but with a vast fund of wit and mother-wit. But that Francis did wish to create a native clergy is shown by his taking two young Japanese with him to Goa, where they were to be trained in the local college.

Francis had learned a great deal in Japan. He was convinced of the immense possibilities of the country, and he now needed new men for the mission. But he had persuaded himself that, before he could make real headway there, he would first have to enter China. The Japanese, he thought, had such a vast respect for Chinese culture (from which their own was derived) that, if he could only win China, Japan would fall into his lap like a ripe fruit at a touch. It was therefore not in disappointment with the rather meagre results of his work that he left, as is sometimes said, but only in order to plan his campaign in a different fashion. He was undoubtedly misinformed as to the effects that a successful Chinese mission would have in Japan, but the lines of his attack at least prove that he was calculating carefully and not plunging in recklessly without thought of consequences.

So also with regard to the problem as to how to obtain admission into China, a land then absolutely closed against all Europeans. Francis believed he had solved it while on the return journey to Malacca, for he discussed with the owner of the ship on which he was travelling, Diego Pereira, a scheme under which Periera was to be appointed ambassador to the Emperor of China from the King of Portugal — with an eye to trading possibilities once the country was opened up — while Francis was to go with him as a member of his entourage. The plan would have worked, had it not been for one small accident that nobody could foresee.

There was no time to refer the matter to the King of Portugal, but the Governor at Goa gave Pereira the necessary credentials, so that Francis, after having seen to missionary affairs in India, sailed for Malacca in the early spring of 1552. It was there that everything was wrecked by the newly-appointed Governor. He simply forbade the embassy. Francis might go alone, if he wished ; Pereira was not to go.

The commandant was one of the many sons of the great Vasco da Gama, and he had some obscure grudge against Pereira or Francis, or against both. That at any rate is the usual explanation of his motives, though it is possible that he felt that he should have been consulted in this appointment, and now wished to show that he possessed authority. Francis in all likelihood would have been upheld, had he appealed to Goa ;

but this of course was not certain, and it would have involved at least a year's delay. Understanding all this, the commandant stood firm, affecting to believe that the appointment of Pereira as ambassador must refer to some other Pereira ; it could not be this fellow who was given such an exalted office. And when Francis threatened the commandant with excommunication, saying that he was the papal nuncio, again there was a pretense of disbelief. Until that time Francis had never used his authority as nuncio, or had even let people know that he possessed it. And he had left the attesting documents in Goa.

Nothing could be done, except that Francis might go to China alone, and to attempt to obtain admission there, as everyone knew, would be to attempt the impossible. No Portuguese ships were allowed to enter any Chinese port, though their presence at Sanchian Island, opposite Canton, was winked at by the mandarins. Nevertheless he determined to go there and to trust to some ingenious stratagem for getting to the mainland. And this though he fully realized arrival there might cost him his life, probably in hideous tortures.

He was not dismayed by that prospect ; the difficulty was that of finding a ferryman bold enough to carry him from Sanchian Island to Canton. Even the lay-brother by whom he was accompanied, Anthony Fereira, was so shaken by fear that he withdrew from the undertaking — and was expelled by Francis from the Society. After that nobody was left with Francis except a young Tamil and a young Chinese.

A junkman was at last discovered who agreed to take Francis across the narrow strip of water — at an exorbitant price. Even so, not much trust could be placed in the man ; he might tip his passenger overboard once he had collected the fare. But Francis accepted that risk ; it was the junkman who was in a state of hesitation, and who eventually backed out. Upon this, Francis began to meditate an alternative plan — of going to Siam, as he had heard that every year an embassy was sent from that country to Pekin. Perhaps he would be allowed to accompany it ; after that he hoped that such credentials as he carried would suffice. What he never thought of was giving up his plan and returning to Malacca.

The Portuguese began to leave Sanchian in November, and before leaving they had to dismantle the huts they had put up, as these officially were not supposed to exist. After their departure food ran low, and by the end of the month Francis was seriously ill.

Even so, he would not leave. Therefore the last of the Portuguese crews gave him, before setting sail, a rug and a handful of almonds — strange food for a sick man — and left him in the care of the faithful Chinese youth, Anthony. He crawled under what few ramshackle sticks still stood of a hut, and there he waited his end. Anthony put a candle in his hand, and with his eyes fastened upon his crucifix Francis Xavier died. He had been murmuring Basque in his delirious moments. At the very end he was calm and collected and said as his last words the line from the *Te Deum* :

In te, Domine, speravi ; non confundar in aeternum.

His body was buried in quicklime so as to clean the bones by the time the Portuguese traders came back in the summer ; then they could take his remains to Malacca. When his grave was opened, his body was found perfectly fresh, in spite of the quicklime. In Malacca it was buried again and remained there for eighteen months. Disinterred for the second time, it was still quite incorrupt. When at Goa it was exposed for veneration a certain Isabella de Carom, in an excess of fervour, bit off one of his toes in order to preserve it as a relic. The right hand that had baptized so many thousands of pagans was also cut off and sent to Rome, where it is still kept in the Gesù. But the rest of the body of Saint Francis Xavier lies in a magnificent reliquary in the Church of the Bom Jesu at Goa. There it is exhibited once every ten years. The face of the Saint now appears to be mummified, and looks like terra cotta, but the whole body is incorrupt to this day — perhaps the most remarkable instance of this phenomenon ever to have occurred.

In conclusion let me quote the opening of Father James Broderick's brilliant book, *The Origin of the Jesuits*. Ignatius Loyola has been touched upon here, though of course not adequately. But as Francis Xavier should always be remembered with him, and he with Francis Xavier, I present Father Broderic's linking of the two men : "It was Xavier's good fortune to labour far away from the contentions of Europe, and to die young, so the world, Protestant and Catholic alike, has agreed to overlook the fact of his having been a Jesuit and to love him as a man. Loyola, on the other hand, whose very name has come to sound like a challenge, lived out his days and often a good part of his nights at the G.H.Q. of the Catholic crusade for the soul of Europe. In a sense, he personified the crusade, and the other side, whose attempts at expansion he was largely the means of thwarting, have never forgiven him. Even now, a measure of cold respect, tempered with polite suspicion, is all that he can look for in history books. People who do not much believe in God have discovered a new formula for him ; they compare him to Lenin and leave it at that. But it is only necessary to study the many extant letters of Ignatius and Francis to see that in the broad essentials of character they were wonderfully alike, Basque to the bone, intense, practical, stead-fast, uneffusive, completely self-forgetful. Their passionate orthodoxy and their clear-cut vision of human life as a battle-ground of God and the devil were inheritances from the age-long struggle of Spain against the Moslem. Francis as much as Ignatius bears the stamp of his proud country and tumultuous age, and Ignatius as much as Francis is a star in the eternal where there are no countries and no ages."

VIII

SAINT TERESA

There has never been a woman who has received the title of Doctor of the Church, though so far as I know, women are not disqualified by their sex for that honour. It is no more than reasonable to suppose that Saint John, to whom Our Lord committed His mother while He was dying on the cross, and who was to be the great exponent of the doctrine of the Incarnate Word, learned it from Mary, Mistress of Theology. And Saint Teresa, though she has never been declared a Doctor of the Church, like her disciple Saint John of the Cross, has recently received posthumously from a Spanish university the degree of Doctor of Theology. Surely no woman ever merited it more, though there have been many women who have been more formally learned — even in the purely speculative departments — than was ever the untrained (but of course immensely brilliant) Teresa of Avila. Pastor in his *History of the Popes* does not hesitate to say that she, "a woman, and alone of her sex, may be compared with the great doctors of the Church." On another page he writes : "In mystical theology she is an authority of the first rank in the Catholic Chuch ; no one before her had described the various mystical states so profoundly, or so clearly and distinctly, and no one since her time has substantially added anything new to the descriptions which she gave ; at the utmost. . . St. John of the Cross may be placed in this respect side by side with his teacher."

You need not fear, however, that I am going to turn this chapter into a close analysis of mystical experience. For that my qualifications are even less than for an exposition of dogmatic theology or the subtleties of philosophy. Yet obviously it will be impossible to talk about Saint Teresa without making at least some reference to such matters. What I promise you is that they will be introduced only in passing and subordinated to the facts of her life and character. But so as to give you some taste of these things, I turn for a quotation at this point, not to Saint Teresa herself but to Saint John of the Cross. And as his prose works are hardly more than an explanation and amplification of his extraordinary poems, I quote one of these as translated by Arthur Symons by way of offering a distillation of his experience. It shows his mastery of Biblical imagery, in the same way that his writings, taken as whole, show his mastery of the writings of the Fathers and the thought of Saint Thomas Aquinas. So here is his poem, which presents with marvellous psychology and under the analogy of love between man and woman, the love which subsists between God and the soul.

THE OBSCURE NIGHT OF THE SOUL

Upon an obscure night
Fevered with love in love's anxiety,
(O hapless-happy plight !)
I went, none seeing me,
Forth from my house where all things quiet be.

By night, secure from sight,
And by the secret stair, disguisedly,
(O hapless-happy plight !)
By night, and privily,
Forth from my house where all things quiet be.

Blest night of wandering.
In secret, where by none might I be spied,
Nor I see anything ;
Without a light or guide,
Save that which in my heart burnt in my side.

That light did lead me on,
More surely than the shining of noontide,
Where well I knew that one
Did for my coming bide ;
Where He abode none might but He abide.

O night that didst lead thus,
O night more lovely than the dawn of light.
O night that broughtest us,
Lover to lover's sight,
Lover with loved in marriage of delight.

Upon my flowery breast
Wholly for Him, and save Himself for none,
There did I give sweet rest
To my belovèd one ;
The fanning of the cedars breathed thereon.

When the first moving air
Blew from the tower and waved His locks aside,
His hand, with gentle care,
Did wound me in the side,
And in my body all my senses died.

All things I then forgot,
My cheek on Him who for my coming came ;
All ceased, and I was not, —
Leaving my cares and shame
Among the lilies, and forgetting them.

That is an astonishing poem. And there can be no doubt that it perfectly conveys the experience of Saint John of the Cross and other mystics. Yet one sometimes wonders whether mystical experience is uniform. It was, I think, La Rochefoucauld who remarked that few people would fall in love were it not for literature ; and I am sometimes troubled by a suspicion that because some mystics travelled a Dark Night of the Soul it has become almost axiomatic that every mystic must do the same thing. Yet that would not appear to be so. Saint Teresa's contemporary, Saint Philip Neri, was a very great mystic and ecstatic, and he went through nothing of the kind. So while validity may be admitted to the broad classification of the Purgative, the Illuminative and the Unitive Way, I am not at all so sure about the Dark Night of the Soul, although I fully admit that even to express such a doubt may prove me a hopeless ignoramus. I repeat, however, that there cannot be the slightest question that in the lines just quoted one of the greatest of mystics embodied what was his personal experience. The poem's passion and candour impart an instantaneous conviction. And this is equally true of what Saint Teresa herself wrote. No writers on mysticism have ever surpassed these two great Spaniards in their insight into the mystical process.

Having said this, perhaps I may be allowed to say that we need not be too scared of the word mysticism. Though it is one of the most abused of all terms and has been applied to all kinds of vague moods, and (worse still) to downright charlatanry ; and though this very fact has led others to give it a too severely technical significance — one that would allow it to apply only to the very loftiest degrees of union with the divine — it may legitimately be used, it seems to me, so long as due caution is maintained, for all experience of God, however imperfect that experience may be. After all, every Christian is a member of the Mystical Body, all are branched in the Vine, all draw through the sacraments a supernatural life. The anonymous author of the fourteenth century *Cloud of Unknowing* insists that the achieving of a union with God is not something reserved for a few élite souls but is open to everybody. And the seventeenth century Carmelite, Leon of Saint John, following the Teresian tradition, wrote : "There is no Christian, whatever anyone may say, who is not bound by the duties of his profession at the baptismal font, to undertake and study the practice of mystical theology."

While Saint Teresa did not believe that it was necessary for all her nuns to become contemplatives, she held that many people are called to contemplation who do not respond. That many are called and few chosen means, in actual fact, that most of those called decline to choose themselves — in this as in other matters. Whatever our state now, if we are going to get to heaven, we must prepare to live in an eternity of contemplation, of an intellectual intensity utterly inconceivable on earth by even the most exalted of mystics. The mystical experience cannot ever be the same thing as an anticipation of the Beatific Vision ; nevertheless it may be an anticipation of some part of it, for while on earth we may have a foretaste in turn of hell and purgatory and heaven. It may be said with truth, I think, that some anticipatory gleams of God, as actually experienced, are given to a large number of people, however much those gleams vary both in kind and degree. It is somewhat analogous to the poet's inspiration — which not even the greatest poet has at command, but which even the simplest and humblest human being shares in more fully and more often than is usually supposed. The mystics do perhaps tend to scare us — as we are sometimes scared even by poets — but properly understood, there is no occasion for this. Least of all is there any occasion to be scared of Saint Teresa.

As a human being she is one of the most interesting in the world's history. And the first thing to note of her is that she was completely devoid of nonsense. Of women in general many men think that they are not very candid, but are instead full of guile ; and I have heard that a not dissimilar opinion is held by women of men. Perhaps this shows no more than that the two sexes have different mental processes, which the opposite sex usually does not take the trouble to understand. However this may be, I do not believe it would be possible to find a more candid woman than Teresa. One does feel indeed that she tended to exaggerate her sins — about which more in a moment — but one never feels that she is indulging in the kind of deliberate (and somewhat unctuous) exaggeration to which pious people are sometimes addicted. So obvious are her candour and truthfulness — I mean of course her *subjective* truthfulness — that some writers have even wondered whether it would not be safest to take her word for it and believe that she really had been the wicked person that she said she was. The only trouble with this is that nothing much can be made of her confessions, nor have the enemies she managed to create been able to rake up anything against her. She herself does not specify any sins of peculiar enormity, but the way she

admits having striven to obtain the good opinion of the world
— something about which she came to be quite indifferent —
is touching in its frankness. Even in this matter, however,
Teresa is honest : she makes her admissions candidly, and at
the same time makes the qualifications which truth demands.
I quote : "I managed that people should have a good opinion
of me, though I did not act in this way purposely — to counter-
feit piety ; for as regards hypocrisy and vain-glory, I thank God
that I do not remember to have offended Him therein." To
this she at once adds ; "I was rather much troubled, that they
should have a good opinion of me, considering what I knew of
myself privately." Her so-called autobiography — which
does give us many biographical details but which is really a
study in mysticism — opens with the charmingly disarming
words : "As I had virtuous parents, and such as feared God,
this would have been sufficient, together with the other favours
Our Lord bestowed upon me, to have made me good, if I had
not been so wicked."

It is this rich, racy — and I might also say, salty — personality of Teresa's that has exercised such a great fascination, and
one by no means confined to Catholics or even pious
Protestants. One feels about her not only that she had something very important to tell the world, but that she was a
person well worth knowing. Before proceeding further,
therefore, I touch briefly on a few of the recent books in which
she has figured. Well, in the *Grey Eminence* of Aldous
Huxley, she is hardly more than mentioned, but he does have
something to say about her there and in some of his other
books. And the interest his strange mind shows is itself
interesting. But valuable as is his analysis of mysticism, it is
clear that he is a man without faith, and that he looks upon

mysticism as merely a technique, and one that can be used equally as well by the sceptic as by the believer. "To the non-Christian," he says plainly, "this seems the supremely important, the eminently encouraging fact about mysticism — that it provides a religion free from unacceptable dogmas." His conclusion is that : "The mystics are channels through which a little knowledge of reality filters down into our human universe of ignorance and illusion. A totally unmystical world would be a world totally blind and insane." But what reality is Mr. Huxley does not pretend to say.

Aldous Huxley is a writer who is always serious, in spite of his frequent impishness and flippancy. One hardly knows what to make of Gertrude Stein's opera *Four Saints in Three Acts*. One of the saints is Ignatius ; Teresa is split in two to provide another couple ; the fourth saint is presumably Gerty herself. I am not sure about which saint — Saint Teresa or Miss Stein — the lyric goes :

> *To know to know to love her so.*
> *Four saints prepare for saints.*
> *It makes it well fish.*
> *Four saints it makes it well fish.*

Yes, that *does* make it well fish — though possibly it also makes it nonsense. And when we are provided with a song that goes, "Let Lucy Lily Lily Lucy Lucy let Lucy Lucy Lucy Lily Lily Lily Lily let Lily Lucy Lucy let Lily. Let Lucy Lily. Let Lucy Lily," I am perfectly willing to let Lucy Lily and Gertrude Gertrude Gertrude — or anything else they want to do. In this case Saint Teresa is nothing but a convenient opportunity for Miss Stein to display the virtuosity of her humorous egotism ; but it is rather remarkable that a writer of this sort should have dealt with Saint Teresa at all.

We have had still more recently that study in contrasts by Miss Sackville-West published under the title of *The Eagle and the Dove*. The two Teresas are considered together — the Little Flower and the mystic of Avila ; and though the book may not add very much to our factual knowledge, it does give an excellent brief account of the two saints, and one written throughout with sympathetic admiration.

Finally there is William Thomas Walsh's *Saint Teresa of Avila*, which I suppose is the best general account that has been written in English. Though the book is a solid piece of scholarship and its copious translations are admirably made, Dr. Walsh does not always know when to refrain and when to omit, but in spite of this there can be no question that his book is a very notable piece of biography.

But now to come back to Saint Teresa herself. Her mother, a very beautiful person — Teresa praises her for not being vain of her beauty or putting it to any improper use — married at the age of fourteen, bore nine children, and then died at thirty-three. She was not only beautiful and gentle and kind ; she was also good. But though Teresa brings her accusation very mildly, she makes it clear that her mother had a great fault : she was given to the reading of romances, much to the displeasure of her sober-minded husband. Teresa acknowledges that the reading of these books did her mother no harm, but says that it did her young daughter a vast amount of harm. In fact, the reading of such fantastic tales of adventure almost wrecked her career at the outset — or so she would have us believe. The other children in the household — there were some by her father's first marriage as well as the nine Teresa's mother bore — were all virtuous, except of course Teresa her-

self. She and one of her brothers, of about the same age as
herself, used to go about inciting one another to remember
eternity. "Forever, forever, forever !" these were the words
always on their lips. And in order to get to heaven quickly
the two children decided that they would run away and go to
the country of the Moors, so as to obtain martyrdom. They
had enough good sense to lay in a little stock of provisions for
their journey — if only of raisins — but fortunately they were
found by a search-party before they had gone very far.
Enthusiastically her English disciple, the poet Crashaw, exclaimed, "She's for the Moors and martyrdom !" but Teresa
looked back upon the episode with characteristic humour.
She explained that she was wanting to get to heaven by paying
a bargain-basement price. To have had one's head cut off
would have been much easier than a long life of the Christian
warfare.

If the reading of romances was a danger to Teresa, a still
greater danger was the company of a cousin. This girl was
not regarded as a suitable companion, for she was frivolous and
may have been something worse ; but as she was a cousin and
nothing definite could be pinned on to her, Teresa's mother
could not altogether forbid her the house, much as she was disapproved of. Just what the cousin did or said we do not know ;
these are Teresa's words : "With this person . . . I delighted
to entertain myself ; with her I held conversations and inter-
course, because she helped me to pass the time in everything I
wished, and she even enticed me into them, and gave me an
account of her conversations and vanities. Up to the time
when I began to be familiar with her (I was then about fourteen
years old, and I think a little more), and she made me

acquainted with all her affairs, I do not think I had offended Almighty God by any mortal sin, nor ever lost His fear, though I dreaded more the loss of my honour."

Teresa makes a great deal of this unhealthy friendship, and it must have created a problem because, after the death of her mother, Teresa's father was at a loss as to how to deal with her. He wished her to get married and settled, and in the meanwhile sent her to visit a married sister. On the way she spent some little time with an uncle, and in his house she was introduced to a very different kind of reading from that of her favourite romances — probably rather stodgy "good" books. Concerning this, Teresa tells us : "These books he made *me* also read ; and although I had no great liking for them, yet I pretended I had ; for I always took the greatest care to give pleasure to others."

The solution of this problem was that Teresa's father sent her to be educated in the Augustinian convent at Avila, and there she remained a year and a half. About this Teresa is a bit puzzling. "During the first eight days I was in the monastery," she writes, "I felt very unhappy, and the more so because I suspected that my vanity was now discovered, and not so much because I was placed in the monastery." We gather that she felt herself to be in disgrace, though we may be sure that no humiliation was intended. In any event, she soon got over that feeling. "All the religious were glad to be in my company ; for in this respect Our Lord gave me the particular favour of always pleasing persons wherever I might be, and thus I was beloved." That is almost an understatement and is made at all only because Teresa wishes the truth to be served. She did indeed exercise an extraordinary fascination on everybody she met — the fascination of her natural charm as well as (later) the fascination of her evident holiness, a holiness that heightened rather than diminished her gifts of nature.

But though she came to like the convent and was glad to see that it contained so many good religious, she had as yet no intention of becoming a nun herself. Very slowly was she led to her vocation. In the first place she had, as she said, a fear of being married — going no further into the subject than that. But in the second place (perhaps it was really the first place) she recognized how dangerous was her condition. "I had just reason to fear, if I died in my present state, I should be sent to hell. But though my will did not wholly incline me to be a nun, yet I clearly saw it was the better and more secure state ; and so little by little I forced myself to embrace it." The considerations, as you see, were purely practical and far from being on the loftiest plane.

But once Teresa had reached her decision, she acted in a fashion quite her own. She knew that her father would be opposed to her plans, and so — presumably by way of softening the blow by distributing its impact — she persuaded her brother, the one who had previously sought martyrdom with her, to join the Dominicans on the same day that she joined the Carmelites at the convent of the Incarnation. The result was what might have been expected : the superiors at both institutions at once got in touch with the children's father to let him know what was afoot, and the boy was promptly packed home. In the case of Teresa, however, her father raised no objection. He would have preferred to see her settle down with a husband, but he may well have considered this solution as good as any.

The convent of the Incarnation was a very large one, containing at this time about a hundred and forty nuns. In addition to these there were a number of lady boarders, all of whom freely received their friends in their apartments and even gave parties for them there. If it comes to that, many of the nuns, though pious women, seem to have looked upon the convent as a comfortable club, for each of them had a bedroom, sitting-room and oratory, furnished according to her own tastes. The punctilio of rank was carefully observed, and no people were more particular about such things than the Spaniards; and though it would seem that the meals were sometimes meagre, this was not out of deliberately sought austerity but because the Incarnation, in spite of being socially extremely select, was not very wealthy. When the nuns felt in need of a good dinner they could always go to the house of a friend to get one. It was a situation common enough in Spain and other Catholic countries of the time; monasticism was not corrupt but it was often relaxed. Such was not Teresa's idea of the best means of saving her soul. It was to be her great work to reform the Carmelite Order.

There is a Carmelite tradition which places the founding of the order on Mount Carmel in the Holy Land at the time of the school of the prophets, about which we read in the Old Testament. In fact this school is more or less identified with the Order. Nobody of course seriously maintains anything so fantastic today. What is true is that we hear of some hermits on Mount Carmel, but not until the middle of the twelfth century; and in Europe the Carmelites appeared at a date only slightly later than the Dominicans and Franciscans, and as part of the general emergence of mendicant friars.

Originally perhaps the most austere of all orders, by degrees mitigation and decline came upon the Carmelites, so that by the time of Saint Teresa there was little attempt on the part of either the men's or women's branches to carry out the severities of the rule, even as revised by Saint Albert. Reconstruction was to be brought about by Saint Teresa, and though she could hardly have brought it about except with the backing her nuns received from the Discalced friars, it was she who gave the first habit of the reform to Saint John of the Cross ; it was she who remained the soul of the movement.

So violent was the opposition that some of the Discalced actually went in fear of being poisoned by the Calced brethren. Probably such fears were wildly exaggerated, yet it is historic fact that Saint John of the Cross was scourged and imprisoned by fellow-Carmelites, though we should remember that both modes of punishment were in those days canonically provided for in the case of the recalcitrant. More often the friars of the reform encountered nothing much worse than suspicion and opposition. Thus when Saint Teresa introduced John of the Cross as a confessor at the Incarnation the nuns, upon going into his confessional, not being quite sure who was there, would enquire anxiously, "Are you Discalced ?" — whereupon Saint John used to draw his habit over his feet and answer, "I'm Calced." After which of course everything was all right.

There is no need for me to attempt even the briefest account of the Carmelite reform. But perhaps I may be permitted to quote Pastor : "The new Orders, as a necessary consequence of the conditions of the times, were all intended for the care of souls, and to exert an influence upon the world ; the older methods could no longer be employed to the same extent, and they were obliged to make up for them by an increase in the life of interior prayer ; in the place of vocal prayer in the choir more attention was devoted to interior prayer and contemplation." In short, the importance of Saint Teresa lies in her mysticism, and the importance of her mysticism was in its nourishment of the active life. The reform was intended to pass on to the world the spiritual benefits the individual had received ; it was the reaffirmation of Saint Thomas's *Contemplata aliis tradere*. The Carmelites were destined to be a great missionary and apostolic force — and this in spite of subsequent efforts to keep everything confined to the cloister and (so far as possible) to Spanish soil.

Saint Teresa, like her friend Saint John of the Cross, happened to be not only a mystic but to possess a marvellous gift of literary expression. She wrote hurriedly, and late at night, sitting upon the cold floor of her cell before a window through which the wintry winds blew ; and work done under such conditions suffered, or would have suffered had she not been an inspired writer. "I know not what I am saying," she wrote characteristically, "for I am writing this as if the words were not mine." Even more characteristically she opens the second chapter of *The Interior Castle* with : "God help me ! how I have wandered from my subject ! I forget what I was speaking about, for my occupations and ill-health often force me to cease writing until some more suitable time. The sense will be very disconnected ; as my memory is extremely bad and I have no time to read over what is written, even what I really understand is expressed very vaguely, at least so I fear." There are, in truth, a good many digressions and repetitions, and even some faulty grammar ; yet in spite of the defects caused by haste, Teresa's force and pungency and vividness of phrase are apparent on every page. "Why do they want me to write ?" she exclaimed to Father Gracian. "Let learned men write, who have studied, for I am a fool and won't know what I am saying. I will use one word in place of another, and I will do harm. There are plenty of books on matters of prayer. For the love of God, I wish they would let me spin my flax, follow my choir and duties of religion, for I am not fit for writing, nor have I health or head for it." Why she was held to her task all the world now knows : it was because nobody was better qualified for it.

The Spanish temperament has always been heroic and often extravagant. And this inevitably shows itself in Spanish asceticism. Saint Peter of Alcántara, the Franciscan who was the first strong directive influence in Teresa's life, lived in a cell only four and a half feet each way, where he could never lie down, and in which he slept no more than an hour and a half each night. Only once in three days did he eat, and he wore a kind of belt of pointed wire under his habit. Yet in spite of this, he was very agreeable, we are told. This spare old man, who seemed to be made of the roots of trees, was just the person Teresa had been looking for, though we do not hear of her imitating his austerities. On the contrary, she warned that going without sleep could bring about a state similar to ecstasy, and as she disapproved of false ecstasies even more than genuine ecstasies, she advised those seeking the spiritual heights to take all the sleep they required.

Compared with such a man as Peter, or even with the famous woman hermit, Catalína de Córdoba, Teresa seems to be almost easygoing. Austerity she practiced, but with discretion ; and when sending her brother hair shirts, she also advised him not to overdo their use. Her letters contain many references to rose-water and oranges and jam, and poverty she accepted gaily rather than sought dourly for its own sake. She had much to say about detachment from relatives, yet she displayed an intense interest in the smallest details affecting her brothers and sisters and their children. "God deliver me from gloomy saints!" was among her favourite exclamations; and to make sure that her nuns did not become gloomy — or perhaps to provide an outlet for her own natural high spirits — she would dance on feast days to her tambourine, which may still be seen in the convent at Seville.

Her good sense, and a humour that was at times a bit tart, are evident in her books and her letters. She had scant patience with any nun who, as she put it, stayed away from choir one day because she had a headache, and a second day because she had had a headache, and three more days in case the headache might return. She herself was ill most of her life, but she paid little attention to her ailments, though the account she gives of them is horrifying.

Another thing that should be noted is her admiration for learning and intelligence. She appears almost to have preferred these qualities to piety, though of course she always wanted them joined to piety. This is Father Ribera's testimony on the point: "Next to their having a vocation, what she cared for most in those she accepted as novices, even if only as lay-sisters, was a good understanding. People who knew her holiness and love of prayer were careful to praise the fervour and prayerfulness of the candidates they brought her, thinking this would make her accept them. But she seemed to care to know only whether they were sensible and apt." As for confessors, she wrote in her autobiography, "I have found by experience, that it is better for directors, who are virtuous and full of holy manners, to have no learning at all, rather than little." She had so often been misdirected by such men. But she adds, "I was never deceived by any truly learned man." Time after time she reverts to this point, and the following sentence sums up her views : "I believe the devil is exceedingly afraid of learning, provided it be accompanied with humility and other virtues, for he knows he will be discovered and suffer loss."

She had special need of expert spiritual guidance if for no other reason than that at the beginning of her career she had been greatly troubled in mind over the manifestations of mysticism that occurred in her — ecstasies and levitations and so forth. These she always did her utmost to prevent. Her nuns were told to hold her down when they saw her being lifted into the air, or she would cling to a railing, to anything firmly fixed, so as not to be drawn up. Like all the mystics, she attached no value to these external phenomena of mysticism, and was even terribly afraid that they might be a delusion of the devil until she found a way of putting him to flight with derision. "Goose !" she discovered to be an insult he did not relish ; but she also used the gesture of the "figs," whose meaning it must be surmised she did not understand. It was highly effective.

The devil could attack her in this way ; he could also stir up opposition to her work, and that was much worse. However, she came to realize early in life that the devil does not always need to intervene in such cases, as there are usually a number of well-meaning but dull people ready enough to do his work. Concerning this Dr. Walsh has a passage worth quoting. Speaking of the Carmelite Provincial, De Salazar, he says : "He was a good mediocre man who, lacking the genius of Madre Teresa for sublime conceptions and bold execution, must have everything running smoothly, always, of course, for the highest ends. . . Human nature being what it is, his type is common, necessary, and by no means indefensible. But he is always and everywhere the instinctive foe of genius, which perplexes and irritates him beyond measure. These are the good stupid people who persecute poets, heroes, and saints (except dead ones, whom they honour inordinately, having nothing more to fear from them) and thus unwittingly provide for them the suffering necessary to all great achievement."

With regard to her visions, Teresa said that her conscious imagination worked so feebly that, however hard she might try, she was unable to picture even our Lord's humanity. She made it clear that she never saw Him with her physical eyes, or heard Him with her physical ears. Concerning this she did her best to explain : "They are certain words well formed, but they are not heard with corporal ears, but are understood more plainly than if they were so heard; and not to understand it, however one resists, is out of the question. For when we do not wish to hear in this world, we can stop up the ears or turn to something else, so that even if it is heard it is not understood. In this conversation that God has with the soul there is no remedy, no, none, but they make me listen in spite of myself, and [make] the understanding so perfect to understand what God wishes we should understand, that it is not enough to like and not to like it. For He who can do all things wishes us to understand that that which He wishes has to be done, and shows Himself truly our Lord."

The voice of God heard in the soul is common in human experience, though few hear it as frequently and distinctly as Teresa did. But her visions and ecstasies, not to mention the intimacy of her communion with the Divine, have such a character as to lead many people to suppose that Teresa can have very little to tell ordinary people that will be within the range of their comprehension. This however, is not so. Why, the second half of *The Way of Perfection* is hardly more than a commentary on the Our Father! In the case of that prayer it is surely possible to imagine a soul to whom even its opening words might be brought with such force as to suspend the mind and make it unable to go any further. Or should one be able to proceed, it is equally conceivable that any later word or group of words — "In heaven," "Thy kingdom come," "Forgive us," "As we forgive" — might have the same power of transporting us. Though in reading Saint Teresa we are all too likely to get out of our depth very quickly, we shall also find that, difficult as are many of the things she has to say, they are not without relation to us.

I turn for illustration to *The Interior Castle*. The book, as you know, is an elaborate allegory that describes the various spiritual states. But where does Teresa begin? Which is the First Mansion? Even the very lowest state one might suppose would be something extremely exalted. And so Teresa assures us it really is. Yet for a moment the vividness of her description makes us wonder if this is not hell itself, for though there is light, it is the light that is semi-darkness, and it reveals at first snakes and noxious reptiles. "Though the room itself is light," she explains, the person entering it "cannot see because of his self-imposed impediment." Regarding this Abbot Butler comments in his *Ways of Christian Life* : "It is wonderfully consoling, especially as coming from Saint Teresa, to know that this Mansion, though those in it are running on the very lowest gear of Christian life, still contains great riches and treasures. But after all, it is sound theology and New Testament : every baptized soul free from mortal sin is a Temple or Sanctuary of God, and has the Holy Ghost as indweller, spreading abroad in her love of God and the sevenfold Gifts."

One reads on, ascending step by step, through the Seven

Mansions of mystical experience. And here perhaps some help is given to our perplexity by the first of the encylicals on the Ordering of the Christian Life — that issued in January, 1923 — in which Pope Pius XI assures us that "holiness is not a privilege of a few to the exclusion of others, but that all are called to it, and that the obligation rests on all." Which is only to put in other words what Saint Francis de Sales said : "Prayer and mystical theology are the self-same thing."

Not many of us are likely to pass through all these Mansions, or can have much hope of getting further than the Third, which is about the same stage Saint Francis de Sales describes as that of the Devout Life. But at least the thing is not beyond our comprehension, any more than is the analogous experience of the poet. Listen to the familiar lines from "Tintern Abbey" :

> *That serene and blessed mood,*
> *In which the affections gently lead us on, —*
> *Until, the breath of this corporeal frame*
> *And even the motion of our human blood*
> *Almost suspended, we are laid asleep*
> *In body, and become a living soul :*
> *While with an eye made quiet by the power*
> *Of harmony, and the deep power of joy,*
> *We see into the life of things.*

Wordsworth checks himself with an "almost" in his description of what might pass for mystical rapture, and in neither case is it the manifestation that matters but the substance of what is achieved — a perception of "the life of things," the ultimate reality. What Teresa provides is an analysis, extraordinarily searching in its psychological precision, of the process by which the soul may ascend. However obscure her mean-ing may sometimes be concerning the various degrees of prayer, she has encouragement to give us : "God deliver you, sisters," she writes, "from saying, when you have done some-thing that is not perfect, 'We are not angels, we are not saints.' Though we are not, it is the greatest help to believe that with God's help we can be. This sort of presumption I want to see in this house, for it makes humility increase ; always have courage, for God gives it to the strong and is no respecter of persons, and He will give it to you and to me."

One of the most frequently recurring images in her work is that of water. "Come ye to the waters," is her constant burden. And in the autobiography she applies this imagery in a homely and effective way. "It seems to me that [the soul] can be watered in four ways : either (1) by drawing the water out of a well, which is a great labour for us ; or (2) with a wheel and buckets for hoisting it with a windlass (I have sometimes done it) is less trouble than the others and brings up·more water ; or (3) from a river or *arroyo* — this irrigates much better, for the ground remains full of water and it is not neces-sary to irrigate so often and it is much less work for the gardener ; or (4) with a good rain by which the Lord irrigates it without any effort on our part, and this is incomparably better than all I have said."

Or take this similar passage from *The Interior Castle* : "Let us imagine we see two fountains with basins which fill with water. I can find no simile more appropriate than water by which to explain spiritual things. . . These two basins are filled in different ways ; the one with water from a distance flowing into it through many pipes and water-works, while the other basin is built near the source of the spring itself and fills quite noiselessly. If the fountain is plentiful, like the one we speak of, after the basin is full the water overflows in a great stream which flows continually. No machinery is needed here, nor does the water run through aqueducts.

"Such is the difference between the two kinds of prayer. The water running through the aqueducts resembles sensible devotion, which is obtained by meditation. We gain it by our thoughts, by meditating on created things, and by the labour of our minds ; in short, it is the result of our endeavours. . . The other fountain, like the divine consolations, receives the water from the source itself, which signifies God : as usual, when His Majesty wills to bestow on us any supernatural favours, we experience the greatest peace, calm, and sweetness in the inmost depths of our being ; I neither know where nor how." This is something not at the mystic's command, any more than the poet's inspiration is at command. And just as — from one point of view — everybody is a poet, and, from another, even the greatest poet is only a poet during the visitations of the Muse, so, from one point of view, all Christians partake of the mystical life, and from another, the most exalted of mystics are unable to live continuously on the heights. In each case the experience comes and goes, but is shared more widely than is generally imagined, even though the vast majority of people catch no more than an occasional glimpse of it.

Let us see what Saint Teresa has to say about the Fifth Mansion, that of the Prayer of Union. None should despair of entering it, she tells us, because they have not received supernatural gifts, "for its chief value lies in the resignation of our will to the will of God." There is the "short cut" of mysticism, and there is the longer and more painful road of asceticism. She goes on to say of this : "I own that the work will be much harder, but it will be of higher value, so that your reward will be greater if you come forth victorious ; yet there is no doubt that it is possible for you to attain to this true union with the will of God."   Then the great mystic makes a very touching admission : "This is the union I have longed for all my life, and that I beg our Lord to grant me.   It is the most certain and the safest."   In other words, she maintains that the ordinary road of asceticism is more meritorious and more secure than that of special spiritual graces.   Mysticism — Aldous Huxley and yoga to the contrary — is not a technique but a special privilege that holds, as do all special privileges, its special risks.   It cannot be refused when God gives it, but it is not to be sought for.   What matters is the union of the will with God's will and not the enjoyment of mystical delights.

The graces God gives are according to His good pleasure and for reasons that we cannot hope to understand.   Yet when they are given they can be analyzed for us, as Saint Teresa analyzes them, very much to the profit even of those who are unlikely ever to have them fully conferred.   It is, however, because they are frequently given — though in the vast majority of cases in a fragmentary, imperfect and occasional manner — that mysticism has a meaning for all of us.   The Catholic Church has always stressed the dangers that lie in these things.   The safe and plain and laborious way — that is what God appoints in His mercy to all except a chosen few.   And when those chosen few write about their experiences, it is as much in warning as in excitation.

What is significant is that the great age of mysticism, the sixteenth and seventeenth centuries, should be also that of the Counter-Reformation.   Indeed, the very fact that an increased intensity of external activity was then called for summoned forth a more intense contemplation. The Carmelites made of prayer an apostolic work, or the nerve of that work. Pastor, the most up-to-date and learned of ecclesiastical historians points out that "in the foundation of Propaganda, as well as of the seminary of missions in Paris, the most influential missionary body of modern times has been conspicuously that of the Carmelites." This is all the more remarkable when we recall that the second General of the reformed Carmelites wished them to be strictly contemplative and tried to prevent any further extension of the order outside of Spain. Had he succeeded, he would have largely undone the work of the reform, which did not aim merely at the observance of a more austere rule but at making the contemplative life feed the life of activity. Fortunately it was through a convent that he himself founded at Genoa in 1584 that his own policy was in the end defeated. "On Italian soil," writes Pastor, "the Carmelite order developed entirely on the lines laid down by Teresa, and thenceforward took on a new character and attained to new and greater importance."

I began by stressing Teresa's place as a writer and a thinker, though she would have denied that she had any such place at all, and denied it in very salty language. In some ways it has been a little unfortunate that she was first introduced to English readers by the magnificent but also somewhat lush and turgid poems of that seventeenth-century Anglican admirer of hers, Richard Crashaw, who became a Catholic and eventually a priest. Even the famous passage I am about to quote emphasizes, I fancy more than Teresa would have wished, the ecstatic note. But Crashaw did not fail to give her her due as a great mind as well as a great heart. "By thy large draughts

of intellectual day" — there we have it all.   Now for the concluding lines of "The Flaming Heart" :

> *O thou undaunted daughter of desires !*
> *By all thy dower of lights and fires ;*
> *By all the eagle in thee, all the dove ;*
> *By all thy lives and deaths of love;*
> *By thy large draughts of intellectual day,*
> *And by thy thirsts of love more large than they ;*
> *By all thy brim-filled bowls of fierce desire,*
> *By thy last morning's draught of liquid fire ;*
> *By the full kingdom of that final kiss*
> *That seized thy parting soul and sealed thee His ;*
> *By all the Heaven thou hast in Him*
> *(Fair sister of the seraphim !) ;*
> *By all of Him we have in thee ;*
> *Leave nothing of myself in me.*
> *Let me so read thy life, that I*
> *Unto all life of mine may die.*

IX

SAINT PHILIP NERI

There are many figures in the period of what is commonly
called the Counter-Reformation who are better known than
Saint Philip Neri, yet there is hardly one who did a more far-
reaching work. Saint Ignatius built up an organization that
gave to the religious life a discipline and a cohesion unknown
before. Saint Teresa of Avila, working with her friend and
disciple Saint John of the Cross, sytematized mysticism. Saint
Francis Xavier lit a flame of missionary enthusiasm which still
inspires thousands of ardent hearts. And these three saints
— along with another of whom few people have heard, Isidore
the Farmer — were canonized on the same day with Philip.
But though these three great souls attracted more widespread
an attention than Philip, his work was, in one respect, even
more important than theirs : this was because it effected the
reform of the Church at its centre, the Roman Curia.

There is another aspect of what Saint Philip did which has
often escaped adequate notice. Without intending anything
of the kind, he introduced a new method into community life.
I say this was done without intending it, because nothing was
farther from his thoughts than the founding of a new religious
institute ; and when it did come into existence, it was in spite
of Philip's own wishes but was forced on him by circumstances.
Even so, he would never regard himself as the "General" of a
new religious order, and in fact was not the General of the
Oratorians. He was even opposed to extending the Oratory
beyond Rome, and if other houses were established, this was

because his hand was forced. But most important of all, he introduced what has been the model for most of the religious congregations founded since the sixteenth century.

We have already seen that the Benedictines, strictly speaking, do not constitute an order, but follow a way of life in which every abbey is autonomous. The Rule of Saint Benedict set the form of monasticism that prevailed until the thirteenth century. At that time a new idea modified monasticism. Where the monk had been attached to a particular house, in which he made his profession and lived until he died, the friar was attached only to his province. He followed many of the older monastic practices, especially in regard to the saying of the Office in choir, but he had a greater mobility and was therefore enabled to penetrate into places which the stabilized monks could not reach. The third great innovation was that made by the Jesuits ; the choral Office was abandoned, even though several Popes tried to oblige them to take this upon themselves. But with Saint Philip Neri a fourth and highly novel concept came into being. The Oratorian was not a religious at all but a secular priest. He was unbound by vows. He could keep any private property he possessed. And he was at any moment completely free to leave the Congregation.

Yet in some respects there was a reversion to the Benedictine idea. The Oratorian was not definitely obligated to stability, yet he was, in effect, attached to a particular house. Something was also taken from the Dominicans, at least in a democratic form of government. But there was at the same time a reaction against the centralization that was characteristic of all the orders except the Benedictines. In particular was there a reaction against the military mode distinctive of the Society of Jesus.

Further modifications were to occur, as no doubt still others will occur in the development of religious life. Saint Vincent de Paul insisted upon what was a startling anomaly : the Fathers of the Mission were technically secular priests (like the Oratorians), yet they were bound by vows. But though these were only simple vows, and taken privately, they were to have the binding force of vows taken publicly before the superior. Perhaps even more revolutionary was the creation of the Sisters of Charity, women who lived like nuns, yet who were not nuns, uncloistered, with a uniform instead of a true habit, and whose vows expired every year.

It is easy to see how these later developments originated in, or were at least deeply affected by, what Philip initiated. Without seeking to introduce anything new, and while steadily resisting the pressure of some of his disciples who would have turned the Oratory into a worldwide organization, patterned somewhat along the lines of the Jesuits, he did in fact think of something entirely new, something that has widely affected religious life.

Perhaps the most striking thing of all to record of Philip Neri is that he accomplished what he did not through an organization but by purely personal influence. This influence was so intensely personal that it could be exercised directly upon only a few men : the Fathers of the Oratory themselves and those others, priests and laymen, who frequented the Oratory. It was as a confessor that Philip did his work. He rarely preached, at any rate not in later years, though several sermons had to be provided every day. But from morning to night he heard confessions, or advised people, or served God by his brilliant and amusing conversation. He may be said to have served God even by his extraordinary antics, his fantastic jests.   Yet all the time he was a mystic — one of the greatest of mystics — but a mystic in motley.

One sees him as a "character," one unique in the history of the saints.   Many of them had a keen sense of humour ; so much so, that one is almost tempted to say that it is hardly possible to become a saint without it.   But Philip's humour was a thing quite exceptional.   And it appeared in the strangest places and at altogether unexpected times.   Yet the quaint penances he imposed upon his disciples and the clowning he was himself willing to do in the full gaze of the world were not "tacked on," as it were, to the man but formed an integral part of his holiness.   Here was an ecstatic who was unable to say Mass unless he first brought himself down to earth by reading a joke-book or playing with a monkey.   Not until the very end of his life was he able to dispense with these precautions.   Then, when he was at last free to indulge himself — the Pope having by then given him special permission to say Mass in private — he had to be left by his server after the *Agnus Dei*, and for two hours he remained alone in the darkened little chapel, from which he would at last emerge white of face and exhausted after nobody knows what mystical experiences.

But here I am running too far ahead : I had better tell you something of his story before returning to his engaging and eccentric character.

He was born in Florence in 1515, just after the Lutheran storm had broken.   His father was an unsuccessful notary, and Philip himself was destined for a business career.   To begin it he went in 1532 or 1533 to San Germano — the present Cassino, if there *is* any Cassino now — to work for his father's cousin, Romolo Neri, who was a fairly successful merchant there.   The understanding was that he was to inherit "Uncle Romolo's" business.

He was a charming and utterly innocent boy, called by everybody the "good Pippo," but he had never shown the slightest inclination for the priesthood or the religious life, though he was on terms of close friendship with the Dominicans at San Marco in Florence and with the Benedictines at Monte Cassino.   On the other hand, his business career lasted only a few months ; he could not have spent much time in Uncle Romolo's counting-house, for he was constantly in the little chapel, hung like a bird's nest in the rocks of Gaeta — a circular chapel only seven yards wide overlooking the sea.   It was there that his decision was reached : it was to become a hermit.

Yet in becoming a hermit, he did not retire to the desert or the mountains.   Instead he went to Rome, and there he was a hermit of the streets, wandering everywhere, but as yet talking to nobody.   There were a number of such odd figures at the time, who are remembered merely because they were odd. To Philip's oddity was added a practicality which eventually emerged and set him to his great life's work.

For a time — at most for two years — he studied philosophy and theology, though with no idea of preparing himself for the priesthood but only in order to quicken his own interior contemplation.   A day came soon enough when he found that his studies had served this purpose ; he was unable to fasten his attention on what the lecturer was saying because he was drawn almost to rapture by the sight of the crucifix in the lecture halls.   He therefore sold what books he had, gave the proceeds to the poor, and returned all the more fully to the eremitical mode that his studies had only partially interrupted.

As soon as he arrived in Rome he had obtained the use of an attic room in the house of a Florentine who was the head of the custom-house. The same man gave him a small quantity of corn every year, and this was turned over to a nearby baker who undertook to supply him with a daily roll and a handful of olives. This was his only food ; a cup of water from the well was his only drink. In return he tutored his patron's sons. But he was not often in his lodgings ; most of his time was spent in the catacomb of Saint Sebastian, a place where he could find absolute retirement, as the catacombs had been virtually forgotten and were not rediscovered until some years later. Active work — and who was to be more active than Philip ? — was something that was still far off.

By degrees, however, he was drawn into something like active life, or something that at least hinted at the activity about to come. The hermit, though continuing to spend most of his nights in prayer in the catacombs, began to spend part of every day in getting acquainted with the young men employed in the banks and goldsmiths' shops. He played games with them ; he entertained them with his jests ; by such means he brought many of them to God.

About 1538 or 1539 he got to know the newly-arrived Jesuits. They were as yet free-lances like himself and, as such, frequenters of the hospitals. It would appear that he was introduced to Ignatius by Francis Xavier, that it has been conjectured that he wished to join them. This could hardly have been the case. No two men were more dissimilar in character than Ignatius and Philip. So far from the Jesuits refusing Philip, Ignatius complained that he was like the bell in the tower that calls men to church but never enters the

church. Already Philip was sending men to the Society —
and into other religious orders and the priesthood. But he did
not want to become a priest or a religious himself. Had he
been left alone, he would have gone on to the day of his death
as the hermit of the Roman streets.

Fortunately he was not left alone. In 1544, when he was
nearing thirty, while he was praying during Pentecost Week
in the catacomb of Saint Sebastian, he had an extraordinary experience about which he said nothing until late in life. A ball
of fire descended from heaven and penetrated his body, fling-
ing him to the ground. When he lifted himself up, he had not
only a great access of spiritual fervour but a physical manifestation of it which everybody noticed but which was not explained
until the autopsy that was performed on his body after his
death. Then it was discovered that two of his ribs had been
broken and forced outwards, giving the appearance of a tumor.
Ever afterwards the slightest emotion made him tremble to such
an extent that sometimes the bed on which he sat, the table on
which he leaned, even the whole room, shook violently. He
said he was always able to control these palpitations, but he
often made no attempt to control them. While he was giving
Communion, or hearing confessions, or speaking of God, his
heart beat like a hammer. Everybody knew of this physical
peculiarity ; everybody also knew that it was in some way intimately connected with his spiritual life. There have been
over a hundred well-authenticated cases of the stigmata ; there
has never been but one case of what happened to Philip Neri.

Yet he still showed no sign of being anything but the hermit
of the streets. The change in his manner of life was brought
about by his joining Persiano Rosa, his confessor, in founding a
confraternity. This was in 1548, four years after he had been

struck with fire from heaven. The confraternity consisted of a group of twelve or fifteen men who met in a church for pious exercises. One feature of this confraternity was that it introduced from Milan the devotion of the Forty Hours. And on these occasions it was Philip Neri, the layman, and not Rosa, the priest, who did most of the preaching. He was there all day long, and all night too, coming every now and then to the front with a little *ferverino*. One of the notable marks of the subsequent Oratory was a similar preaching on the part of laymen. Later on, when reform involved a stricter regimentation, this practice had to be abandoned ; but so long as it was tolerated, Philip used the possibilities to the full.

From this confraternity of his emerged a remarkable piece of what would now be called social service. For the jubilee of 1550 it provided a hostel for pilgrims and, after the pilgrims had departed, a small hospital for convalescents. But Philip was no director of charity, no Vincent de Paul ; he was more than content to leave that project in other hands after having started it. God was calling him to other things. The Confraternity of the Pilgrims and Convalescents developed later into a vast organization. Popes and princes were to wait upon the poor in the hostel Philip had founded. He himself retired from the work and can be described as being at most an honorary member of the undertaking he had initiated.

It was through this confraternity that he passed to the priesthood. Rosa insisted that he take holy orders, and Philip obeyed. The requirements for ordination were in those days slight enough, and many men were made priests who had hardly more learning than was necessary for the saying of Mass. Compared with them Philip was well equipped. And though he was never much of a student, he had a phenomenal memory and the keenest and quickest of wits.   In his later years professional scholars were astonished at the scholarship of this man who had had so very little formal schooling.   The truth is that he was not learned ; he was merely a man of genius.

Immediately after ordination Philip took up quarters in the Church of San Girolamo della Carità.   It was a former Franciscan monastery and housed a number of priests, some of whom had pastoral duties or were attached to the Confraternity of Charity, which operated from this centre, while others, like Philip himself, lived there unfettered by any obligation.   It was just the sort of arrangement that suited him.   He received no salary, and he wanted none.   What he did want was to retain his independence.

As a free-lance, he began to gather disciples around himself, a group of about eight young men, most of them Florentine goldsmiths.   These would meet every afternoon in his room for conversation followed by a walk and then an hour of prayer.   About all that Philip did was to read a page or two from a book and invite comments from those present.   He was the presiding spirit, the soul of the gathering, but there was no formal association of any kind.

Even so, it was enough to excite opposition from those in charge of the church, particularly from the medical officer of the confraternity.   No doubt the comings and goings of young men at all hours tended to disturb the place, for there were not only meetings in the afternoon but Philip could be sought at any hour of the day or night by young men who wanted to go to confession.   He was encouraging his constantly widening circle of disciples to go to confession to him every day.

This sort of thing struck the authorities — not of the Church itself but those in power at San Girolamo — as extravagant and a bit unhealthy. Already the place housed one eccentric, an elderly priest named Cacciaguerra, only recently ordained, who was promoting daily communion — something unheard of in those days. The man had once been immensely wealthy, and immensely dissolute. His conversion was effected only after he had twice seen Christ following him bearing His cross. When at last he broke from his sins he was aging, shattered in health, with his face ravaged by scars from his duels and his dissipations. Now he was gathering a following, mostly of women, who perhaps found him all the more of a romantic figure because of his lurid past. That now there should be a priest at San Girolamo who encouraged daily confession, in addition to a priest whose dubious specialty — it was considered extremely dubious — was that of daily communion, was more than could be borne by sensible people. There was an attempt to eject Philip by the time-honoured device of making his life miserable.

But Philip hung on. He was not to be got rid of in this way. His disciples increased, so that they had to hold their meetings in the attic over the church. In the end he won over his opponents. It was in this fashion that the Oratory — that is, the Oratory in the sense of the gatherings of young men — was founded. The Congregation of the Oratory was not to come into being until many years later.

Who were the men who frequented the Oratory ? Well, the first group were of no special note ; in fact then, and afterwards, some were of the poorest and most humble classes. But before long Philip began to attract a number of brilliant and highly placed young men. One was Giambattista Salviati, the brother of a cardinal and a grand-nephew of Leo X and a cousin

of Catherine de' Medici, the Queen of France. He was a favourite victim for Philip's fantastic penances. He was often
selected to sweep the streets in front of a church, or to take out
the slops and make the beds in a hospital, or to carry Philip's pet
dog through the jeering streets. Francisco Maria Tarugi, still
a layman but a future cardinal, was mortified by similar tasks.
He was perhaps the most gifted of all those Philip drew to himself. Another future cardinal, one less brilliant than Tarugi
but of more solid parts, was a young law-student named Baronius. Though he was only twenty, Philip set him to giving
daily lectures on Church history, keeping him to that task for
thirty years. Not till then did Philip order the Father of
Church History whom he — though himself no historian —
had begotten, to write the celebrated *Annals*. He was a man
who could have been elected Pope after Philip's death, had he
not clung to the pillars and refused to be dragged to the waiting
throne.

Then there were the musicians who gathered around Philip.
He gave them an opportunity for performing their compositions at the meetings, compositions of a new kind that were to
eventuate in the musical form of the oratorio, whose name
shows where it originated. The greatest of these men were
Animuccia and the still more famous Palestrina. The best music of the musical centre of the world was available — all for
nothing. Many went to the Oratory for that reason alone ; to
all it was a refreshment and a kindling of religious zeal.

Philip's work was an apostolate for men, and especially for
young men ; we can still more sharply describe it as for young
laymen. But it was a work in which those who were minis-
tered unto were expected to do some ministering. Among the
most acceptable preachers during the first phase of the Oratory

were the physicians Antonio Fucci and Giambattista Modio. And of those who later became priests — men like Tarugi and Baronius — the majority had preached as laymen at the Oratory.

But as might be expected, the ecclesiastical authorities came to look upon the proceedings with some suspicion. The vernacular hymn-singing — Jacopone da Todi providing many of the poems set to music by Philip's composers — and the lay preaching were not viewed with favour by the new Pope, Paul IV, the zealous but high-handed Carafa who came to the throne in 1555. It seemed for a while as though the meetings would be suppressed. Philip was in fact suspended for a short period in 1559. The fate of his work was hanging in the balance.

This may have something to do with a project he formed for going out as a missionary to India. Twenty of his disciples — including the two doctors who have been mentioned — were prepared to accompany him, and some of these men were ordained priests for this very purpose. The letters of Francis Xavier, Philip's old acquaintance who had died in 1552, had inflamed their imaginations. Only when a Cistercian monk whom Philip consulted told him that he was to find his Indies in Rome did he give up the notion of India. And Rome did prove to be his India. Never once did he leave the city from the time he arrived at eighteen till he died at eighty. He was the Apostle of Rome.

If his work survived this was because Paul IV died at the end of 1559 and was succeeded by the milder Pius IV. Paul had made himself and his family so detested that a reaction set in. The Carafa Pope was personally a very good man, but he strangely combined a passion for drastic reform with nepotism at its worst. His nephews, unknown to him, had been committing the vilest of crimes, for which they were to be punished under Pius IV. It probably did Philip good rather than otherwise to be known as one who had been persecuted under the former rigorous and obnoxious régime. Be that as it may, his difficulties disappeared, and by the time the fifth Pius came to the throne Philip enjoyed the prestige of a saint and the Oratory was everywhere recognized as a remarkable instrument for improving conditions in Rome.

Even so, there gradually came about some modification of the Oratory's original practices. To silence criticism, laymen were no longer put up to preach — though it must be remembered that this preaching of theirs, unlike that done by the young Philip, was not in the church itself but in the room occupied by the brothers of the Oratory. So as to indicate just how the meetings were conducted, I quote the account given of them by Baronius: "It is certainly by the divine disposition that we have seen, in great part, renewed in the city of Rome what the Apostle recommended to be done for the profit of the Church, in the method of discoursing of the things of God to the edification of the hearers." Then, after specially mentioning Philip and Tarugi (but carefully making no mention of himself) Baronius goes on: "After some time spent in mental prayer, one of the brothers read a spiritual book, and in the middle of the reading, the Father who superintended the whole discoursed upon what was read, explaining it with greater accuracy, enlarging upon it, and insinuating it into the hearts of the readers. Sometimes he desired one of the brothers to give his opinion on the subject, and then the discourse proceeded in the form of a dialogue ; and this exercise lasted an hour, to the great consolation of the audience. After this one of his own people [one of the Fathers of the Oratory] at his command mounted to a seat raised a few steps above the rest, and without any adornment of language discoursed upon some approved lives of the saints, illustrating what he said by passages of Scripture or sentences of the fathers. He was succeeded by another, in the same style, but on a different subject ; and lastly came a third [this was Baronius himself] who discoursed upon ecclesiastical history. Each of them was allowed only half an hour. When all this was finished, to the wonderful contentment as well as the profit of the hearers, they sang some spiritual canticle, and so the exercises finished. . . It seemed as though the ancient and apostolical method of Christian assemblies was renewed." Even that, however, describes the later procedure and not the primitive phase, though in that Baronius had taken part as a layman.

Now this may not sound very exciting when put in Baronius's sober words, but it attracted all that was best in Rome. And there were features of the Oratory's activity that Baronius does not mention. Philip organized pilgrimages to the Seven Churches, and these were festive as well as pious occasions. Sometimes as many as two thousand men were in the party, music being provided all the way, and a picnic lunch after Mass, when they ate their cheese and hard-boiled eggs and drank a little wine in some open space, while the trumpeters from Sant' Angelo and the other instrumentalists performed. There were even gala occasions when women were allowed to attend. Then a boy would be put up to preach a sermon he had learned by heart, greatly to the delight of everybody.

These boys should never be forgotten. Philip always had them around him and let them make as much noise as they pleased in his rooms, even to the extent of playing tennis against the walls. When complaints came from some of the studious

Fathers in the house about the infernal din, Philip always took
the boys' part and told them to go on playing. "They may
chop wood on my back," he used to say, "if by that means I
may keep them from sin."

We are sometimes led to wonder how the boys and young
men about him found any time for work or study. The gentlemen of leisure among them were few, so it would seem that
those who had an occupation could not have taken it very seriously. For not only were there the long exercises at the
Oratory, but as soon as these were over in the afternoon Philip
would go out into the streets, always accompanied by a crowd.
The explanation must be that there was a good deal of coming
and going, people being present only for an hour or so and then
departing, and with the attendance itself changing from day to
day. But how Philip himself found time for all this is a cause
of astonishment. From noon until late at night he always had
a group of men with him, and in the mornings he was likely to
have a stream of visitors. In fact, even before he was up in the
morning — and he rose very early to go straight to his confessional — sometimes men would go to his room for confession.
For the convenience of such early callers he used to leave his
key under the door, so that they might enter without ceremony. And though he had built a balcony above his room to
which he could retire to pray — he loved to commune with
God in a place where he could have his eyes over his beloved
Rome — instructions were strict that he was to be summoned whenever anybody wanted him. This was, he used to
say, only leaving God for God. Such inroads on his time, so
far from lessening as he grew older, increased as his celebrity
spread. He was at everybody's beck and call. There was no
urchin in Rome who did not know Father Philip, and among

his penitents were half the Sacred College and some of the popes themselves. If Philip had nothing else to do he would take a group of boys to a meadow to play ball and take a hand in the game himself. At any rate he used to take a hand at the start of the game, after which he would withdraw a little way to meditate ; but he was always ready to go back to his boys if one of them came up, as they often did, begging him to do so.

Along with all this went a most intense spiritual life. The phenomena connected with mysticism were of frequent occurrence with him, greatly to his embarrassment. He was so afraid of going off into an ecstasy that, when he went into a church, he would not as a rule stay longer than the time required for the saying of an Our Father and Hail Mary. Though he had no system of mysticism, he thoroughly concurred with such experts as Saint Teresa and Saint John of the Cross that external mystical manifestations had little or no value. He was often seen in levitation, but he did his best to conceal these happenings and to prevent them. In order to throw people off the scent he would do ridiculous things, wearing his clothes inside out or even having his beard trimmed in church. On that great day in 1590 when the relics of some martyrs were translated to his new church, he successfully warded off a mystical seizure by going up to one of the Swiss Guards present and, in the full gaze of the public, stroking the man's luxuriant beard. As for his own beard — which was as white as ermine on a face like alabaster — he sometimes had it cut off on one side and exhibited himself in that state to excite derision. There was one occasion, when he was visited by several Polish noblemen, on which he deliberately disedified them by making them wait while he had his favourite joke-book read to him. Every now and then he would turn to them and exclaim, "You see what capital things I study !" When he was admonished for this afterwards, he was quite impenitent and returned, "If they come back I shall behave in an even worse manner." And he would have done so too ; he had such a horror of being thought a saint that he disguised himself in the character of a buffoon.

This was of course partly due to Philip's humility. But I am sure he enjoyed the situations he created, when he played the fool himself or made others play the fool. Fine gentlemen were sent out into the streets in fantastic garments. A lay-brother was told to go into the refectory, while the community was assembled there, carrying a monkey on his shoulder. Another lay-brother was frequently summoned — especially when cardinals or other dignitaries were present — to sing patois comic songs or to dance a jig. Nor was it any use for the Fathers to try to hide the brother at these times ; Philip would ferret him out and make him give his performance. Baronius, being a somewhat solemn fellow, was a darling victim of Philip's sense of humour. Once when he and Philip were guests at a wedding, Philip took it into his head to make Baronius intone the *Miserere*. Another day he sent Baronius with an enormous bottle to buy a minute quantity of wine. He had instructions first to sample the entire stock. Then, after making the wine-seller wash out the bottle, he had to tender a gold coin and demand change. When the historian, after publishing a volume of his *Annals*, took it to present it to Philip, instead of getting the commendation he expected he had imposed upon him the obligation of serving thirty masses. It was by such means that the Saint made other men saints. But in doing so, he also had a good deal of fun.

For thirteen years Philip had been living at San Girolamo.

He still had no community or any organization except that of the Oratory meetings. And when he was pressed to become the Rector of the Florentine Church at Rome, he refused to live there himself, though he sent priests to look after it. Not even when the exercises were transferred to the Church of the Florentines would Philip take up residence in that place.

This was because he did not want to appear in any position of authority ; but it was also because he was afraid of doing anything that might seem like establishing a religious institute. Even when a disagreement with the trustees of the Florentine Church necessitated the building of what is still called the Chiesa Nuova, and the creation of the Congregation of the Oratory, Philip continued to live apart in his old rooms at San Girolamo. Not until eight years later — and then only because he received a direct order from the Pope — would he transfer himself to the Oratorian Church, although the Congregation had been founded since 1575.

When at last he did so, of course he made an occasion of it. Anybody else would have had his belongings carried to his new lodgings by some conveyance. Not so Philip. Accompanied by his disciples he walked there, all of them bearing kitchen pots and pans. And he was delighted when the jailbirds in a prison they had to pass yelled jovial insults at them. "Fry us some pancakes, Father !" they shouted. The person least embarrassed was himself.

There was no doing anything with such a man. Saint Charles Borromeo, when he was Secretary of State under his uncle, did his best to make Philip comport himself with more dignity. Philip's own subjects tried to make him behave — the only result being that he behaved worse than ever. They had to put up with his eccentricities ; he had become a privileged character.

Only narrowly did he escape being made a cardinal. When Gregory XIV was elected Pope in 1590 and Philip called upon him to tender congratulations, he found himself in the papal embrace ; and the red biretta which Gregory had worn as a cardinal was placed upon his head with the words, "We create you cardinal." Philip got out of it that time by treating the whole affair as a joke. Clement VIII also tried to make him a cardinal, and was with difficulty resisted. But Philip knew what was in store for Tarugi and Baronius. Though they too escaped during his lifetime, he divined that they would not always escape. So everyone who entered Philip's rooms saw hanging there two cardinalatial coats-of-arms, on which, instead of the ordinary bearings, skulls had been drawn. Philip never explained what he meant by them ; only when Baronius and Tarugi were commanded to accept the red hat did they understand. But as for the red biretta Gregory had sent Philip, he would sometimes use it as a football, especially if any of the Fathers suggested that he should submit to the proffered honour. Or he would throw the biretta in the air and exclaim, "Paradise ! Paradise !" What did he want with dignities ?

He kept as much out of sight as possible, even after he went to live with his community in 1583, for he did not want to appear as superior. He usually took his meals in his own rooms, except when he had guests. Nor did he often attend the recreation of the Fathers. In the very bosom of his family he was at once a recluse and the most accessible of men. Anybody might see him at any time, but he hated to preside over the smallest function. Though he had absolute control over his subjects, he rarely gave an order ; a suggestion or a request was so much more effective.   When he was asked how it was that he was so perfectly obeyed, he answered that it was because he commanded so little.   He had the secret of ruling by love.

Saint Philip was undoubtedly a character, an eccentric ; but he was of course a great deal more.   Goethe was so fascinated by what he heard of him when he lived as a young man in Italy that he lingers affectionately over him as the humorous saint. But though this humour must not be separated from Philip's sanctity, it was his sanctity which, after all, was the important thing about him.   Rather it was through the combination of both qualities that he put such a deep mark upon others, and that he still does.   Possibly no two men could have been much less like one another than this very Italian Italian and that very English Englishman, John Henry Newman.   Yet Newman was one of the greatest of his sons.   He would have been the last man to go in for Philip's antics, but in no man is Philip's spirit more clearly discernible.

Philip's greatest effect upon his own time was that he drew to himself all the élite of Rome.   Particularly was this true during his later years, when the Oratory was crowded with members of the papal court.   The Pope had, indeed, induced Philip to choose the Vallicella, because of its accessibility to his courtiers.   Even so, Philip never set himself to cultivate the highly placed, and the poorest of men continued to be as welcome as nobles and prelates.   Yet it was through the influence he exerted over the Curia — something absolutely without parallel — that, without any intention of being a reformer, he actually became one of the most effective instruments for the reform of the Church.   Individual lives, these were all that he wished to remould.   But as he had among his disciples cardinals and bishops and papal functionaries and even popes, what he did for them was carried through ever extending circles. He was no Saint Ignatius, sitting in a little room and from there directing worldwide operations. Nor was he like his friend Saint Charles Borromeo, who was so largely the means for putting into operation the decrees of the Council of Trent. It is no detraction from what they did to say that the effect of Philip upon his age was hardly less.

His, however, was always the purely personal touch. And this is illustrated in the charming stories of his encounters — brief and casual as they were — with the students of the English College at Rome. This was in the same street as the Church of San Girolamo and as Philip wandered about so much, he was continually running into the young Englishmen. It was his custom to raise his hat and salute them with *Salvete, flores martyrum*. They knew that they were all destined to die on the scaffold, something that was borne home to them every day by the grisly and realistic pictures in their refectory and lecture-halls. When these men were ordained and about to leave for England, they all went to Saint Philip to receive his blessing — all, that is, except one, who for some reason neglected to go. He, according to tradition, escaped martyrdom, but only by apostatizing. Those who did kneel before Philip, asking his blessing, to a man died upon the scaffold.

Equally charming, but more intimate, were Philip's relations with the Dominicans, who made him a kind of tertiary of the order, as did the Franciscans, though it would appear that he was not formally a member. But he was almost a second novice-master at the Minerva, and as such he often used to take the novices out on picnics, when he would entertain them with his stories and jokes, and edify them with his spiritual conversation. On these occasions, though he was himself the most abstemious of men, he used to urge the young friars to eat and grow fat when the hampers of food were unpacked. "Eat, eat !" he would exclaim. "It makes me fat to see you eat." In spite of which he remained a little wisp of a man, delicate and ethereal. The official novice-master, like the prior at the Minerva, well understood how much benefit their charges derived from these merry outings.

There is another instance, of a very different kind, of his strong friendship for the Dominicans. He championed the cause of Savonarola when there was a question, at the end of Paul IV's pontificate, of putting his writings on the Index. That this was prevented cannot be said to have been due to any influence Philip had with the papal court, for he was at that time somewhat under a cloud. But he used his influential friends, and he prayed. At the very moment when the decision in favour of Savonarola was reached, but was of course not yet known, the Dominicans found Philip in ecstasy ; coming out of it, he told them that they had won their case. Savonarola's writings had escaped condemnation, though, in order to satisfy those who had been pressing for it, a few of his sermons were placed upon the Index for their excessive violence but not because they contained anything heretical.

Even that cannot be called an intrusion into ecclesiastical politics. Still less did Philip meddle in secular affairs, though as there was a solitary exception to this, it should be noted. It came at the very end of Philip's life and was his intervention on behalf of Henry IV of France. The King's profession of Catholicism was viewed, with some apparent justification, as not quite sincere, and Philip of Spain, who looked upon himself as being more Catholic than the Pope, vigorously opposed

Henry's being received back into the Church, in his case with motives that may well be viewed with suspicion. St. Philip, on the other hand, was convinced — by supernatural illumination, he said — that Henry should be reconciled, as this would be for the good of Christendom. He not only argued in this sense with Clement VIII, but when the Pope still hesitated, he went so far as to threaten to withdraw Baronius from his office of papal confessor. The issue was not decided during Philip's lifetime, and it would be altogether too much to claim that it was solely or even mainly due to him, but he undoubtedly had a considerable part in it ; and he showed that he was correct in his judgment, whether or not we believe in his enlightenment from on high. But apart from this matter, Philip never exercised his influence directly, even when he might legitimately have done so. Never would he ask anything for himself or for his congregation. From a succession of popes who were his personal friends, and who always treated him as though he were the cardinal he refused to become, he asked nothing, and he accepted nothing. He was absolutely at their service, but he jealously guarded his own independence. It was enough to be a saint, and to make other men saints.

We hear of all kinds of marvels in connection with him. Three hundred miracles or supernatural manifestations were attested to at the time of his canonization, and however freely it be admitted that many of these things are susceptible of a natural explanation, we are still left with a number of incidents not easily to be accounted for. Philip himself used to be annoyed with the reports in circulation about him. "What's all this talk about miracles ?" he used to protest. "How should a sinner like myself perform miracles ?" And to Baronius he confided, "Cesare, I assure you that it is a great subject of regret to me that people take me for what they do ; I constantly pray to God not to do anything through my instrumentality, which may give them occasion to esteem me for what I really am not ; and believe me, if at times anything has happened of a supernatural character, it has been through the faith of others, not through my merits."

That of course is only what one would expect him to say. But let us look at what happened to him in 1592, when he was thought to be dying. It was something attested to by a number of people who were present, including a couple of doctors. The curtains had been drawn around his bed, and the priests and the physicians there were talking, if at all, in hushed tones. Suddenly they heard the dying man saying loudly, "Oh, my most holy Madonna ! My beautiful Madonna ! My blessed Madonna !" The doctors ran to him and drew back the curtains. There was Philip kneeling, suspended in air. He appeared to be embracing someone whom nobody else could see. He was weeping and saying, "No, I am not worthy ! Who am I, O my dear Madonna, that you should come to see me ? O Virgin most beautiful and most pure, I do not deserve a grace so great ! Why have you come to me, the least and lowest of your servants ? Who am I ? O holiest Virgin ! O blessed among women !"

The doctors spoke to him, asking what was the matter, and he answered, "Did you not see the Mother of God come to visit me to take away my pain ?" At this he came to himself, and sinking back on the bed, he drew the covers over his head and burst into floods of tears. The fact is that he had been instantly and completely cured, as the doctors were able to bear witness. One of them, Angelo da Bagnorea, went home and at once wrote down an account of the whole matter before any of the details could slip his mind.

Philip lived three more years, years spent in almost unbroken prayer. For in 1593 he insisted on resigning the office of superior and Baronius took his place. After that he was free from all cares and duties ; the many friends who still came in a steady stream to see him did not disturb his union with God but were rather witnesses of it.

It is worth remarking that never in the whole life of this mystic do we hear of anything even remotely like the "dark night of the soul" which seems to be so common in the road of mystical experience. Perhaps this was because Saint Philip never had any system. More likely it was because he was devoid of introspection. His simplicity bore the fruit of a joy that was always radiant, always visible upon his face. Yet he left a distinct mark upon the new school of mysticism that was about to arise. Questionable as it may be whether St. Francis de Sales ever met him when he was in Rome in 1591, it is easy to recognize Philip's spirit in him. And it was this that Francis passed on to Jeanne Francis de Chantal and Vincent de Paul. Philip wrote nothing, however, except for tossing off an impromptu poem now and then ; and with the utmost reluctance would he bring himself to pen so much as a letter. The continuous labour necessary to the composition of a book was at complete variance with his temperament. Preaching itself he had long given up after one or two experiences when he was so overcome as to be unable to proceed. At the Oratory exercises in later years he did no more than ask a question or make a correction. What he imparted was entirely through conversation. We know what was the effect of that — and of his personality — upon others. It was in this way that he reached people.

He died on May 26, 1595, eighty years old, at one in the morning, on the day after Corpus Christi. He knew that he was dying and foretold the exact hour. Yet to the end he was seeing friends and hearing confessions. Nobody expected him to die just then. When those who were made aware that something was amiss rushed to his room, they found him sitting on his bed. It was sitting there that he died.

At once there was a demand for his canonization. The formal Process was begun two months after his death, but before that his picture was being sold in the streets of Rome aureoled and with his name printed under it as "Blessed." His was really the last instance of a saint who was canonized by popular acclaim. The *ex votos* were arriving in bales, and unofficially Philip's cultus had already begun, but with the full knowledge of the Pope. The Process was looked upon as hardly more than a technical formality. That the beatification took as long as it did was because Clement VIII, though holding Philip to be a saint, did not want to press his cause, lest the Jesuits feel that favouritism was being shown. Ignatius had been dead thirty-nine years in 1595. Moreover, the enquiry had to be delayed so as to allow the Process for Charles Borromeo to be completed. Even so, the matter was pushed through with unusual speed. Paul V pronounced the decree of beatification on May 25, 1615, and canonization came on March 12, 1622, during the pontificate of Gregory XV.

On that same day four saints were canonized together with Philip. All the others were Spaniards — Isidore the Farmer, Teresa of Avila, Ignatius Loyola and Francis Xavier. The witticism was that the Pope had canonized four Spaniards and

a saint. Loyola and Xavier would not perhaps have relished
being called Spaniards, for they were Basques ; but the people
of Rome ignored that distinction. They did not like Spaniards and, as they believed, for good reasons. But Philip Neri
was their own. He had spent all but eighteen years of his
life among them. Thousands of people were alive who had
known him. Long before the Pope acted they were all quite
positive that Philip Neri was a saint.

X

SAINT VINCENT DE PAUL

Vincent de Paul offers us, even more than do most of the great men who, while seemingly simple are actually highly complex, a number of rather startling contrasts. To begin with he was, as my namesake, the Abbé Maynard remarks, "the most positive and efficient organizer the world has ever seen." And men of that type, though they are very necessary to the orderly operation of the world, are not usually very attractive. Yet the charming personality of Vincent so struck men's imagination that few saints — surely no saint of modern times — has had so many legends cluster about his name. Though such stories have to be removed from the realm of historical fact, we shall not see him truly unless we recognize that he was the kind of man about whom legends are told. The average person does not think of Vincent as the organizer but as the kind old man who took the place of a galley-slave and who used to go out into the streets of Paris gathering up deserted babies in his cloak. Those things never happened at all ; as to that we can now be perfectly certain. But it is instructive to note that it was the administrator and the efficient man of whom people said they did happen.

These stories are conclusively shown to be legends by Père Coste, the Vincentian, whose definitive edition of Vincent's letters and conferences and his three-volume biography — the most scholarly of all lives of saints — prove them to be without foundation. Yet while Père Coste was writing his monumental work a number of his older colleagues shook their heads and believed that he must be losing his faith. However, as Père Verdier, the Superior General of the Congregation of the Missions, wrote an Introduction, the biography has now to be accepted as official Vincentian history. Père Verdier is a little sad about the whole thing, but concludes "There is nothing so beautiful as truth" — in spite of which we may be sure that all the statues and paintings of Vincent will continue to show him with his babies.

The second point of piquant contrast is that Vincent was a peasant and yet spent most of his life among aristocratic and even royal personages. He did have a good deal of peasant shrewdness to the end, but there could have been nothing of the country bumpkin about him. Even the tale about his appearing at court in ragged clothes has nothing to support it except that Cardinal Mazarin, who did not like him, one day drew attention to the slightly frayed band of his soutane. Though he was the reverse of a fashionable abbé, he much more than held his ground among such people. Whatever his birth, he was a natural gentleman.

Again we might notice that, though the Congregation of the Missions had as its original purpose — one never abandoned — that of giving missions in country districts, this was only one of the Vincentian purposes. And this particular work was undertaken at the insistence of the Comtesse de Joigny. When Vincent had once begun his work he found himself surrounded by the highest-born ladies in France, and he set them hard at work for him. The Sisters of Charity came into being only as an auxiliary group of strong peasant girls who could do the rough tasks beyond the powers of his delicately nurtured Ladies of Charity.

Finally we must observe the contrast between his careful

planning and the way his schemes materialized with apparent spontaneity.   He accepted other people's advice, or at least listened to it ; and he took his time ; but the decisions reached in the end were his own.   This is his explanation : "The good which God wishes to be done is done as it were without our thinking about it ; that is the way in which our Congregation came into existence, the way the missions and the retreats for ordinands began, the way the Company of the Daughters of Charity arose, the way the association of Ladies to assist the poor in the Hôtel-Dieu and the parochial poor was established . . . the way in which all the works of which we now find ourselves in charge first saw the light.   Not one of these works was deliberately undertaken by us but God, who wished to be served on these occasions, brought them about imperceptibly and, if He made use of us, nevertheless we never knew to what they were going to lead."   That is perfectly true : the founding of the Congregation of the Mission was not his idea, and when he formed his little scheme of getting assistance from country girls, he did not know to what it was going to lead.   But this has to be said : the organization of any project sprang naturally and inescapably from something that he had already done.   And when the organization was effected, though it was always on a modest scale, it was always so well based and so elastic as to be capable of almost indefinite extension.   He did not begin any of these works of his until relatively late in life, and it was only because he lived to a great age that he managed to put his finger into so many pies.   But one undertaking inevitably prepared for the next, and nothing he ever started was abandoned by him.   It was hardly even a question of adding something new, while leaving the old still functioning as before : one would be nearer the truth to say that nothing new was ever added, but that everything was an unfolding from the central plan with which he started, and that that plan itself was hardly more than the meeting of every situation as it arose with the commonsense which would make charity operative.

Vincent's was a life of intense activity, and he made it plain that those whom he attracted to himself were to serve God in the active life. But because he was a saint he understood that external activity has to be nourished by interior devotion. To the Vincentian Fathers he used to say : "Prayer and study should resolve themselves into action ; the light in the mind should become a fire in the heart." It is the principle that we encounter over and over again, though applied in varying ways, and with differing degrees of emphasis laid upon it, in all the characters presented here : those who are to be described as contemplatives regard contemplation as the mainspring of work, while those who are most deeply immersed in work find that they cannot do it fruitfully without contemplation. Mary and Martha are sisters — one might almost say twin sisters — and they are hand in hand.

A word about the Vincentian biographers before coming to Vincent himself. The first of the lives, one written in three substantial volumes, was produced by a man who had known Vincent intimately ; this was Louis Abelly, the Bishop of Rodez. At the time he wrote there were in existence about thirty thousand of the Saint's letters, and upon these he was able to draw freely, though it would seem that some of them were "doctored" by the Congregation before being handed over to the biographer for his use. Despite the fact that it may be charged that Abelly in each volume told Vincent's life over again, each time from a different point of view, there can be no doubt that the real Vincent emerges from his pages. There has been no need for any subsequent biographer to correct the main lines of the portrait he painted, whatever need there has been of correcting some incidental mistakes, and of making some amplifications.

Pierre Collet, who wrote in 1748, does not improve upon Abelly, from whom indeed he draws most of his material; and Louis-Emile Bougaud does not add a great deal to our knowledge, either, though he handles his material more skillfully than do his predecessors. But the Abbé Ulysse Maynard, whom the magazine. *Newsweek* announced was my uncle (which would make me very venerable, as the first edition of his four-volume work appeared in 1861) thought and (with charming modesty) said that he had superseded all previous biographies. If his opinion of himself was rather too high, his opinion of the other biographers is correspondingly low. Collet is called, "Cold and dry, after the fashion of too many theologians." Bougaud is similarly attacked. And Abelly is accused of having only fathered a work actually written by the Vincentians themselves. A good popular life has been produced by the Duc de Broglie, and a brilliant study by Henri Lavedan, though this has unfortunately suffered from his uncritical attitude. Pierre Coste's biography would be perfect if it were but a little more readable. Yet it is only fair to say that it is a mine of carefully tested information. I can think of no saint whose story has been examined with an equal degree of scientific precision, unless it be the one on Philip Neri by Ponnelle and Bordet.

A serious error that is decisively disposed of in the pages of Coste — and one wonders how it escaped so long — is that of Vincent's birth. Here there was a case of quite deliberate falsification : it was given as 1576 instead of 1581. Abelly in putting down the earlier date may have done so in good faith ; it is possible that Père Almeras, Vincent's successor as Superior General, may have misled him. At the same time, as Abelly was often in Vincent's company and as Vincent spoke freely of these matters, it might be supposed that he heard the correct date from the Saint's own lips. A mistake of this sort often occurs, and is sometimes of no great importance. Unfortunately this was no mistake but a calculated untruth. It was put into circulation in order to conceal the fact that Vincent had been ordained before he was nineteen, five years before the canonical age for ordination. One can only suppose that Almeras wished to hush that up so as to avoid giving a handle to the *advocatus diaboli* when Vincent's cause for beatification was being examined. It might also have given a handle to the Jansenists, who would have been quick to point out that this old enemy of theirs, this reformer of the French clergy, was himself at fault in a grave question of ecclesiastical discipline. Therefore the lie was told with good intentions, as lies often are ; there can be no denying that a lie was told.

Vincent de Paul was born of a peasant family, poor but not abjectly poor. In later life he was accustomed to say that it would have been better for him had he never climbed beyond that position. This was something he felt so strongly that as an old man he would give no help to a nephew who wished to become a priest. Yet he may have seen that the youth was more moved by ambition than convinced of any divinely conferred vocation. Be that as it may, it is clear that Vincent believed that the humble and obscure life of laborious poverty is the safest that man can have.

Vincent was led out of obscurity by strange and devious

paths, at once to exalted social circles and the heights of spirituality. He could hardly have imagined that many others would have encountered the dangers through which he had successfully passed. But he did not forget that, though he had been a well-behaved boy, he had sought priesthood, not so much because of a supernatural motive as to rise in the world. He himself had been well on the road to promotion and affluence — for despite his peasant origins he had made extremely useful connections — when by the grace of God he turned back. It is true that his ambition was never inordinate, for even when he was beginning to acquire abbeys *in commendam* and similar benefices, he wrote to his mother to say that he hoped for an honourable retirement so that he might spend the rest of his days near her. Even so, that was to prefer his private good to the vocation to which he was about to be summoned ; and he realized that the danger of ambition lies not so much in its magnitude as in permitting ambition to be a motive at all. After that, nobody was less concerned about advancement than was Vincent. But when he was at school, he once refused to see his father, who had come a long way on foot to make this visit, because he did not want to be embarrassed by acknowledging himself to be the son of this shabbily dressed peasant. That was an offence he sorrowed over even in old age.

By dint of hard work and some patronage he obtained a decent education, taking his theological studies at the University of Toulouse, as there were as yet no seminaries in France. And if he was ordained before he was nineteen, it must be said in his defence that he was much better trained than were most of the priests who were ordained in those days, and that the decrees of the Council of Trent were not promulgated in

France until 1615. Nor can he be severely blamed if his object was merely that of securing a reasonably good ecclesiastical job, for that was almost universally the object of the clerical profession. All one can say is that, had he secured it, we should never have heard of him again.

In this, however, he was for the moment disappointed. Instead he had to console himself with a small legacy. As it consisted of a debt due from a young man living in Marseilles to the lady who made the bequest, Vincent at once set out to collect the money. In order to get to Marseilles he sold a horse he had hired, and which did not belong to him, though he intended to straighten out that little matter upon his return. However, I suppose the transaction did make him a kind of horse thief, and his procedure in Marseilles was hardly that of a saint : he had the debtor arrested and thrown into prison so as to compel him to disgorge. He clearly had an eye wide open to the main chance, and was not particularly squeamish in pursuing it.

Just then a fortunate calamity happened. He was persuaded to make the return journey by sea instead of going overland again. This resulted in his being captured by Barbary pirates, taken to Tunis, and sold as a slave.

Now comes a curious reflection. Had Vincent been brought up by the sea and so grown accustomed to boats, he would probably have lived the rest of his days as a slave. But he was *not* accustomed to boats and became seasick whenever he got in one. Because of this the man who had purchased him — a fisherman — found that Vincent was quite useless and therefore disposed of him to another master.

His second owner turned out to be an alchemist, and with him the slave had a rather amusing time. Vincent apparently took his alchemy quite seriously, and when he at last escaped, he carried back with him two of the prize exhibits of his master, a mirror of Archimedes — whatever that may have been — and a skull which opened and shut with a spring and seemed to talk, ventriloquism probably being part of the trick. If this dabbling in magic did not last long, it was only because the alchemist was summoned to Turkey by the Sultan, whereupon Vincent was sold again.

The third master was a Christian renegade, a former Franciscan friar named Gualtier, one who was then availing himself of the privilege given by the Prophet and living with three wives. That Vincent had a power over women had already been shown by his having had a lady leave him a legacy ; it was now shown again in the kindness of Gualtier's wives towards their slave. But that this power of his was by no means limited to women appears in his converting his master and escaping in his company to France. There the vice-legate was so excited by the story the two men had to tell that he took them with him to Rome, where the talking skull was exhibited to the admiration of the college of cardinals and where Gualtier retired to a monastery. Vincent, taking up the dropped threads of his life, started to look once more for a comfortable benefice.

Eventually he landed in Paris and fell in with the famous Pierre Bérulle, soon to be the founder of the French Oratory and eventually a cardinal. He was one of the most remarkable and influential men of his time. At once his keen eye penetrated beneath the worldly veneer — probably it was hardly more than a varnish — of his new acquaintance ; from that moment Vincent's true vocation was decided. Or, if its final shape was still indistinct, Bérulle perceived that in Vincent he had encountered a man for whom God had great designs. He made no attempt, however, to rush Vincent along altogether new paths. That would come but could be brought about only by degrees. If Vincent had Gascon vivacity, he had a certain stubborn peasant obstinacy which required careful handling. Therefore Bérulle at this stage thought it sufficient to find him a position — it must be presumed to have been obtained through Bérulle — as almoner to Margaret of Valois, the ex-wife of Henry IV. She had married him in 1572 but the marriage had been annulled in 1599, whereupon she was replaced by the florid and foolish Marie de' Medici. As Margaret's almoner, Vincent was rewarded with the *commendam* of a Cistercian abbey, and was sure that he had at last put his foot on the first rung of the ladder of success.

Queen Margaret was something of a character. She was kindhearted and (in her own style) pious ; but she was also eccentric. She had, for instance, built a circular chapel where a community of Augustinian canons had the duty of singing in pairs throughout the day hymns of her own composition. At any rate these hymns were officially hers, though as she had the well-known poet François Maynard as a member of her establishment, one suspects that he touched up her verses.

This went on until 1611, when Bérulle, whose eye had all the time been keenly fastened upon him, found his friend another job — something more useful than hanging around an eccentric ex-queen. Vincent was appointed Curé of Clichy, now a suburb of Paris but then a small village. So easily were his modest ambitions satisfied that he would have contentedly remained there until he died, had this been permitted.

It was not permitted. Bérulle again had a job for Vincent. He asked him to become tutor in the household of the Gondis

— and with this, though nobody knew it as yet, Vincent's chance had come.

The Gondis were an immensely rich and powerful family. For several generations every Bishop of Paris had been a Gondi, and one of the boys Vincent tutored was destined for that position. This was Henry, the younger of the sons, who used to inform his elder brother that when he became a cardinal, like his uncle, this would give him precedence over a mere count. This elder brother, however, went a little further than that, for he was the future Duc de Retz. As for the boastful Henry, he met a fatal accident, so clearing the ecclesiastical road for a boy born to the Gondis while Vincent was in their household. He is remembered in history as the highly entertaining but equally disedifying Cardinal de Retz. It is most unlucky that the first two hundred and fifty pages of his *Memoirs* were lost ; they probably contained some spicy comments on the tutor. However, the Cardinal had later on a great respect for Vincent, and Vincent showed him indulgence, expressing the opinion that this scamp was not far from the kingdom of heaven. It is no more than just to add that the Cardinal did end his days well, and that he had entered the priesthood for no other reason than that his father and mother insisted upon it, in the belief that as a priest this precious son of theirs would be, even at the worst, considerably less vicious than in any other walk of life. Also, of course, they had no intention of renouncing the bishopric of Paris as a family preserve.

The Comte de Joigny, the head of the family, was general of the galleys, another hereditary Gondi office. Hence there came about Vincent's appointment as chaplain-general of the galleys. Although this was only one of his many activities, he

took it seriously and accomplished a great deal for the allevia-
tion of the lot of the men condemned to the oar.   It was with
the Gondis that he was to be associated for a number of years ;
it was the Gondis who opened out to him his career — one
very different from what he had sought.

At this point I must make a personal confession.   All
Vincent's biographers have lavished praise upon the Comtesse
for her sweetness of character and saintliness ; I find her an
exceedingly tiresome person.   She was an egotist and a
spiritual hypochondriac — a good woman no doubt and well-
meaning, but one who took it for granted that her exalted rank
entitled her soul to special attention.   What she demanded
from Vincent was, in effect, that he should sit beside her and
take her pulse every half hour.   When we add to this the fact
that the Gondi boys, according to their aunt, were little devils,
we can understand why, after four years of this life, Vincent,
feeling that he could stand no more of it, simply fled.

He was, it is true, later persuaded to go back to the Gondis,
but the breathing-space he obtained gave him the opportunity
to make his first beginnings in works of organized charity.   He
had gone to Châtillon-les-Domes in Bresse (again through
Bérulle) to build up a decayed parish, and it was there that he
founded his first Confraternity of Charity.   He discovered
poor people ; he preached about their needs ; and the response
was so great but also so haphazard that he saw the need of
putting everything upon a well-ordered basis.   From that
starting-point these confraternities of his — first of women
and then, less successfully, of men — eventually spread over all
France.   But probably this extension would not have come
about had not the Comtesse, by pulling wires with Bérulle and
the Cardinal of Paris, her brother-in-law, induced Vincent to

return to her house. Her great argument, in a letter to Vincent, was : "If after all this you still refuse, I will charge you before God for all that may happen to me. . . There are few who are capable of assisting me. . . I know, that as my life only serves to offend God, it is dangerous to place it in peril. . . I shall probably soon be in a worse state, and the mere fear of it would cause me such pain that I think it would bring about my death." Then of course she would be damned, and Vincent would be responsible.

Well, Vincent did go back to her, and he stayed with her until she died. But he went on his own terms, and he cured the Comtesse by setting her to work. This discovery of his of the value of work to a sick soul was to be very useful on many similar occasions. On the Gondi estates, which were many and scattered throughout France, his first missions were preached and new confraternities were established. He was soon finding work not only for Marguerite de Gondi but for scores of rich and fashionable women. They were sent out to help the poor, greatly to their own advantage as well as that of the destitute.

But if Vincent forced the hand of the Comtesse, she forced his hand as well. She and her husband gave him forty-five thousand livres — a very large sum in those days — for endowing missions to country people. In vain Vincent suggested that it be given instead to the Jesuits or the Oratorians ; she would listen to nothing else than that he found a congregation for this purpose. Then as soon as he had agreed to do so, she died, and as her husband joined the Oratory, Vincent was completely free. The Collège des-Bons-Enfants and the huge priory of Saint-Lazare came into his hands, so that he — or rather his poor — were handsomely endowed. The tiresome

and insistent Comtesse had, after all, insisted upon the right
thing.

It would be impossible to deal here with all of Vincent's
multitudinous activities. But some of them must be touched
on. One of the most important was the founding of the Ladies
of Charity. The list of their names is like a social directory.
The one who gave most freely to further Vincent's plans was
Cardinal Richelieu's famous niece, the Duchesse d'Aiguillon,
nor was she the one among them who did the least hard and
thankless work. Other duchesses were those of Nemours,
Ventadour and Verneuil. Then there were the Princesse de
Condé, the mother of the "great" Condé, Louise-Marie de
Gonzague, before long Queen of Poland, the Marquise de
Vigean, whose daughter married the Duc de Richelieu, the
Comtesse de Brienne, the wives of Marshal Schomberg and
President Herse of the Court of Requests, and the Baronne
de Renty. And these were only a few of the great ladies
whom Vincent set to work for him. Work, real work, was
demanded of them. Oh, he could always use their money in
his charities, but he expected them to go in person to the poor
in the hospitals and in the parishes. He even had the idea of
a kind of super-fraternity under the presidency of the Queen,
silly but goodhearted Anne of Austria. Among these people
he made virtue fashionable.

One of these Ladies of Charity deserves more than passing
mention. She was Louise de Marillac, known then as
Mademoiselle de Gras, for though she had been married, her
husband was not of the rank to entitle her to be known as
"Madame." He was, however, very well connected, and for
uncles she had the Chancellor and the Marshal Marillac.
When Vincent first encountered her she was somewhat like the

Comtesse de Joigny, in that she was scrupulous and fussy and tiresome. And so she would have remained, had Vincent allowed it. As she had nothing in particular to do now that she was a widow, he employed her as one of his official visitors for the country Confraternities. It was in this way that he formed her into Saint Louise de Marillac, and it was under her direction that the Daughters — or Sisters — of Charity were placed.

At first there were only three, and then a dozen, of these sturdy peasant girls, all of whom lived in Louise's house in Paris, their duty being to assist the Ladies of the Confraternity in the rough work that was beyond the strength of dainty hands. But as they grew in numbers they had to have a rule, and this was something that taxed Vincent's ingenuity. How to fix their status was a nice question. It must be remembered that in those days nuns were always cloistered. For though Saint Frances of Rome had founded a house of Benedictine Oblates who, though living under rule, were only Oblates, unbound by vows and without a cloister, such an arrangement did not accord with French ideas. Whether or not Vincent had ever heard of this community I do not know, but he must have been aware that Saint Francis de Sales, a close friend of his, had started the Visitation with the intention that its nuns should work among the poor, a plan that came to nothing precisely because of the association between the concept of "nun" and "enclosure." Very well, as this was the situation, the Sisters of Charity should not be nuns at all ! They would simply be pious women living together, doing any kind of work, under no vows, and not wearing a religious habit, though for the sake of convenience they wore their peasant costume, and in Paris this constituted a kind of uniform. It has since developed into a habit, and the familiar cornets have been added ; but in Vincent's time it was not that at all. Nor were they in the beginning even allowed to take the yearly vows that were afterwards permitted.

All this was a startling innovation and to many people it seemed one that was full of dangers. Nuns were under the protection of the state, with a definitely recognized canonical and civil position, but these Sisters had to go anywhere and do anything. Imagine what it was to send them out as nurses — something unheard of — during the last stages of the Thirty Years' War and the disturbances of the Fronde ! Yet Vincent accepted the risk and asked them to accept it — and everything turned out a tremendous success.

But note, please, the very curious relationship of Louise de Marillac to these girls. She did not wear the peasant's costume but her widow's weeds. And though she directed them, she did so merely as a Lady of Charity. Moreover the original intention was that, when Louise died, another Lady of Charity would take her place. Fortunately the ailing woman lived long enough for that situation to be clarified and for a rule to be approved by Rome under which a canonical status was given to the Sisters of Charity, under which "Mademoiselle," as she was always called, could be succeeded by a member of their own group.

There was a similar innovation with regard to the Fathers of the Congregation of the Mission. Vincent insisted upon things that appeared to be irreconcilable. His priests were to be seculars, yet they were to be bound by vows, though vows constituted them religious. Vincent was equal to that difficulty, too : the vows were to be taken privately and not before the superior. At the same time, those vows were to have the binding force of solemn vows publicly pronounced. It is small wonder that he was kept waiting a long while before he received papal approbation for so radical a departure from all previous concepts of the religious life.

What was the work of these Fathers ? First and foremost it was that of preaching country missions. Under the contract entered into with the Gondis this had to be done on all the Gondi estates. But it was extended to many other places. And the preaching was to be of the simplest kind, according to what Vincent described as the "little method." The pulpit oratory of the age was of a somewhat ornate and ostentatious character, and that would not do for illiterate peasants. But, if it comes to that, Vincent would not permit his Fathers to use any other method even when they were preaching before cultivated city audiences. For though something more is needed for preaching than being understood, one should at least start there. The instant a man begins to show off in the pulpit — or anywhere else, for that matter — people begin to doubt his sincerity ; and when that happens, he might as well stop talking and go home. Vincent's was not a novel discovery, but it is one that has to be insisted upon over and over again, so prone are egotistical men to exhibit themselves. That is why Saint Philip Neri had allowed only a direct conversational style in the preaching at the Oratory in Rome, That is why, too, a reaction had set in in France against ornateness. Even on the stage and in poetry simplicity was beginning to be accepted as the best of mediums. Any art that is too elaborate, or too artificial, is rightly distrusted ; and this is above all true of the arts whose effect must be instantaneous. Vincent put everything in a nutshell when he said that his missionaries "will speak to convert and not to be esteemed, and if men are to be converted they must understand what is said."

The giving of missions was, however, only one part of the work of the Fathers. Another part of the work was what was done for the clergy. Ecclesiastical seminaries were still so rare as to be all but nonexistent, so in order to provide at least some idea of the new state of life that was being taken on by those about to be ordained, retreats were given them. But Vincent did not stop there : that he might steadily operate upon the spiritual condition of the clergy, Vincent instituted, first in Paris and then in other places, his famous Tuesday Conferences. Yet as even they could not supply all that was needed, Philip founded seminaries, encouraging his friends the Oratorians and Jean-Jacques Olier and Saint John Eudes to work along much the same lines. How badly this was needed is shown from the fact that another friend of Vincent's, Adrian Bourdoise, confined himself to giving practical instruction in the external duties of the priest, without bothering about theological training, as this, after all, could be obtained elsewhere. This is what Vincent says : "Good Monsieur Bourdoise was the first person whom God inspired to set up a seminary in which men should be taught how to administer the sacraments and carry out the rubrics ; before him, men scarcely knew what a seminary meant ; there was no special place in which these things were taught ; a man after his theology, his philosophy, his minor studies, and a little Latin, went to a parish and administered the sacraments there just as he fancied." But though Vincent established seminaries, he did not on that account give up the retreats for the ordinands. For those who could not go to a seminary — still the vast majority — the retreat was better than nothing ; for those who had attended a seminary, a retreat would add to their spiritual good.

Another of the ways in which Vincent de Paul did a great service to the Church in France — and to the Church universal — was the part he took in obtaining from Rome the condemnation of the five propositions in Jansen's *Augustinus*. The danger here was very considerable. For Jansenism, whatever may have been the learning and zeal of many Jansenists, was operated upon, however unconsciously, by the spirit of Calvinism. Thus two of the five propositions were that God's grace was irresistible and that Christ did not die for all men but only for the elect. We see at once the same distorted emphasis that Calvin laid upon God's foreknowledge in relation to predestination, and also the virtual denial of the freedom of the human will. But where Jansen's book had been no more than a thesis that might be debated at leisure by theologians in the universities, the new Jansenists made a practical application of its principles which was devastating to Catholic life. Antoine Arnauld, the brilliant brother of Mère Angélique, the superior of the Cistercian abbey of Port-Royal, wrote a book in which he discouraged frequent Communion on the ground that it was hardly conceivable that anybody could ever receive the Eucharist worthily. In those days not even very good Catholics ordinarily went to Holy Communion more than two or three times a year, for Communion as frequent as it is now was then far from being encouraged by the Church. But there was a wide difference between prevailing practice and what Arnauld advocated. The Jansenist school was paralyzing the soul with scrupulosity and making scrupulosity a sign of an exalted spiritual state, basing everything upon a theology that was highly, though subtly, heretical. Had the Jansenists succeeded, as they very nearly did, in capturing the better minds within the Church, they would have made the ruin wrought by the Reformation final and complete.

The theological controversy passed into other hands, notably those of the Jesuits. But the first phase of the matter, the condemnation of the five propositions, was brought to a successful close largely through the instrumentality of Saint Vincent. The answer of Arnauld was disingenuous : while he professed to agree that the propositions condemned were worthy of condemnation, he denied that they were to be found in the *Augustinus,* this because the terms of the condemnation did not cite specific passages, but instead covered the general substance. Under cover of this subterfuge the heresy was able to propagate itself all through the seventeenth and eighteenth centuries, and though as formal theology it is now dead, it is still to be encountered as a spirit of rigour, Puritanical and very un-Catholic.

But though Jansenism lingered on, the condemnation did have a decidedly deterrent effect, and this we owe to Vincent de Paul. Jansenism was no longer able to parade itself as super-orthodoxy and super-spirituality. If Vincent was able to bring this about, it was because of his unique position of influence among the French bishops. As a member of the Council of Conscience he had a good deal to say about the appointment of men to high ecclesiastical posts, and Louis XIII vowed on his death bed, where he was attended by Vincent, that if he lived he would see to it that nobody was ever nominated to the episcopacy unless he had first attended Vincent's Conferences for at least three years. In all kinds of ways, indeed, this simple priest exerted a deep influence over Catholic life in France, and as France, in spite of all the shortcomings of many of its clergy, was producing what were by far the most vigorous intellectual movements in the Church, the Vincentian influence spread and has lasted until this day.

The activities of Vincent continued into his extreme old age. His Congregation was extended to Italy and Corsica and Poland, and Vincent sent missionaries to Ireland and to Scotland — so saving the Faith in the highlands and the Hebrides — and the heathen of Madagascar were evangelized by his men. Though he could not send missionaries who avowed themselves to be such to Tunis, he did manage to attach a number of priests as chaplains to the consulates there, and through them no less than twelve hundred Christian captives were redeemed at a cost of well over a million livres. Vincent had not forgotten that he himself had once been a slave in that country.

Apparently Corsica, though supposedly Christian, needed missionaries as badly as did any heathen. The vendetta was so sacred that Corsican priests carried weapons even into church. We are told of one of them who was vesting for a procession of the Blessed Sacrament sticking a couple of pistols into his girdle. When one of Vincent's priests remonstrated with him the Corsican cleric relented to the extent of saying, "All right; I'll take only one pistol today." Yet in that wild island the work of the Fathers brought at least some Corsicans to acknowledge the virtue of Christian forgiveness.

In a less spectacular way the founding of charitable institutions went on — almshouses, country schools, the famous foundling-hospital of Paris, and asylums where the insane could be humanely looked after. Until Vincent appeared, the condition of these unfortunates was beyond words. Though there was still a long way to go to the modern science of psychiatry — if there *is* such a thing — it can at least be claimed for Vincent that he was almost the first to understand that nothing could be accomplished except by kindness. For the mentally deranged he had a special tenderness of heart.

These great works of his, and I have mentioned only a few among them, continued to the end and were constantly being added to, and Vincent did not cease directing them even after he was no longer able to move his own body about on its former labours. Some time before death actually came for him it was apparent that it could not be far off. Even though we cannot allow him the extra five years that were given to his age by those who moved back the date of his birth, he was very old, close on to eighty. And all his life he had toiled without ever sparing himself.

Now in 1660 the first of his disciples, gained while Vincent was still Curé of Clichy, died. This was Antoine Portail. A month later, as Louise de Marillac lay dying, since Vincent was unable to go to her, he sent her word that they would soon be meeting in heaven. She remained her scrupulous self to the last, and stopped the priest who was about to give her the Apostolic Benediction for the hour of death. He must wait, she told him ; her time had not yet come. A few minutes later she was demanding it. By the end of September of the same year Vincent himself was dead.

I began by remarking certain contrasts. Let me conclude by indicating a few more paradoxical things about him. He was a man of action, yes ; yet he moved very slowly. He was extremely deferential to others, yet very sure of his own mind, once he had made it up. He was a great innovator, yet he would seem to have had little originality. Certainly in his own spiritual life he leaned heavily on Bérulle and Francis de Sales. All that we know about his method of prayer is that he made the practice of the presence of God. But he made this very perfectly and (as was characteristic of him) in a most methodical fashion. Every time he heard the clock strike the quarter-hour he was at pains to recollect himself. Absorbed as he was in external affairs, he was still more recollected in God.

De Broglie has claimed for him that he merits a high place among the French authors of the seventeenth century, and, with a greater reserve, Père Coste makes a similar claim. That he could have been an author had he wished is true, but he wrote no books at all, and in his thousands of letters no attention is paid to anything except making his meaning clear. However, I am not disposed to undervalue that as a literary gift, nor can I believe that perfect lucidity is possible without some sense of style. But Vincent cannot be called a conscious artist.

His letters he usually signed, "Vincent, Unworthy Priest of the Mission," or, if he was in a hurry, with initials which stood for that formula. It is in these letters that we see him. Still more clearly, perhaps, does he appear in the conferences he gave to the Sisters of Charity and which they managed to take down word for word without his ever suspecting it, for his humility would never have permitted them to make a stenographic report. His conferences to the Fathers were not taken down nearly so fully ; men are less careful in such matters than women. But when in his old age he had Brother Ducornau as a secretary, even the Fathers got something more than a bare summary. In these utterly spontaneous and improvised talks — all *en famille* — he was intimate and racy and humorous. We can catch the very tone of his voice, almost the twinkle in his eye. Perhaps it is as well that he did not aspire to formal authorship, in which he would have been obliged to revise and edit himself. We have his words just as they fell from his lips, fresh and unstudied and unpretentious.

He could, however, rise to real eloquence, when the occasion demanded it. The greatest of French orators, Bossuet, often spoke at his Tuesday Conferences and was one of his disciples. But not even the rolling thunder of Bossuet was more effective than the simple words Vincent addressed to the Ladies of Charity when they were on the point of giving up the foundling-hospital: "So now, Ladies, sympathy and charity led you to adopt these little creatures as your children. You have been their mothers according to grace, ever since their mothers according to nature abandoned them; reflect now upon whether you, too, intend to abandon them. Cease to be their mothers and now become their judges. Their life and death are in your hands. I am now about to collect your opinions and votes; the time has come to pronounce their sentence and see if you still have desire to have mercy on them."

After such an appeal of course the work was continued. How could even the hardest of hearts have resisted those words? But that Vincent had power of this sort shows that he was a good deal more than an administrator and an efficient organizer. Though I have stressed this aspect of him by way of counterbalancing the legendary picture of Vincent, that picture does, after all, contain its truth, a truth that perhaps only legend can convey.

XI

COVENTRY PATMORE

One reason — perhaps the main reason — why Patmore has often been regarded a little askance by those of his faith is that, to put it somewhat crudely, his central theme is that of sex. This has tended to make Catholics nervous and even suspicious, as many of them are nervous and suspicious of the greatest of their novelists, Sigrid Undset. Such an attitude is of course of recent origin, and springs from that fussy and arid rigourism unknown among Catholics until the Reformation. Therefore, though Patmore considered himself, to use the biblical phrase, to be "digging again the wells which the Philistines had filled," he was well aware that what he wrote would "scare the devout with paradox."

Concerning all this, I shall have more to say. But I think that even if you are not prepared to accept Patmore as a Pillar of the Church, you may at least be willing to accept him as a gargoyle on one of the pillars. Surely Catholic universality is wide enough to include him.

Yet at this point I will argue against myself. The man Coventry Patmore is not one that I particularly like. Moreover, though I hold that his doctrine is immensely valuable — when dealing with it he is always illuminating — it must be admitted that he had a habit of extravagant and violent statement which often undid his effect. And he was a bundle of prejudices, of a literary, political and personal sort.

These things simply have to be tolerated, and Patmore makes our toleration all the easier by using language so fantastic that it is evident that he does not intend to be taken quite literally. It was so when he told Edmund Gosse that Cardinal Manning was "the worst type in history of the priest-ridden atheist." Probably all that this meant was that Manning, many years before, had used the wrong type of argument in his attempts to convert the first Mrs. Patmore. And the ode "1867," which opens

> *In the year of the great crime,*
> *When the false English Nobles and their Jew,*

is merely part of Patmore's aristocratic pose, concerning which Quiller-Couch has commented : "Somewhere and somehow Patmore had picked up a conception of himself as a stern unbending aristocrat, abandoned by the cowards of his own order, but erect, mailed, and defiant among the ruins of that fairer England he and his had ruled so long for its own good." These things to me are amusing rather than startling ; I do not find it difficult to condone them. What does affront me much more is the man's extraordinary arrogance, his conviction of his supernatural superiority. This Gosse explains charitably : "He would never have admitted it in words, perhaps because he would expect no sensible person to deny it. He was serene and kindly, but aloof ; he was like a king in exile." Of Patmore it may be said, with more truth than Mr. Schlesinger said of Orestes Brownson, that humility was the one Catholic virtue he did not possess.

Yet even here we may suspect that Patmore had much more humility than he would ever have confessed. He certainly had a good deal of humour, and that is hardly possible without humility. Thus when he asked Basil Champneys what he thought of the Sargent portrait of himself and Champneys answered that, if it had only been extended downwards there must have appeared the handle of a whip and that he would have been revealed as a sort of Southern planter on the point of thrashing his slaves and exclaiming, "You damned niggers !" Patmore was delighted and asked, "Is not that what I have been doing all my life ?" He was in truth what Gosse calls him, "the latest and fiercest of our English prophets" ; he was fittingly chosen to sit for Sargent's portrait of Ezekiel in the Boston Public Library : the prophet's fierceness of manner was necessary to prevent him being charged with being too dainty and sugary. In mere self-defence the poet had to offset this with intimidating growls and glares. The famous arrogance probably at bottom amounts to little more than that.

Patmore offered his distinctive doctrine to the world as one of universal applicability. It was therefore, to put it mildly, extremely paradoxical that he should have expressed so withering a contempt for the multitude. He more and more tended to state what was universal, what was catholic as well as Catholic, with an air of mystery. In rejection he withdrew into an esotericism tinged with bitterness. This, however, does not alter the fact that what Patmore was offering was an explanation of the most fundamental of human experiences.

He knew that his explanation would not be generally accepted. "Alas, and is not mine a language dead ?" he asks. But his greatness lies in the power he has over the minds of those willing to read him attentively and with understanding. The very shape of such minds he is able to change, for he comes upon them with the force of a revelation. Alice Meynell, his chief disciple, was too cautious a critic to commit herself, as did her protégé Francis Thompson, to the opinion that Patmore was the "greatest genius of the century," but she would not, I be-

lieve, have seriously dissented.   And that Thompson was not
giving vent to an unguarded burst of enthusiasm appears from
the fact that in two of his odes he elaborates on the same theme.
In one Patmore is

> *This strong*
> *Sad soul of sovereign song.*

In the other we get a portrait and a fine piece of criticism, which
gives to Patmore the place of honour among the Victorian
poets:

> *Last came a Shadow tall, with drooping lid,*
> *Which yet not hid*
> *The steel-like flashing of his armèd glance ;*
> *Alone he did advance,*
> *And all the throngs gave room*
> *For one that looked with such a captain's mien.*
> *A scornful smile lay keen*
> *On lips that, living, prophesied of doom ;*
> *His one hand held a lightning-bolt, the other*
> *A cup of milk and honey blent with fire ;*
> *It seemed as in that quire*
> *He had not, nor desired not, any brother.*
> *A space his alien eye surveyed the pride*
> *Of meditated pomp, as one that much*
> *Disdained the sight, methought ; then, at a touch,*
> *He turned his heel, and sought with shadowy stride*
> *His station in the dim,*
> *Where the sole-thoughted Dante waited him.*

First let me run over the main biographical facts before coming to a consideration of Patmore's doctrine.   He was born in

1823, the son of an author who got an unsavoury reputation, never lived down, because of having been mixed up in a fatal duel. As though that were not bad enough, the elder Patmore later ruined himself by speculation and was obliged to live abroad, leaving his brilliant son to shift for himself. And if the father was not a very pleasant person, Patmore's mother was even less attractive. That the boy's father and grandfather showed him partiality was enough to estrange her from him. When his first book of poems was published she refused to read a page of it.

Young Patmore was brought up by his father as an atheist. But he records in the autobiographical fragment included in Champneys' biography that, when he was eleven or twelve, he picked up some little book of devotion and had the thought strike him, "What an exceedingly fine thing it would be if there really were a God with whom I could be on terms of love and obedience." It was the first flicker of spiritual light.

Suddenly plunged to poverty from affluence, young Patmore had to do all kinds of literary odd jobs to earn a meagre living until he obtained through Monckton Milnes a position in the British Museum reading-room. This gave him his chance. In 1844 appeared his *Poems*, of which I possess a copy containing corrections in the poet's own hand. Though it is not very good, it was thought to show promise and it brought him the friendship of Tennyson and afterwards that of Browning, Ruskin, Carlyle and Rossetti. And in 1847 he married for the first time.

By now he was in the full tide of his career. Though "Tamerton Church Tower," which appeared in 1853, was again a somewhat unsatisfactory poem, it at least clearly pointed at what was to come. And in 1854 and in 1862 he showed what this was to be by publishing the two parts of *The Angel in the House*. About this more in a moment. Just now I continue with the biographical facts, putting them down baldly for the sake of fixing the points before proceeding to commentary.

In 1862 his first wife died and two years later he married again. Then in 1881 he married for the third time, and in his old age had a son. There were five children by the first marriage but none by the second. This youngest son one day said to him, when he learned that his father had been married three times, "Why, Papa, you're half as bad as Henry VIII!"

The year 1877 saw the publication of the complete collection of the Odes gathered under the title of *The Unknown Eros*, and in 1878 he published *Amelia*, the poem he regarded as his masterpiece. To it were added "Tamerton Church Tower" and some of the pieces of the 1844 volume, all of them revised. With that his poetic life closed. When his poems were reprinted in 1886 it was with a preface which said : "I have written little, but it is all my best ; I have never spoken when I had nothing to say, nor spared time or labour to make my words true. I have respected posterity ; and, should there be a posterity which cares for letters, I dare to hope that it will respect me."

After that time he gave himself to the writing of essays, of which we have the two volumes *Principle in Art* (1889) and *Religio Poetae* (1893). And in the year before his death he gave the world a little book called *The Rod, the Root, and Flower*, which is a kind of anthology of extracts from his prose writings, a distillation of his thought. "After all," he remarked about this time, "all the greatest things have to be said in prose." It is not true, and perhaps least of all true of Patmore himself. But with these proud sad words he did his best to comfort himself. Though he had enjoyed in early life a ringing poetic triumph, he was well aware that the world had rejected him.

For the rest, his life was largely a story of broken friendships. Even with Alice Meynell there was some mysterious quarrel in the end, though when news of his death reached her, she at once went into a room, in which she sat with shutters drawn for hours brooding upon her friend. One can understand his feeling that Rossetti had been unfaithful to his gifts, and dropped him on that account, for Patmore considered him as spiritually the most richly endowed of his contemporaries. But Patmore dropped Tennyson as decisively, and for no reason that anyone has ever been able to discover. The most that one can make out is that there was a fancied slight and that when, years later, Patmore made an advance towards reconciliation, Tennyson, again without intending it, reopened the old wound.

In general it may be said that Patmore, after his conversion to the Catholic Church, tended to withdraw from the circles in which he had formerly moved, feeling that his Catholicism would not be understood and fearing a rebuff. Yet he never found many equal friendships among Catholics, though his acquaintance with Gerard Manley Hopkins might have ripened into one had circumstances been favourable, and though he obtained the fervent admiration of Francis Thompson in his last years. It was at this time that he took up men a good deal younger than himself, and of these the closest to him were Edmund Gosse and Basil Champneys.

He did, however, still occasionally meet friends of his earlier years. Thus he left an account of a visit to Carlyle, writing : "When I bade good-bye to him, Carlyle, with his hand on the open door, and without any connection with our previous conversation, said to me : 'Why don't you write a history of the Anglo-Saxons ? You are the only man in England who could do it.' I have not the least idea what he meant, for I know little of history, and never professed to have any particular interest in the Anglo-Saxons."

Such meetings were hardly more than the encountering of a ghost from the past, and show only the more clearly how solitary a figure Patmore had become. Gosse describes the occasional visits that the poet made to London during his Hastings and Lymington years. Then his friends were always glad to see him but hardly knew what to do "with this grim pilgrim who would sit there for hours, winking, blinking, smoking innumerable cigarettes, and saying next to nothing." But Gosse goes on to say that they found that the best means of handling him was to give a dinner or luncheon for him, "for though he would sometimes say scarcely a word, or would wither the conversation by some paradox ending in a crackle and a cough, it was discovered that he believed himself to have been almost indecorously sparkling on these occasions, and would long afterwards refer to a very dull, small dinner as 'that fearful dissipation.' "

His capacity for making enemies has already been noted. As Patmore was also given to the use of vitriolic phrases, there is no wonder that this recoiled upon him. Father Hopkins, writing to him on December 6, 1883, protested against the "Their Jew" in the ode "1867," writing, "*Jew* must be a reproach either for religion or for race. It cannot be justified for religion here, for Disraeli was not by religion a Jew ; he had been baptized young and had always professed Christianity. . . It must then be for race." And he went on to point out that Lord Beaconsfield had as a statesman been devoted to the hon-

our of England.   To this the impenitent Patmore immediately
replied, "I hate (in all charity) Lord Beaconsfield more, if possible, than I hate Gladstone, and 'Jew' or *any* stone seemed
good enough to throw at such a dog."   The sequel came in
1892 when Patmore was suggested to Gladstone, who was then
Prime Minister, for the laureateship.   Gladstone had a long
memory and replied coldly, "Patmore died a long time ago."
But of course even without Gladstone's hostility, Patmore, as a
Catholic, was hardly in the running.

Little of this, I am aware, shows Patmore in a very agreeable
light.   He was undoubtedly harsh and even savage at times,
and he flaunted his arrogance.   Yet there was in him, after all,
an essential humility.   Like the Jesus of Blake's poem, he was
humble to God, haughty to man.   The fact that he became a
Catholic would itself show that he was basically humble.   So
would his pathos, in which quality (or in the power to express
it) he has perhaps never been excelled.   His confidence was
not so much in Coventry Patmore as in the truth, whatever may
have been his exalted estimate of his own position as a prophet
of truth.   Thus his "Magna Est Veritas" is a vastly more
humble poem than is its better-known counterpart, Arnold's
"Dover Beach" — a piece of quiet despair, though that too is
not wholly desperate.

> *Here in this little Bay,*
> *Full of tumultuous life and great repose,*
> *Where, twice a day,*
> *The purposeless, glad ocean comes and goes,*
> *Under high cliffs, and far from the huge town,*
> *I sit me down.*
> *For want of me the world's course will not fail:*

When all its work is done, the lie shall rot ;
The truth is great, and shall prevail,
When none cares whether it prevail or not.

That little poem comes late in Patmore's poetic life.   Its beginning, if we set aside the trial-flight of the *Poems* of 1844,
really came with Patmore's marriage in 1847 to Emily Augusta
Andrews — the most important fact in the poet's career, with
the exception of his conversion to Catholicism, with which it is
closely connected.   It was she "by whom and for whom" he
became a poet, and the *Angel*, for all its decorous moderate
low-Church tone, shows clearly enough in what direction his
face was already pointed.   For if Emily made him a poet she
also largely helped, without being aware of it, to make him a
Catholic.   The main influence, as he recorded after her death,
"was not that of supernatural grace in me but the natural love
of the beauty of supernatural love as recalled in her."   Or, as
he said more generally in the *Angel* :

> *The faithless, seeing her, conceive*
> *Not only heaven but hope of it.*

Though Patmore used to get rather annoyed with the identi-
fication of Emily with the Honoria of the poem and of himself
with its hero, Vaughan, there can be little doubt that in
Vaughan Patmore depicted himself as he would have liked to
be, and still less doubt that Honoria was the actual Emily.   It
is true that Patmore did not set out to draw a portrait as such
and that relatively few passages describe Emily specifically ;
yet Champneys did find a diary of Patmore's and in it the head-
ing, "Passages of 'The Angel in the House' which more particularly describe or apply to her."   That the poet did not write

out these passages probably means only that on looking them over he saw that they were of a composite character. At any rate, he wrote to his second wife, alluding to the Honoria of the poem :

> *I could not love thee, dear, so much,*
> *Loved I not "Honor" more.*

Her portrait was painted by Millais and her medallion made by Woolner. And as though that were not distinction enough, it was in her album that Browning wrote the lines he afterwards published under the title of "A Face" :

> *Painted upon a background of pale gold,*
> *Such as the Tuscan's early art preferred.*

Because of her nonconformist upbringing, she had a considerable horror of the Catholic Church and a dread of her husband's joining it. Aubrey de Vere had brought in Dr. Manning to convert her without success, or apparently without getting very far with her husband. Yet she divined what was already happening in his mind, and said to him sadly on her deathbed, "They will get you when I'm gone."

The second marriage, which occurred two years later, made a great difference to Patmore's material conditions. He encountered in Rome a Catholic lady named Marianne Caroline Byles with whom he fell in love and to whom he proposed. Only after he was accepted did he discover that she was an heiress, and so took to flight, lest he should seem a fortune seeker. It was with some difficulty that he was persuaded to accept his good luck sensibly.

This Miss Byles was a convert, as was now Patmore himself, and Champneys has put into circulation the story that, in her

Anglican days, she was thought of as the one who was going to succeed the first Mrs. Manning, Dr. Manning being then still Archdeacon of Chichester. It has even been suggested that Patmore's dislike of Manning took its origin from this. Champneys, however, admits that Patmore's letters to the Cardinal show that during her lifetime he had been quite ignorant of any engagement, if there ever was one, and Wilfrid Meynell seems to have cleared this up by venturing to ask the Cardinal point-blank whether there was any truth in the story, and by this means obtained a flat denial. It was Manning who performed the wedding ceremony, though regretting "the sacrifice of her vocation," for until she had met Patmore she had intended to join a religious order.

She strikes one as rather demurely nun-like as a wife, reserved and self-effacing and somewhat shadowy. Champneys said she had a good deal of "old-maidishness" about her. But she was sufficiently happy with her husband, even if she may have suffered by comparison with her predecessor, and her wealth made the poet comfortable. He was able to give up his work in the British Museum and to turn country-gentleman at Heron's Ghyll in Sussex, Hastings and Lymington in succession.

She bore the poet no children. Of the five that Emily had, two possessed considerable poetic talent — Henry, who died young, and Emily Honoria, who also died young, as a nun of the Holy Child order. Her life, which culminated in a beautiful ecstatic death, has been written by an American nun of her order, the late Mother Saint Ignatius, who generally used her secular name of Louisa Wheaton for her literary work but who in this instance wrote anonymously. "What he tried to say, she was," is how Emily Honoria's biographer sums it all up.

After the death of his second wife in 1880 Patmore married a woman much younger than himself, Harriet Robson, who long outlived him. She also was a quiet and self-effacing person. The only one of the three wives who appears greatly to have impressed people, or to have had much to do with the development of the poet's gifts, was the first. But she made up for them all by her fascinations and the deep indirect imprint she left on English poetry. The only disparaging thing we hear about her is that Mrs. Carlyle once accused her of trying to look like Woolner's medallion — a somewhat catty remark to make, but perhaps to be accounted for by the life poor Mrs. Carlyle had to lead.

Now for the writings of Patmore.

I think I will start with the short idyll, "Amelia," though that belongs to his middle period, because this was the poem of his that Patmore rated highest. It does not tell us anything about his doctrine, though perhaps it does reveal something about the poet. It starts with a charming picture of Hastings, where he was living at the time :

> *The little, bright, surf-breathing town,*
> *That showed me first her beauty and the sea,*
> *Gathers its skirts against the gorse-lit down,*
> *And scatters gardens o'er the southern lea.*

He had always wanted to live in the Mansion there, and though he was unable to purchase it, he did succeed in renting it — he supposed for the rest of his life.

I must confess that, while I recognize that the poem is full of beautiful lines and that it does completely carry out the poet's intention, its central idea strikes me as a bit comical. Patmore hesitated to say that the man of the poem was going with his betrothed to visit the grave of his dead *wife*, and he was careful to remove the circumstances of the poem from those of his own life. Yet we cannot help remembering that his first wife had written in her will, "I leave my wedding-ring to your second wife with my love and blessing. . . If in a year or two you are able to marry again, do so happily, feeling that if my spirit can watch you, it will envy her who makes you happy, and not envy her the reward of a part of your love, the best years of which I have had." So Amelia, on a visit with her lover to Millicent's grave, receives there a band of pearls from him and drops a rose upon the sod covering her :

For dear to maidens are their rivals dead.

Somehow that does not seem to me quite to come off. And, the reason is, that the lover had not hit upon a very exciting mode for entertaining his betrothed. Surely he ought to have been able to think of a lot of better ways of giving a girl a good time than that !

And now at last I am belatedly free to come to an examination of Coventry Patmore's doctrine of love. It is adumbrated rather than clearly stated in *The Angel in the House,* though anyone who turns back to that poem from the Odes and the essays will find its implications everywhere. By way of providing a corrective to those who might think him too "spiritual," he indicates that he preaches a complete normality which includes the physical as well as the spiritual. If he labels the three types of Love as Platonic, Anacreontic and Vaughanian, may we not make those types clearer by using instead the labels of "Dante," "Ovid," and "Patmore" ? But here is the brilliant little poem :

I saw three Cupids (so I dreamed),
Who made three kites, on which were drawn,
In letters that like roses gleamed,
'Plato,' 'Anacreon' and 'Vaughan.'
The boy who held by Plato tried
His airy venture first ; all sail,
It heavenwards rushed till scarce descried,
Then pitched and dropped for want of tail.
Anacreon's Love, with shouts of mirth
That pride of spirit thus should fall,
To his kite linked a lump of earth,
And lo, it would not soar at all.
Last my disciple freighted his
With a long streamer made of flowers,
The children of the sod, and this
Rose in the sun, and flew for hours.

The story Patmore has to tell is rather Trollopian, but is none the worse on that account, or should not be regarded with less esteem in days when Trollope in some quarters is regarded as the best of the Victorian novelists.   But the *Angel* is not much read at present, nor was it very successful upon its first appearance.   Browning, however, wrote to Patmore to assure him, "I do not say that it will be now, or soon ; but, some time or other, this will be the most popular poem that was ever written."   It proved to be almost that during Patmore's own lifetime.   As Gosse says, "Just about the time when their reviews began to tell them not to admire *The Angel in the House*, readers found they had formed a passion for it."   Every well brought up young lady, every curate, perhaps every bashful pair of lovers found that their affairs, which others were only too likely to treat with amusement, were receiving serious treatment from a great poet. A quarter of a million copies sold, not counting a cheap reprint — surely enough to satisfy anybody. If Patmore was far from satisfied, this was not on account of his sales, but because the disposition was to look upon him as a sportive lambkin whose tail was tied with pink ribbon. An intelligent reading should have given warning that this poet was really a sardonic and saturnine person, and that the connotations of his poem were not quite what they imagined. But as few of his readers were intelligent, he was as embittered as much by undiscerning praise as by total neglect.

The *Angel* is a wonderful achievement, though not by any means the greatest thing that Patmore was to do. Its verve and brilliance and its psychological insight remain, and certain lapses into bathos should not blind us to these merits. As for the descriptions of Victorian manners and millinery and upholstery, these are things which will eventually appear less old-fashioned than they do today. Browning's prophecy was fulfilled ; it is sure to be fulfilled again.

In *The Victories of Love* Patmore attempted the converse of the earlier story. Here instead of handsome and well-born and wealthy people very much in love, and with the way of marriage made as smooth as it can ever be, we have an account of the marriage into which the naval lieutenant, Frederick, drifts with a very plain Jane after he had been disappointed by losing the heroine of the *Angel*. There is little romantic love at first, and still less money ; almost too carefully Patmore stacks the cards against the couple, giving them dull routine and commonplace domesticity instead of the bed of roses he had built in the *Angel*. The implication is obvious : that the success of marriage does not depend upon its external circumstances but upon the fidelity of the husband and wife to their duties. Indeed, Patmore comes closer to his theme here than in the earlier unfinished poem. Yet the *Victories* has never been read much, and probably never will be. This may be due to the fact that the story is told in the form of letters ; or it may be due to something else — perhaps to the rather depressing setting given to it. But nowhere does Patmore exhibit more often his power of pathos and his wit :

> *Faults had she, child of Adam's stem,*
> *But only heaven knew of them.*

No epigram was ever more pointed or profound. And as an instance of the pathos, take this :

> *Too soon, too soon comes Death to show*
> *We love more deeply than we know !*
> *The rain, that fell upon the height*
> *Too gently to be called delight,*
> *Within the dark vale reappears*
> *As a wild cataract of tears ;*
> *And love in life should strive to see*
> *Sometimes what love in death would be !*

> * * * *

> *No magic of her voice or smile*
> *Suddenly raised a fairy isle,*
> *But fondness for her underwent*
> *An unregarded increment,*
> *Like that which lifts, through centuries,*
> *The coral-reef within the seas,*
> *And lo ! the land where was the wave,*
> *Alas ! 'tis everywhere her grave.*

The same octosyllabic couplet is used in "The Wedding Sermon," preached by Dean Churchill of Sarum Close when he married his daughter Honoria to Vaughan.   In it we are told :

> *The love of marriage claims, above*
> *All other kinds the name of love ;*

and

> *Though love is all of earth that's dear,*
> *Its home, my Children, is not here :*
> *The pathos of eternity*
> *Does in its fullest pleasure sigh.*

But perhaps the most interesting passage in some ways is that in which the Dean expounds the doctrine of vocation as applied to marriage.   After remarking that, though ghastly doubts will come as to whether the choice made was really the best, the Dean continues :

> *Could it be else ?   A youth pursues*
> *A maid, whom chance, not he, did choose,*
> *Till to his strange arms hurries she*
> *In a despair of modesty.*
> *Then simply and without pretence*
> *Of insight or experience,*
> *They plight their vows.   The parents say*
> *'We cannot speak them yea or nay ;*
> *The thing proceedeth from the Lord !'*
> *And wisdom still approves their word ;*
> *For God created so these two*
> *They match as well as others do*
> *That take more pains, and trust Him less*

Who never fails, if asked, to bless
His children's helpless ignorance
And blind election of life's chance.

"Love," says Patmore in one of his *Aurea Dicta*, "is a recent discovery and requires a new law.   Easy divorce is the vulgar solution.   The true solution is some undiscovered security for true marriage."   He believed he had found it, and it is implied in the passage just quoted.   Perhaps this may be elucidated by what Saint Thomas Aquinas has to teach regarding vocation — with religious vocation in mind, but enunciating a principle which fits equally well any walk of life and especially the vocation of marriage.   Saint Thomas is far less rigorous in this matter than Saint Alphonsus Liguori, who seemed to assert that in the right choice of a vocation, one's salvation or damnation is inevitably bound up.   Now obviously few people can be quite sure on such a point ; seldom does a voice speak from heaven ; the decision has to be made in the dark.   Well, Saint Thomas says that a man who enters the religious state for a bad motive — let us say ambition or expectation of an easy life — lacks the grace of a vocation, even should he take religious vows.   But he goes on to say that, should he later repent, the grace will be given him.   On the other hand, one who really is without a vocation but acts in good faith, receives a vocation upon taking his vows.

Surely this applies to marriage as well as to the cloister.   In both cases good-will is what matters, not special insight.   Not the shrewdness with which we choose but the humility and fidelity with which we bind ourselves is the important thing. Therefore

The bond of law
Does oftener marriage-love evoke
Than love, which does not wear the yoke
Of legal vows, submits to be
Self-reined from ruinous liberty.

With "The Wedding Sermon" perhaps I can now come to an exposition of the main theme.

When Patmore first came into the Church he was a little afraid that the *Angel* might not be quite in harmony with Catholic doctrine and that he would have to repudiate it. Later he wrote, "It has been with a sense of wonder that I have since read many passages of that poem, passages in which, when I was writing them, I fancied I was making audacious flights into the regions of unknown truth, but in which I have since found out that I have given exact expression to what may be called the more esoteric doctrines of the Catholic Faith." The term "esoteric" may be objected to ; there *are* no esoteric doctrines ; there are only mysteries. But Patmore is surely right in his contention that "The Catholic Church alone teaches as matters of faith those things which the thoroughly sincere person of every sect discovers, more or less obscurely, for himself, but dares not believe for want of external sanction." To which one might add his saying : "Fidelity does not *discover* dogma, but only enables the faithful, in proportion to their faith, to confirm it with absolute personal assurance." In the case at least of people of spiritual insight, revelation is a confirmation of already existing intuitions. One of his *Aurea Dicta* is, "Great is his faith who dares believe his own eyes."

Patmore's doctrine, though clearly implied in nearly everything he wrote, never received full and explicit statement. But that this was so was due merely to an incalculable accident, the criticism he received from Father Gerard Manley Hopkins. The friendship between them, one carried on almost wholly by correspondence — the two men writing to one another as "My dear Mr. Hopkins" and "My dear Mr. Patmore," though Patmore towards the end began to sign himself "Yours affectionately" — gave Patmore a high opinion of Hopkins's critical acumen. On October 31, 1883, Patmore wrote : "Your careful and subtle fault-finding is the greatest praise my poetry has ever received. It makes me almost inclined to begin to sing over again, after I had thought I had given over." Patmore took in the same spirit the severe judgment that Hopkins passed on his prose style. On October 20, 1887, he was told : "At bottom what you do and what Cardinal Newman does is to think aloud, to think with pen to paper." Hopkins went into further detail, accusing both writers of too great a conversational looseness in writing and not enough attention to composition. He adds : "But the style of prose is a positive thing and not the absence of verse-forms and pointedly expressed thoughts are single hits and give no continuity of style." Patmore admitted the justice of this judgment but explained : "There are two reasons for my not attempting to make my prose what I know prose might, and on certain subjects, should be. First there is little audience for such writing ; secondly, I could write in verse, with little more difficulty, and much more effect."

This purely technical criticism should, I think, be borne in mind in what follows, for it is this — and Hopkins's own poetry ("To me," Patmore wrote to Robert Bridges in 1884, "his poetry has the effect of veins of pure gold imbedded in masses of impracticable quartz") — that made Patmore far more willing to listen to this Jesuit, where literary judgments were concerned, than he would have listened to any other priest. So when Hopkins was on a visit to Patmore and was shown the *Sponsa Dei*, a prose work in which the poet had set forth his doctrine concerning the relation between man and wife as illustrating the union of God and the soul, Hopkins returned the manuscript saying, "That 's telling secrets" and suggesting that the author should consult his confessor before publishing it. Upon this Patmore burnt the *Sponsa Dei*, though the few people who had seen it pronounced it to be his masterpiece. After the destruction had been made and Hopkins knew of it he wrote in great distress to Patmore on May 6, 1888, saying that he wished he had been more guarded in offering his reflections, which he did not consider final. We therefore get Patmore's doctrine only as hints scattered throughout his poetry and prose — hints that are clear enough, and from which his system may be inferred, but which do not state his system as a rounded whole. As to this he quoted Aristotle's reply to Alexander who had complained that the philosopher, in one of his books, had published "secrets." "They are published and not published," said Aristotle, "for none will learn from my book anything but that which he already knows."

I shall never forget how Alice Meynell said to me one day, "*I* am the repository of Patmore's secret doctrine." When I told about this in an article I wrote after Mrs. Meynell's death, her son Everard wrote to me : "I cannot agree that my mother ever said that in her had been confided Patmore's 'secret' doctrine. He did tell her everything, so that she would say that what he had hesitated to publish he had confided to her — his *full*, or *ultimate* teaching, or rather complete definition of divine Truth. But 'secret doctrine' has a very unfamiliar sound in that connection — as between two persons so extremely orthodox ; it smatters rather of occultism or new religions." Well, to that I can only answer that Alice Meynell did use those very words, though I never attached any unorthodox connotation to them. But it seems to me that it can hardly be denied that there was a touch of the esoteric about Patmore, possibly something that was not much more than the prickly and defensive attitude of a sensitive man, for it was obviously at complete variance with the universality of his theme.

Perhaps it was impossible, or at any rate inadvisable, for Patmore to publish his full thought to the world. Yet he is quite definite, so far as he goes, and uses what is almost a scientific precision of language. He realized that all would not receive his doctrine — in fact, that the vast majority would not — and that many would even be scandalized by it. Therefore it had to some extent to be hidden, "Lest shameless man cry 'Shame !' "

It was nevertheless not only the shameless whom he had to fear, but still more the squeamish. And though this squeamishness may not then have been more prevalent within Catholic circles than outside them, it was naturally among Catholics that Patmore most often encountered it. Therefore he wrote to Hopkins in 1887 : "I find that there are not a few *Protestants* who jump at such hints ; but that Catholics, as a rule, can make nothing of them. . . It is of no use writing for 'Catholics.' I have turned myself to the Gentiles." He even came to think of his writings as a kind of irenicon, a means of insinuating into all spiritual minds something of Catholic truth in a non-controversial form.

What he was expounding was the all but infinite series of

corollaries between human and divine love. He constantly insists on their identical nature, and that one is the preparation for the other. "The natural first, and afterwards the spiritual," was one of his favourite quotations. It would seem that he was the first to modify Pope's line into "The proper study of mankind is woman." On this Osbert Burdett writes : "The path which she reveals to most men is the same path, according to Patmore, as that which the contemplative pursues without her help. It is not a path different from his, nor, Patmore insists, is the end to which it leads other than that which it is the special privilege of the contemplative to follow."

The mystic and the lover, he fully concedes, are on different planes, but the road each is following is the same and leads to the same goal. The lover is, indeed, for Patmore a mystic ; or it is only one who is something of a mystic who can attain even to the understanding of the true nature of human love.

Patmore's prose has been even more neglected than his poetry, perhaps because it is there that most of his extravagances occur. Gosse even finds in some of the essays, "the aimless violence and preposterous paradox of failing power in a very brilliant mind." Though this judgment is, I believe, mistaken, nobody would give Patmore's prose a value equal to that of the odes of *The Unknown Eros*. What his prose does is to amplify what even the most daring of his poems only gives in hints. Gosse is, however, probably correct in attributing to the burning of the *Sponsa Dei* the great change that came over the poet — a silence that sometimes alternated with explosions of bitterness — during his last years. But Champneys, too, is also probably substantially correct in believing that parts of the destroyed work were preserved in such essays as "Dieu et ma Dame." In these, though there is no attempt at any systematization, it is evident that some of the ideas of the *Sponsa Dei* were given to the world. Accordingly the essays should be studied by all who wish to know Patmore's mind.

In one of the essays — that entitled "Ancient and Modern Ideas of Purity" — Patmore records a little girl who had been brought up in one of the best convent schools in England saying to her father, when she heard him praising the institution of marriage, "Why papa, I thought that marriage was rather a wicked sacrament!" That little girl was of course his own daughter, as I suspected on first reading the essay but as to which Mr. Meynell definitely assured me. Naïve as her remark was, it does convey in its innocence the shocked reaction Patmore often met with among contemporary Catholics. Not until Emily Honoria became Sister Mary Christina did she enter into a complete sympathy with her father's thought.

A catena of quotations may perhaps best serve to illustrate what it was that Patmore held : "Everyone who has loved and reflected on love for an instant knows very well that what is vulgarly regarded as the end of that passion, is, as the Church steadfastly maintains, no more than its accident. The flower is not for the seed, but the seed for the flower. And yet what is that flower, if it be not the rising but of another flower, flashed for a moment of eternal moment before our eyes, and at once withdrawn, lest we should misunderstand the prophecy, and take it for our final good ?"

"All religions have sanctified this love, and have found in it their one word for and image of their fondest and highest hopes ; and the Catholic has exalted it into a 'great Sacrament,' holding that, with Transubstantiation — which it resembles — it is unreasonable only because it is above reason."

"The whole of after-life depends very much upon how life's

transient transfiguration in youth by love is subsequently regarded. . . . The greatest perversion of the poet's function is to
falsify the memory of that transfiguration of the senses and to
make light of its sacramental character."

"What love does in transfiguring life, that religion does in
transfiguring love. . . Love is sure to be something less than
human if it is not something more."

"Nuptial love bears the clearest marks of being nothing
other than the rehearsal of a communion of a higher nature."

"Man, then, as soon as he is made by grace a participator of
angelic and celestial powers, stands between God and woman,
and, as he pleases and when he pleases, can take aspect of Bride
to Christ or bridegroom to woman, the Priestess of the Divine
Truth or Beauty to him, as he is priest of the Divine Love or
Power to her."

Finally I take these quotations from the little book Patmore
published just before his death, *The Rod, the Root, and the
Flower*. He gives us only isolated paragraphs, sometimes only
sentences, and these would remind us of Pascal's *Pensées*, were
it not that Pascal was making notes for a larger work projected
by him whereas Patmore was to some extent culling from what
he had already written. It might be noted that, while this book
also contains what I have described as his distinctive "doctrine,"
he is now more mystical than ever, and seems to be in direct
contemplation of the object he had formerly been illustrating
rather than regarding it as it is in itself. Here are a few extracts, taken just in the order in which they appear :

"Men would never offend God, if they knew how ready He
is to forgive them."

"Many a Lover must have said to himself, 'There are suffer-
ings far worse than hanging for a few hours upon a Cross.

What is that, beside the fact that one's destined Bride is in another's bed ?'   But has not Christ suffered this ?   Lies not the
soul, the Miranda of His desires, contented in the bed of Cali-
ban, so long as she prefers the world to Him ?"

"What a Lover sees in the Beloved is the projected shadow
of his own potential beauty in the eyes of God.   The shadow is
given to those who cannot see themselves in order that they may
learn to believe the word : 'Rex concupiscet decorem tuam.' "

"The power of the soul for good is in proportion to the
strength of its passions.   Sanctity is not the negation of passion
but its order."

"Religion is not religion until it has become not only natural,
but so natural that nothing else seems to be natural in its presence ; and until the whole being of man affirms, 'Whom have I
in heaven but Thee, and what on earth in comparison to Thee ?'
and 'To whom shall we go if we leave Thee ?' "

With a passage from "The Wedding Sermon" I conclude,
quoting this because it shows how free Patmore was from that
false mysticism of the dim religious light and the crystal bowl.
In him is none of the romantic paraphernalia of artfully con-
trived mystery —

> *Thy Incense sweet*
> *From swinged censer teeming :*
> *Thy shrine, thy grove, thy oracle, thy heat*
> *Of pale-mouthed prophet dreaming.*

Instead he warns :

> *Beware*
> *The Powers of Darkness and the Air,*
> *Which lure to empty heights man's hope,*
> *Bepraising heaven's ethereal cope,*

But covering with their cloudy cant
Its ground of solid adamant,
That strengthens ether for the flight
Of angels, makes and measures height,
And in materiality
Exceeds our Earth's in such degree
As all else Earth exceeds.

That he is one of the true mystics appears here and throughout his work — for the mystic might be defined as one to
whom mysteries have ceased to exist, as he has penetrated them
and has laid hold on Reality.

Now I have no idea as to whether or not I have convinced
you that Patmore has a right to be regarded as a Pillar of the
Church.   I have not really argued at all, but have let Patmore
speak for himself.   At least Patmore has convinced me.   And
there have always been, as it is to be hoped there always will be,
people in every generation who come upon him with a cry of
surprise.   His work is very far from being done, nor is his
force spent.   And though the *Sponsa Dei* was destroyed, the
scattered fragments that remain are sufficient for us to work
them up into a system to ourselves, once we have lit upon the
clue.   Patmore is, in short, an immensely practical person,
with a message for everybody willing to receive it.   Let nobody be scared from him by his haughty manner : to those
who will listen, he has the force of a gospel, a revelation of life,
a revelation of God.

XII

BLESSED FRANCESCA CABRINI

What I am going to give you in this concluding chapter is the story of the first citizen of the United States who will receive the honour of canonization. Beatified since November, 1938, only twenty-one years after her death, she would have been canonized already had it not been for the war. As soon as this ceases and it is possible to bring together in Rome all those who would want to attend the ceremonies, we shall be able to speak of Saint Francesca Cabrini.

On the last day of March, 1889, a ship carrying over a thousand immigrants — nearly all of them Italians — arrived in New York harbour. On board were a group of nuns who had come to work among the neglected Italians of that city. They were led by a slight, diminutive, childlike looking woman nearing forty. She was Mother Cabrini, the General and Foundress of the Missionary Sisters of the Sacred Heart. Neither she nor her companions knew any English ; they were aware of the immense difficulties ahead of them ; they had no money : nevertheless they had come. For Archbishop Corrigan had written assuring them that they would be welcome.

In spite of this their welcome was far from auspicious. The Fathers of the Italian church on Roosevelt Street met them late that evening at the pier, but after dinner had rather lamely to tell them, when they asked to be taken to the convent they supposed would be waiting for their reception, that there was no convent, indeed that there was no place for them to stay. They spent that night — one of horror — in a couple of rooms on the edge of Chinatown, in an indescribably filthy rooming-house.

Worse — or what looked as though it would be worse — awaited them in the morning. When they went to see Archbishop Corrigan he received them at first somewhat coldly. In the first place he was not expecting them just then, for Mother Cabrini had written on February 16th to say that she would arrive in May "if not sooner." He had still to find out that she was a woman impatient of all delays, one given to acting with the utmost speed. But in the second place the Archbishop and an American lady with an Italian title, the Contessa Cesnola, who had been going to establish the Sisters in an orphanage on Fifty-ninth Street, had come to a serious disagreement. He strongly disapproved of the location the Contessa had chosen, and though she had rented the house and had furnished it, he refused to allow the nuns to occupy it.

At this first interview he actually told Mother Cabrini that the only thing he could suggest was that she take the boat by which she had come and return to Italy. Her answer was to produce the letter — it was written by the future Benedict XV and signed by Cardinal Simeoni, the Prefect of Propaganda — authorizing her coming. "No," she said in her high-pitched little voice, "I came here by the orders of the Pope, and here I remain." In face of that there was nothing for it but to allow her to do so.

The Archbishop later became a great friend of Mother Cabrini's, and in fact before that first interview ended he was partly won over. He found lodgings for the nuns at the orphanage conducted by the Sisters of Charity nearby — the building that was subsequently Cathedral College — and three weeks later when he and the Contessa were brought together, his prohibition was lifted.   His main objection was that Fifty-ninth Street was too exclusive a neighbourhood for an orphanage, but when he advanced his second objection — that the five thousand dollars the Contessa had collected would not last long — she went down on her knees before him and reminded him that in the Our Father we ask only our *daily* bread, not for complete security.   When Francesca Cabrini sailed for Italy three months later, she had gathered four hundred little girls in her orphanage, and she had an Italian school in operation in Little Italy.

The official Italian biography of Mother Cabrini by an anonymous nun is, I fear, somewhat disposed to exhibit Archbishop Corrigan in the light of a persecutor.   That he was justified in his objection to the Fifty-ninth Street location is shown by the fact that, a year later, Mother Cabrini, of her own accord, moved to a less expensive place.   But to anticipate a bit, the anonymous biographer says that again in 1894 the Archbishop told Mother Cabrini to go back to Italy.   This is simply not the case, as I am assured most positively by nuns, still alive, who were very close to Francesca at the time.   Moreover, I have gone to the New York archdiocesan archives and have read the letters there written by Mother Cabrini to the Archbishop.   It is clear from them that the relations between him and herself were extremely cordial.   And when she founded her first hospital in New York, it was Corrigan who headed the subscription list and who sent her to local Italians whom he thought would contribute — a fact of which the anonymous biographer gives no inkling.

I shall come in a little while to an account of Mother Cabrini's achievements in the United States and elsewhere.

But first I think you should be told something about the early life of this extraordinary woman.

She was born in 1850 in a village near Lodi on the inland plain of Lombardy, and she grew up a most beautiful, pious but very delicate child. Yet while still a little girl she had a conviction that she was called to be a missionary, a conviction that developed into a certitude that she was to found an order of missionary sisters. Her favourite game as a child was making little paper boats and filling them with violets and launching them on the river. These violets in her imagination were the missionaries she was going to send all over the world. One day in playing that game she fell in the river and was nearly drowned, getting from the experience a phobia against deep water that lasted for nearly thirty years. But even that did not shake her assurance that God had called her to be a missionary. By way of preparing herself for China, she gave up eating candies, as she had somehow got it into her little head that to the Chinese candies were unknown.

She was, however, rather late in being able to carry out her ambitions. Not only that, for a long dark period it appeared that she was going in a direction that would make these ambitions impossible of attainment. After teaching school for a couple of years, she was persuaded by a friend whose name will always be remembered in connection with hers, a Monsignor Serrati, to go for two weeks to try and bring about a measure of order in a small orphanage he had in his parish at Codogno. He begged so strongly and promised so emphatically that it would only be for two weeks — during the summer vacation — that she consented. She was to remain there for six overcast and tangled years.

This orphanage, which was known as the House of Providence, had been established and partly endowed by a woman named Antonia Tondini. But she had so grossly mismanaged the place that the Bishop and the Monsignor believed that an improvement might be effected if La Tondini and two friends who lived with her became nuns. Well, they did·put on a religious habit, but Tondini used to say with cheerful cynicism that she "kept her vows in her pocket." There was no pretence at anything resembling a religious life, though there was nothing scandalous about this strange community except that the friends were always quarrelling and that the funds of the orphanage were handed out to Tondini's scamp of a nephew. Poor Francesca Cabrini — a young laywoman — was given the task of reforming this place. It was more like a madhouse than a nunnery.

Though Francesca had gone to the House of Providence on the strict understanding that it would be only for a fortnight, she felt unable to desert the orphans who so obviously needed her. Three years later she consented to wear the habit of the institute —a simple diocesan establishment limited to this one house. On the day that she took her vows she was summoned into the parlor and appointed superior — Tondini not being so much deposed as ignored. You can imagine the situation — Francesca in tears but obeying, and Sister Tondini in hysterics and attempting physical violence against her new superior.

Things dragged on in this miserable way for another three years, during which time Francesca was, in effect, building up a new order within the House of Providence by training some of the older orphans and inspiring them with her own ideals. Over and over again she assured them that the day would come when they would be missionaries, though there was no indication whatever as to how this could be. It was in the end made possible by Tondini herself, for when she brought legal proceedings against the Bishop, he felt that he had had enough, excommunicated her, dissolved the House of Providence and so gave Francesca Cabrini — who was now thirty — her chance.

She went out at once and bought, with money supplied by Monsignor Serrati, a tumble-down Franciscan friary in the town and founded a new institute, the one that was eventually to be known as that of the Missionary Sisters of the Sacred Heart.

In acting as they did, however, the Bishop of Lodi, and still less Monsignor Serrati, had no real intention of furthering Francesca Cabrini's missionary plans. Her delicate health made them seem out of the question, and they thought that by keeping her quietly occupied in the diocese she could be best employed. Indeed, Monsignor Serrati had seven years before this done a very strange thing. Twice when Francesca had applied to religious orders for admission, he had gone behind her back to advise them to reject her, because of her physical frailty. Had she not been rejected, she would never have been able to do the work to which she was certain that God was calling her. Now at last she had been led by dark and devious ways to her goal. Though she remained a lifelong invalid, this did not prevent her from doing a prodigious amount of work.

The new order was in the beginning far from prosperous, but it grew rapidly, and it found plenty to do at Codogno and in some neighbouring towns, and before long in Milan as well. Yet the Monsignor, instead of being glad that Francesca was having so many young women apply for admission to her community, was all for her refusing to accept more than those she already had. He pointed out that she would have to enlarge the convent, and that she had no money for this. She met the situation by setting her nuns to work as bricklayers, and though that experiment was not particularly successful, at least experience was gained which was afterwards very valuable. In later years in the United States Mother Cabrini often acted as her own contractor.

One of the most striking circumstances in this woman's life is that she never waited until she had all that she needed before setting to work. She usually had nothing, or next to nothing ; yet when she saw a piece of work which demanded to be done, she at once started operations, confident that the necessary means would be supplied by Providence — as they always were. Of what cautious men call prudence she did not have a particle ; she had instead an inexhaustible supply of real prudence, which is trust in God.

Shy and retiring as she was by natural disposition, and though not at all what is called the executive type, she came to show herself an immensely capable business woman. But though she was a notable organizer, she was the reverse of a cold statistician. She could never have told anybody just how many nuns belonged to her order, or how many houses she had founded. Her work was performed without any of the appliances of efficiency — yet with an efficiency that never failed. From one point of view hers is a resounding success story ; it is all the more remarkable because she was to achieve her success in countries whose language she did not know. Even more remarkable is the fact that it was in the United States, the land of big business, that Francesca, arriving without financial backing, made the "hard-boiled" gasp equally at her intrepidity and her skill in affairs.

There were in her, of course — there always had been — unsuspected qualities which the occasion drew forth. But what those close to her had been aware of from the beginning was rather her mysterious gifts, which they could not but look upon as supernatural. Time after time when her convents ran short of bread or milk or wine, she would suggest that the kitchen Sisters look again ; and what was needed was found where ten minutes before it had not been. The same method was employed sometimes when the question was one of finding money for a contractor. Casually Francesca would toss over her shoulder, "Have you looked in that drawer, Sister ? Well then, look." And there there would be a pile of bills. This sort of thing occurred from the first days at Codogno. It was at Codogno too, during the infancy of the order, that the Sister who shared Francesca's room awoke one night to find the room flooded with light. "Mother ! Mother !" the Sister exclaimed. "Did you see that ?" From the other bed came the calm reply, "Yes, I saw it ; it 's nothing." But the next night — and for the rest of her life — Francesca slept alone.

Francesca could bring herself to wait only seven years after the founding of her order before going to Rome to seek papal approval. She was warned against attempting anything of the kind, especially so soon. Monsignor Serrati tried to intimidate her by telling her that she would be sure to fail, and then would have to return as a laughing-stock to Codogno ; when this did not deter her, he said, "Only saints do this sort of thing." Her own bishop was ill at the time and so expressed no opinion, and he died soon afterwards. But the Archbishop of Milan was very positive in holding that she should be content with diocesan approval. Nevertheless, with a single companion and two shabby suitcases and hardly any money, she went to Rome at the end of 1887.

The first thing she did on arrival was to pray at the chapel in the Gesù where the right hand of Saint Francis Xavier was venerated, for she had taken his name in religion — and was officially Francesca Saverio. But the second thing was to seek an interview with the Cardinal-Vicar to ask his permission to open a house in Rome. He was decidedly discouraging. "Religious houses here," he told her, "are like the flowers of spring; we have too many already. Go back to Codogno. There you can do some good. You are not needed in Rome." But so as not to make his refusal absolute, he said he might permit her to stay if she could show that she had half a million lire to spend. Instead of being crushed by this, Francesca said to her companion, "You will see: God will change the Cardinal's heart."

God did change it. A few weeks later, after he had consulted Pope Leo XIII, the Cardinal said to her when she saw him again, "Well, are you ready to obey? Then I cannot allow you to found a house in Rome; you must found two." While she spent from morning to night, fasting and with a fever, at public auction-rooms picking up bits of furniture, she, and the Sisters she had at once sent for, slept on straw; and their refectory table was a couple of planks laid across washstands. When the Cardinal-Vicar, who had by now accepted them as his protégées, visited them, he saw a statue of Our Lady in the hall of the apartment they had rented. It had a crown beside it. "Why have you not crowned her?" he asked. Francesca flashed her answer with a smile, "She is

waiting to be crowned by the one whose heart she has
changed." Shortly afterwards the Rule of her Institute was
approved, and with that the world was opened to her missionary labours.

At this moment there entered upon the scene Bishop
Scalabrini of Piacenza. He had specially interested himself
in the deplorable social and religious conditions of the Italian
immigrants in the United States, and had founded a Congregation of priests to work among them. He tried to persuade
Mother Cabrini also to go, and by way of bringing further
pressure, secured an invitation for her from Archbishop
Corrigan of New York.

Francesca, however, was reluctant to give up her ambition
of being a missionary to China, and she did not at all relish the
prospect of her nuns acting as auxiliaries to the Scalabriniani
Fathers, which was what the Bishop had in mind. When she
asked Monsignor Serrati what she should say in reply, his
characteristically laconic advice was, "Say nothing." He was
still hoping to keep her in Italy.

Just then she had one of those dreams which always seemed
to come to her at moments of crisis. In it she saw a procession
of saints — her dead mother among them — urging her to
accept the American mission. In another dream she got another and more definite letter from Archbishop Corrigan.
When she told Bishop Scalabrini about this in the morning he
laughed, "You and your dreams!" But before the day was
out he came to her carrying a letter that had just arrived from
New York.

She now asked Leo XIII to decide for her. He listened to
the diminutive nun kneeling before him, and gave his answer,

"Not to the East but to the West." After that commission she did not hesitate. It was the beginning of a lifelong friendship between the Pope and herself.

The members of her order nevertheless were greatly worried that she proposed to go to America herself. Some time previously she had been given only a year or two to live. Therefore they begged her at least to see a doctor. His answer was, "If you really want my opinion, you'll die unless you *do* go." Events were to prove that she had nearly thirty years of intense activity before her. And all that time she was incessantly on the move, travelling immense distances in North and South America and in Europe, the centre of her order being wherever she happened to be. Even in the convents visited by her she was only a temporary lodger. From now until her death she was God's gypsy.

She stayed in New York just long enough to get the orphanage on Fifty-ninth Street in operation and to start a school for the Scalabriniani Fathers on Roosevelt Street, using the church itself for the purpose. To support these works she and some of the Sisters had to go out every day begging in Little Italy, for it was evident that the Contessa Cesnola's five thousand dollars would not last very long. Yet undismayed by her lack of means, Francesca returned to Italy after three months to gather recruits, taking with her two Irish girls as postulants. These wrote to Archbishop Corrigan, upon their arrival at Codogno, "It is the desire of our Reverend Mother that we, her first two Americans, shall become saints."

Corrigan had already taken a strong fancy to Mother Cabrini and often used to invite her to go with him when he had to make a visitation outside of New York. On one of these occasions, when they were at Peekskill, he had pointed to the other side of the Hudson and said, "Now *that's* where you should have your orphanage." What he had in mind appeared a little later when the Jesuits let her know that they were giving up their novitiate in the Catskills and offered this to her at a very cheap price. To investigate its possibilities she hurried back to the United States and exclaimed the moment she saw Manresa (now known as West Park) : "Why, this is the very house I saw in my dream !" She also foretold on that first visit that it was the place where she would be buried. Undeterred by the fact that the water supply was inadequate — which was the reason the Jesuits were relinquishing the place — she bought the property and got a wonderful bargain. Even the water the Jesuits had never been able to find she located quickly enough, or said that the Blessed Virgin had located it for her.

But instead of being content to stay quietly in the United States, as soon as she had put things into operation, she projected a new enterprise. In the Fall of 1891 she took twenty-eight Sisters to Nicaragua to open a school at Granada. There she received a flamboyant official welcome from the heads of State and Church but was shocked beyond expression when, on the evening of her arrival, the dinner to which she and the Sisters had been invited by their benefactress was served by semi-nude native women. Still more was Francesca shocked by the moral laxity she found to prevail, and her refusal to accept any illegitimate children in her school caused an uproar. Intimidation was attempted ; for over a week a crowd of hired rowdies howled around the convent every night, and the nuns thought they were all going to be murdered in their beds. But she held her ground and in the end her firmness and courage won respect, so that the school prospered until, a couple of years later, a revolution broke out in Nicaragua and the Sisters were ejected by soldiers almost at an hour's notice.

Long before that, however, Francesca had left Nicaragua. When in the spring of 1892 she returned to the United States, she went by way of the San Juan river to the Caribbean — taking two months for the trip — in order to see the Indians of the Mosquitia Reserve, among whom she intended to open a mission. For she never ceased to be inflamed with the idea of carrying the Gospel to the heathen. This scheme fell through only because of the revolution which, for the time being, wrecked all her work in Nicaragua.

More important than Francesca's little tour among the Indians was her visit to New Orleans which immediately followed. She went there because of a shocking outrage in which eleven young Italians, who had been accused of murdering the chief of police but who had been acquitted, were lynched by the mob. Clearly her oppressed compatriots needed her. After investigating conditions on the spot, she promised to send nuns as soon as possible to open a mission.

She lost little time in doing this. But as she did not have enough money to pay the railroad fare for the nuns all the way from New York to New Orleans, the Sisters had to get out at various towns en route and beg until they had collected enough money to pay for a further stage of the journey. She had told them that, as soon as they saw they were going to succeed, they were to wire her. One day they collected the vast sum of seventeen dollars and thirty cents and sent a telegram, "Success. Please come at once." A few days later Francesca was there, four other Sisters with her.

They lived in two or three rooms in an old-style, sprawling tenement house inhabited mostly by Negroes. They cooked their food in a brick oven in the courtyard, and ate it there too, surrounded by children and dogs. At night the dancing and singing of the Negroes in the courtyard kept them awake. But it was the beginning of the work in New Orleans, and that very tenement on St. Philip Street became the main centre of Italian religious and social life in the city, and is still in possession of the Missionary Sisters. An orphanage, a school and a settlement were all provided, as they always were provided wherever Mother Cabrini went.

Hospitals until now had never had any part in her plans. But the Scalabriniani Fathers had a small one in New York City, on 109th Street, and when this was on the point of closing because of mismanagement Francesca was asked to take it over. She was reluctant to do so, although the Cardinal Prefect of Propaganda told her she would do well to accept this new work, until she had a dream. In it she saw Our Lady walking through a crowded hospital ward helping the sick. When Francesca, recognizing her, ran up to give her assistance, Our Lady said, "I am doing what you refuse to do." After that Francesca refused no longer.

But the hospital landed her in difficulties. The Fathers failed to pay the salary they had promised the Sisters and even expected Francesca to discharge the debts they had incurred. She would have been willing to do even this, if they had made the property over to her and had left her hands free. While the matter was being argued, the owners of the mortgage made a foreclosure, and so Francesca decided to start her own hospital in complete independence of the Fathers.

To found it she had at her disposal the enormous sum of two hundred and fifty dollars. But to speak more accurately, she had nothing at all when she made her decision ; the two

hundred and fifty dollars was what she obtained from Archbishop Corrigan and the men to whom he sent her.   It paid the
rent for a month for two adjoining houses on East Twelfth
Street and for fifteen cheap beds.   These were for the patients
she moved from the uptown hospital ; she and the Sisters were
going to sleep on the floor for the time-being.   The mattresses
she made herself and she cut out the sheets from a bale of
material.

They moved in so suddenly that there was no gas or water
laid on.   The food had to be bought at a restaurant round the
corner and heated on a stove in the centre of the ward.   A
couple of dozen bottles of medicine constituted the whole of
their pharmacy.   A doctor had lent them a set of instruments,
and somebody had given them an ambulance.   Never could
two hundred and fifty dollars have been made to stretch so far.
Even so, Sisters had to be sent out every day begging.   As this
was the fourth centenary of the discovery of America,
Francesca named her hospital after Columbus, the first immi-
grant to America.   Under his name all the Italian factions
could unite.   From this time the anti-clerical opposition to her
began to subside ; so also did the coolness shown her by the
consular officials.   She ended her career by being, to some
extent, subsidized by a government which had to recognize the
social usefulness of her work.   The name "Columbus" —
which she gave to all the hospitals she founded — was an "open
Sesame" to her ; that she selected it was a stroke of genius.

Yet hardly had she taken possession of her hospital than she
was off to Italy.   There she had her centre ; there she had to
train her recruits ; there she needed to withdraw from time to
time for a period of spiritual renewal after intense activity.
She had by now become very intimate with Pope Leo XIII and

saw him often. On one occasion she encountered the eighty-four-year-old Pontiff as he was being carried in his sedan chair. He signalled to her to approach. "Let us work, Cabrini ; let us work, and what a heaven will be ours !" She smiled and answered that she *liked* to work and so wondered whether she would get any merit on that account. "Will work get me to heaven, Holy Father ?" she asked. "Certainly it will," he answered. "Heaven is for those who work like you." When his sedan-chair moved on he turned to her and called again, "Let us work, Cabrini ; let us work !"

In America still larger undertakings were waiting for her. The chief of these was the establishment of her Institute in the Southern continent. After what was for Francesca a long visit to the nuns who had settled in Panama after their ejection from Granada, she went by coastal steamer to Chile from where she was to enter the Argentine across the Andes. By going this way she would have a chance to visit the tomb of Saint Rose of Lima, the patroness of the Americas.

She and her companion had the adventure — which Francesca thoroughly enjoyed, though her companion did not — of crossing the Andes on mule-back. Francesca was at the head of the procession in a huge brown fur-lined cape, which made her look, she thought, like a Capuchin, while the other nun sprawled in terror like a sack of flour on the back of her mount. All the precipitous and snowy way along there were dangers, and once Francesca would have been dashed to pieces in a chasm had it not been for the quickness of her muleteer. But they got to Buenos Aires safely, only to find that the Archbishop who had invited them there was dead.

Fortunately the new Archbishop at once took the nuns under his patronage, as did President Uriburu and the mayor of the city. On Christmas day she took possession of the house she intended to use as a school and by March 1st had the school actually opened. In the interval she had obtained Sisters from Europe and the United States to staff the institution. She had been warned that she could not expect more than seven or eight students for the first two years, but she disregarded all these opinions, and her school was crowded from the outset. Everybody was won by her charm and carried away by her enthusiasm and energy. Early in August of that year, 1896, she was able to sail for Europe.

It was very necessary that she should go there. She saw clearly that, in order to conduct schools in South America, she would need to obtain Spanish-speaking nuns. She therefore planned to make foundations in Spain for this purpose, and her eyes were also fastened upon Paris and London. The time had come to give an international character to her institute.

This she would have done at once had she not been detained in Italy by a long-drawn-out lawsuit. But as soon as she was free, she was off to Paris where, as she was unable to establish an orphanage just then because of misunderstandings with the ecclesiastical authorities, she opened a fashionable boarding house for women instead. The setback proved providential. Through her new circle of aristocratic acquaintances she got to know the Infanta Eulalia and through the Infanta came an invitation to Spain from Queen Maria Cristina. The Queen wanted her to let one of her nuns act as governess for the royal children, and though Francesca would not consent to that, she did gain what she needed in the country — convents that would bring her vocations from well-educated young Spaniards. England too was marked down for conquest, and England conquered her during a brief visit she made to

London. "In other countries they speak of nobility and courtesy," she wrote ; "in England they really practice these things."

While in Italy she had seen Leo XIII again. "How can you do so much work ?" he wanted to know. "I am much older than you [he was eighty-seven], but I am much stronger. I could not work as you do." She smiled and explained that it was because she was his spiritual daughter. On parting, when he gave her his blessing, he put one hand on her head and drew her to him with the other. She said she felt as though she and all her daughters were being embraced by the Church.

The year 1899 was one in which she concentrated upon the founding of schools for Italian immigrants. Of these several — notably the one at Chicago — were connected with parishes and so had some support ; but in other cases, as in Newark and New York, she was obliged to begin by renting empty stores or factories. In one case at least, that of the school at Newark, she began operations with a capital of sixty cents.

Chicago has a special importance, because it marked her first move westwards. She continued by pressing on to Denver, with the intention of striking to the Pacific coast. Between these labours she was darting incessantly back to Europe or to South America, everywhere she went founding a new house, sometimes entering a strange city and getting a school or an orphanage there in operation within a couple of weeks, as she did in London. Her institute was now growing by leaps and bounds.

Wherever she established herself she made it her business to look after the Italian prisoners in the jails. These could not usually be reached by the regular chaplains, who as a rule did

not know Italian.   The Sisters sometimes even had to prepare
the condemned for death.   Once in Chicago they had to remain all day with five men who were to be executed together.
The youngest prisoner, hardly twenty, clung to a Sister, holding her hand in terror to the last.   Another prisoner — this
time at Sing Sing — gave the nuns his crucifix as he climbed
into the electric chair.   If these unfortunates left behind un-
provided children, Francesca saw to it that they were admitted
into one of her orphanages.   She sometimes was also instrumental in obtaining a commutation or a stay of execution.
This was obtained for one man until she could arrange to have
his mother brought over from Italy for a final parting.

At Denver she and the Sisters worked not only in the city
but in the mining camps, often going down the shafts to visit
those working in the mines.   The men there were utterly
isolated, and to them, as to so many scattered groups of Italians
all over the country, she was almost the only person who spoke
of God.   To these miners, as to the plantation workers in
Louisiana and Mississippi, she managed to get priests sent and
prepared the way for the Bishop to administer Confirmation in
the fields or on the hills under the open sky.

At Chicago she opened her second Columbus Hospital in
1903.   A chance occurred to buy the North Shore Hotel,
which was going cheap at $160,000.   When she told Arch-
bishop Quigley that she had a thousand dollars collected he
laughed and sent her out to beg again among the local Italians.
At the last moment the owners attempted to swindle her.
Suspecting this would happen, she had sent out two nuns at
five in the morning to measure the property.   This they did
with pieces of string, to the amazement of the policemen on the
beat.   But the amateur surveyors had done their work well,

and in this way was prevented the slicing off of a section of the property. What was obtained was one of the finest and most valuable locations in the city.

But Francesca's troubles were not at an end. The contractors who were brought in to remodel the building took advantage of the inexperience of the nuns left in charge and had almost gutted the whole interior when Francesca was hastily summoned back. "Mother," the archbishop told her, "if you had not come, in another day or two your nuns would have been sleeping in Lincoln Park." However, she was there, and she took command at once, repudiating all the monstrously inequitable contracts that had been made, and constituting herself her own contractor. Under her direction the work was completed, and with such efficient dispatch that what was estimated to take a full year was done in eight months.

The second Columbus Hospital proved, however, almost too well-equipped an institution. It soon become so much patronized by the well-to-do that an annex which would be entirely free and entirely for Italians — with the staff entirely Italian — was a crying necessity. Francesca provided this by buying a large house facing Vermont Park, much to the annoyance of the other property-owners of the neighbourhood, who feared the lowering of real-estate values if an Italian charitable institution came so close. To prevent this happening, they first cut the water-pipes by way of sabotage, and as that did not scare Francesca away, they tried to burn the place down. She met the challenge by moving in at once, before the renovations were finished, believing that her enemies would not resort to murder. The patients who were admitted were told nothing of what was going on, or they would have hardly ventured into such a place ; as they did not know, they came in such numbers that the little hospital was crowded within a few days. There was no further trouble from saboteurs.

Just how all these projects of hers were financed has always been something of a mystery. She was a powerful beggar and an all but irresistible one. Who could refuse this woman who approached her victims with the firm belief that she was conferring a favour upon them in allowing them to contribute towards her enterprises ? But it does not appear that many people were benefactors on a large scale. Most of the money she collected came from the Italian immigrants, and of these nearly all were sufficiently poor. We must therefore conclude that she drew frequently upon what she called her "heavenly bank" ; it is certain that the money she needed was always forthcoming.

It was not, however, always literally found in a drawer of her desk. Thus at New Orleans, where her work had long outgrown its old headquarters on St. Philip's Street, a retired sea-captain named Salvator Pizzati who had made a fortune in trade, came forward and offered to build her a new orphanage. This happened just at the right moment. While the building was going up the great epidemic of yellow fever struck the city ; by the time it was over, there was a multitude of destitute children needing Mother Cabrini's care. During the weeks the epidemic lasted in many cases the terrified and illiterate immigrants, who got it into their heads that the doctors were deliberately spreading the disease, were unmanageable except by the Sisters. For their heroic work Francesca was officially thanked by the Italian government.

The twenty-fifth anniversary of the founding of the institute found Francesca in Los Angeles, much too busy to think of attending Codogno for the jubilee celebrations. These were deferred until the following year, though the Californians, so as not to miss such an opportunity, insisted upon marking the occasion in their own expansive way. She submitted to this good-humouredly but looked forward to her return to Italy.

She had the secret intention of retiring at this time, and therefore was working very hard in first clearing up all the work in hand. She was getting old, and had always been in delicate health ; she felt that a younger and more vigorous woman was needed at the head of affairs. As for herself, she would settle quietly in Codogno and give herself to the life of complete contemplation for which she had always yearned in the midst of her activities.

This was not permitted her. As soon as the Sisters in Italy discovered what was in her mind, they wrote to all the houses of the institute all over the world and obtained a unanimous vote against her relinquishment of office. On her sixtieth birthday she was summoned before Cardinal Vives y Tuto, who presented her with the formal approval of the rules she had drawn up in their definitive form and then told her, to the delight of the Sisters with her, "Mother Cabrini, as you have carried out your duties as Superior-General so badly, we have decided to give you the chance to do better ; you must be Superior-General in perpetuity."

This was all the harder for her because scarcely more than a year before — in 1909 — she had contracted malaria while on a visit to Brazil. But she reshouldered the burden she had hoped to drop and went forward again, frailer than ever but with her old energy and courage. As most of these last years were spent in the United States she now was able to do what she had always intended to do and take her oath of allegiance to her adopted country.

This happened in Seattle.   In that city, too, she had one of her great triumphs.   It was necessary to find a new location for an orphanage and just when others had given up all hope, she had another of her dreams.   She told her nuns to go out the next day and that they would find precisely what they were looking for and where they would find it.   They protested in vain, "But Mother, we have been there already ; there is nothing suitable in that place !"   The only answer they got was, "All the same go ; then come back and tell me about it." That evening they gave an excited description of a paradise on earth.

Then Mother Cabrini went out to see it for herself.   It was a magnificent estate on a lake with a view of Mount Ranier. The only question was how they could afford such a luxury — a question which was answered when a lady, passing in her car, told her chauffeur to stop and invited the nuns to get in. She turned out to be the wife of the owner ; she became so interested in Francesca's plans that a virtual gift was made of the property.

Francesca could generally get things almost for nothing. At Dobb's Ferry the following year she passed a boys' school and went in offering to buy it.   When she was told that it was not for sale, on her way out she slipped a medal of Saint Joseph into a flower-bed.   "You will see," she told her companion, "Saint Joseph will send those boys away."   A few days later the owner wrote offering to sell on her terms.

Her health was now visibly failing.   Yet she went on working as hard as ever, travelling incessantly and consolidating the undertakings she had already begun and at the same time projecting new plans. The last of these — swinging from victory to defeat and then to final victory — concerned the purchase of the Perry Hotel in Seattle for an orphanage. She discovered that it was owned by a Mr. Clarke in New York and so wired her nuns there to go to him and ask him to give them the hotel. She did not give his address because she did not know it, and she refrained from trying to discover it lest enquiries would reveal what she intended. The Sisters had to unearth Mr. Clarke by ringing up everybody of that name listed in the telephone book. But though when found at last he of course refused to give the hotel as a present, he was prepared to sell very cheap. For $10,000 Francesca got an option, but could not gather more than another $20,000 of the $160,000 needed. She had to write the amount she wanted upon the book in the hand of a statue of Our Lady being taught to read by Saint Anne. "Now she will have to see it there," said Francesca in perfect confidence.

But the local banks refused to lend any money, hoping in this way to prevent the completion of the deal. And though at the very last moment a man was found to advance the sum needed, the Bishop stepped in with an objection. He had approved of buying the hotel for an orphanage, but he did not approve of Francesca's having changed her mind in favour of a hospital. After her long struggle she found that she had only a useless building and an enormous debt. It is true that before she died the Bishop made some concessions, so that the hotel was able to be employed for the purpose for which it was purchased ; but this came a little too late to relieve Francesca of the cares that crushed her. Defeated and worn out she went at the end of 1916 to California.

By the spring she had recovered sufficiently to insist on going

to Chicago, her plea being that she wished to consult the
doctors there, but her real motive being to attend to pressing
business.   Hardly able to stand she got on the train ; hardly
able to stand she got off it.   Yet she went to work on the very
day of her arrival, protesting that a little exercise would do her
good.   Only with the greatest reluctance would she take any
rest at all.   Her compromise was to consent to take a drive
every afternoon.

A little improvement was effected in her condition.   The
malaria was brought under control, and nobody supposed that
her death was near.   Or rather, all the Sisters were so
accustomed to her being near death and then getting better
that they could hardly imagine she would ever die.   She
might indeed have lasted some years longer had it not been for
the disaster of Caporetto which occurred in November and
seemed to grow worse all through December, until Christmas
day, when at last the Austro-German drive was checked.
But that, like the concessions of the Bishop of Seattle, came just
too late to save Francesca Cabrini.

On December 22nd she spent the whole day in doing up
five hundred small parcels of candy for the children in the
Italian school.   This was her personal gift to them.   The next
morning she was too exhausted to get up, but she received
several visits from Sisters in her room and nobody was alarmed
about her.   But a few minutes after the last of her visitors had
departed she died suddenly, and alone.

The rules that call for fifty years to elapse between death
and the introduction of a cause for beatification were waived
in her case.   Twenty-one years after her death she was
beatified.   The two people who were miraculously cured by
her intercession — the two whose cures were officially ac-

cepted at Rome — are still alive ; one of them, a baby blinded at birth but now a soldier in the army, spoke over the radio on the great night of November 13, 1938, attesting to what had happened to him.   Many of Francesca's companions are with us to this day and all speak of her as though she were in the next room.   And Cardinal Mundelein was able to say that he was the first man in the history of the Church who had officiated at the beatification ceremonies for the same person at whose funeral he had also presided.   The immediacy and the intimacy of it all makes Francesca Cabrini's case something unique in the story of our times.

BIBLIOGRAPHY

What follows is of course no more than a list of a few books that the reader might find worth his while to consult, and which he would be most likely to find accessible. In no case, except perhaps that of Coventry Patmore and Mother Cabrini, does the bibliography pretend to be more than a reading-list, and even in these cases periodical literature has been passed over completely. All that has been aimed at is the giving of some little service to those who might like to go beyond the pages of this book. But not all works referred to by me have been included here.

For the general ecclesiastical background the work that is on all scores the best is Ludwig von Pastor's *History of the Popes from the Close of the Middle Ages* (32 volumes to date in the English translation, St. Louis, 1923–41, London, 1891–1940). Horace K. Mann's *Lives of the Popes in the Middle Ages* (18 volumes, London, 1925–32) covers an earlier period in a more restricted way. Works on a smaller scale, though in a wider field, are the Mourret-Thompson *History of the Catholic Church*, of which 5 volumes have so far appeared (St. Louis, 1930–41), and *A History of the Church* by Philip Hughes, but of this only 2 volumes have as yet been published (New York, 1935–40). For those who wish something still more condensed there are Francis Xavier Funk's *Manual of Church History* in 2 volumes, translated from the 5th German edition by Luigi Cappadatta (St. Louis, 1910), and *An Outline History of the Church by Centuries* by Joseph Mc-Sorley, C.S.P. (St. Louis and London, 1944).

Though in the case of almost every one of the "Pillars" treated here a good deal of collateral reading would be desirable, all that is given is a list of some of the more important or useful works of the figure under consideration. To embark upon anything else would involve making this bibliography almost as long as the book to which it is appended.

SAINT BENEDICT

The Holy Rule of Our Most Holy Father Benedict, 8th ed. Atchison, Kansas, 1935.

Butler, Cuthbert, O.S.B. *Benedictine Monachism.* London and New York, 1919.

Chapman, John, O.S.B. *Saint Benedict and the Sixth Century.* London, 1929.

Herwegen, Ildephonsus, O.S.B. *Saint Benedict, a Character Study*, trans. by Peter Nugent, O.S.B. London and Edinburgh, 1924.

Knowles, David, O.S.B. *The Benedictines.* New York, 1930.

Cabrol, Fernand, O.S.B. *Saint Benedict*, trans. by C. M. Antony. London, 1934.

Tosti, Luigi, O.S.B. *Saint Benedict: an Historical Discourse on His Life*, trans. by William Romuald Woods, O.S.B. London, 1896.

McCann, Justin, O.S.B. *Saint Benedict.* New York, 1937.

SAINT PATRICK

Healy, John. *The Life and Writings of Saint Patrick.* Dublin, 1905.

The Tripartite Life of Saint Patrick with Other Documents Relating to that Saint, ed. by Whitley Stokes, 2 vols. London, Rolls Series, 1887.

Bury, John Bagnall. *The Life of Saint Patrick and His Place in History.* London, 1905.

MacNeill, Eoin. *Saint Patrick, Apostle of Ireland.* London, 1934.

Shahan, Thomas J. *Saint Patrick in History.* New York, 1904.

Gogarty, Oliver St. John. *I Follow Saint Patrick.* New York, 1938.

Concannon, Helena. *Saint Patrick: His Life and Mission.* London and New York, 1931.

De Blacam, Hugh. *Saint Patrick, Apostle of Ireland.* Milwaukee, 1941.

THE VENERABLE BEDE

Bede. *The Ecclesiastical History of the English Nation*, together with *The Life and Miracles of Saint Cuthbert* and *The Lives of the Holy Abbots of Weremouth and Jarrow*. London and New York, Everyman's Library.

Browne, G. F. *The Venerable Bede. His Life and Writings.* London, 1919.

Werner, Karl. *Beda der Ehrwürdige und seine Zeit.* Vienna, 1875.

Gasquet, Cardinal. "Saint Bede" in *The Mission of St. Augustine and Other Addresses*. London, 1924.

SAINT DOMINIC

Jarrett, Bede, O.P. *Life of Saint Dominic.* London, 1924.

Lacordaire, Jean-Baptiste, O.P. *Vie de Saint Dominique.* Paris, 1841.

Drane, Augusta Theodosia (Mother Francis Raphael, O.S.D.). *History of Saint Dominic.* London, 1889.

Reeves, John-Baptist, O.P. *The Dominicans.* New York, 1930.

Mandonnet, Pierre, O.P. *Saint Dominic and His Work*, trans. by Sister Mary Benedict Larkin, O.P. St. Louis and London, 1944.

O'Connor, John B., O.P. *Saint Dominic and the Order of Preachers.* Columbus, Ohio, 1916.

SAINT LOUIS

Joinville, Sieur de. *Chronicle of the Crusade of Saint Lewis*, in *Memoirs of the Crusades by Villehardouin and De Joinville*. London and New York, Everyman's Library.

Le Nain de Tillemont, L. S. *Vie de Saint Louis*, 6 vols. Paris, 1846–51.

Wallon, Henri. *Saint Louis et son temps*, 2 vols. Paris, 1875.

Sepet, Marius. *Saint Louis.* London, 1917.

Knox, Winifred A. *The Court of a Saint.* London, 1909.

Saint Thomas More

More, Thomas. *English Works;* reproduced in facsimile from William Rastell's edition of 1557, and with a modern version by W. E. Campbell; with introductions and philological notes by A. W. Reed, 7 vols. London, 1928–32.

———. *Utopia* with *A Dialogue of Comfort against Tribulation.* London and New York, Everyman's Library.

Roper, William. *The Life, Arraignment and Death of that Mirrour of all true Honour and Vertue, Syr T. More.* Paris, 1626, reprinted London, 1903.

More, Cresacre. *Life of Sir Thomas More* by His Great Grandson, ed. by Rev. Joseph Hunter. London, 1828.

Stapleton, Thomas. *The Life and Illustrious Martyrdom of Thomas More,* trans. by Philip E. Hallett. London, 1928.

Bremond, Henri. *The Blessed Thomas More,* trans. by Harold Child. London, 1920.

Hollis, Christopher. *Thomas More.* Milwaukee, 1934.

Sargent, Daniel. *Thomas More.* New York, 1933.

Bridgett, T. E., C.SS.R. *Blessed Thomas More.* London, 1891.

Chambers, R. W. *Sir Thomas More.* London, 1935.

———. *The Saga and the Myth of Sir Thomas More.* Oxford, 1927.

———. *More's Utopia and His Social Teaching.* London, 1930.

Harpsfield, Nicholas. *The Life and Death of Sir Thomas More.* Oxford, Early English Texts Society, 1932.

Hutton, W. H. *Sir Thomas More.* London, 1895.

Mackintosh, Sir James. "Sir Thomas More" in Vol. I of *Lives of Eminent British Statesmen,* 7 vols. London, 1831–9.

Saint Francis Xavier

Monumenta Xaveriana, 2 vols. Madrid, 1900–1912.

Bellesort, André. *Saint François Xavier.* Paris, 1929.

Brou, Alexandre, S.J. *Saint François Xavier,* 2 vols. Paris, 1922.

Coleridge, Henry James, S.J. *Saint Francis Xavier : Life and Letters,* 2 vols. London, 1890.

Cros, L. J. M., S.J. *Saint François Xavier, sa vie et ses lettres,* Paris, 1900.

Maynard, Theodore. *The Odyssey of Francis Xavier.* New York, 1936.

Broderick, James, S.J. *The Origin of the Jesuits.* London and New York, 1940.

SAINT TERESA OF AVILA

Teresa of Avila. *Life of Saint Teresa of Jesus of the Order of Our Lady of Mount Carmel,* written by herself, trans. from the Spanish by David Lewis; re-edited with additional notes and introduction by Benedict Zimmermann, O.D.C. New York, 1932.

————. *Book of Foundations,* trans. from the Spanish by David Lewis; new and rev. ed. with intro. by Benedict Zimmermann, O.D.C. London, 1913.

————. *The Way of Perfection,* edited by A. R. Waller. London, 1902.

————. *Minor Works,* trans. from the Spanish by the Benedictine nuns of Stanbrook. New York, 1914.

————. *Letters,* a complete ed. trans. from the Spanish and annotated by the Benedictine nuns of Stanbrook, with an introduction by Cardinal Gasquet, 4 vols. London, 1920–24.

————. *The Interior Castle, or The Mansions,* trans. from the Spanish by a Benedictine of Stanbrook; rev. with additional notes and introduction by Benedict Zimmermann, O.D.C. 4th ed., London, 1930.

Joly, Henri. *Saint Teresa,* trans. by Emily M. Waller. London, 1918.

Coleridge, Henry James, S.J. *Saint Teresa, Life and Letters,* 3 vols. London, 1887.

Zimmermann, Benedict, O.D.C. *The Life of Saint Teresa of Jesus.* London, 1916.

Sackville-West, Victoria. *The Eagle and the Dove.* New York, 1944.

Walsh, William Thomas. *Saint Teresa of Avila*. Milwaukee, 1944.

SAINT PHILIP NERI

Capecelatro, Cardinal. *Saint Philip Neri*, 2 vols. London, 1882. (The one volume ed., London, 1896.)

Bordet, Louis and Ponnelle, Louis. *Saint Philip Néri et la société romaine de son temps (1515–1595)*. Paris, 1927. English trans. by Ralph Francis Kerr under the title, *Saint Philip and the Roman Society of His Times (1515–1595)*. London, 1932.

Bacci, Pietro Jacopo. *The Life of Saint Philip Neri*, ed. by F. I. Antrobus, 2 vols. St. Louis, 1903. (Another ed. of this was published by F. W. Faber, 2 vols. London, 1847–56.)

Matthews, V. J. *Saint Philip Neri*. London, 1934.

Maynard, Theodore. *Mystic in Motley : The Life of Saint Philip Neri*. Milwaukee, 1945.

SAINT VINCENT DE PAUL

Vincent de Paul. *Saint Vincent de Paul. Correspondance, Entretiens, Documents*. Ed. by Pierre Coste, C.M., 14 vols. Paris, 1920–25.

Coste, Pierre, C.M. *The Life and Labours of Saint Vincent de Paul*, trans. by Joseph Leonard, C.M., 3 vols. London, 1934–35.

Abelly, Louis. *Vie de Saint Vincent de Paul*, 3 vols. Paris, 1891.

Collet, Pierre. *Vie de Saint Vincent de Paul*, 2 vols. Nancy, 1748.

Bougaud, Louis-Emile. *Saint Vincent de Paul*, 2 vols. London, 1898.

Maynard, Ulysse. *Saint Vincent de Paul*, 4 vols. Paris, 1860. (3rd. ed., 1886.)

Lavedan, Henri. *The Heroic Life of Saint Vincent de Paul*. London, 1929.

Broglie, Emmanuel de. *Saint Vincent de Paul*. London, 1898.

Maynard, Theodore. *Apostle of Charity*. New York, 1939.
Sanders, E. K. *Vincent de Paul, Priest and Philanthropist*. London, 1913.

COVENTRY PATMORE

Coventry Patmore. *Poems*. London, 1921.
――――. *Principle in Art, Religio Poetae, and Other Essays*. London, 1913.
――――. *The Rod, the Root, and the Flower*. London, 1923.
Champneys, Basil. *Memoirs and Correspondence of Coventry Patmore*, 2 vols. London, 1900.
Edmund Gosse. *Coventry Patmore*. New York, 1905.
Patmore, Derek. *Portrait of My Family*. New York, 1935.
Burdett, Osbert. *The Idea of Coventry Patmore*. London, 1921.
Page, Frederick. *Patmore : A Study in Poetry*. London, 1933.
Further Letters of Gerard Manley Hopkins, Including His Correspondence with Coventry Patmore, ed. by C. C. Abbott. London, 1938.

BLESSED FRANCESCA CABRINI

Cabrini, Francesca. *The Travels of Mother Frances Xavier Cabrini*. Exeter, England, 1925.
――――. *Parole Sparse della Beata Cabrini*. Rome, 1938.
Una delle sue Figlie. *La Madre Francesca Saverio Cabrini*. Turin, 1928.
La Beata Cabrini. Rome, 1938.
Rosmini, Emilia de Sanctis. *La Beata Francesca Saverio Cabrini*. Rome, 1938.
Vian, Nello. *Madre Cabrini*. Brescia, 1938.
Cigognani, Amletto Giovanni. "Mother Cabrini" in *Sanctity in America*, Paterson, N.J., 1939.
Martindale, C. C., S.J. *Mother Francesca Saverio Cabrini*. London, 1931.
Maynard, Theodore. *Too Small a World : The Life of Francesca Cabrini*. Milwaukee, 1945.

A Benedictine Nun of Stanbrook Abbey. *Frances Xavier.* London, 1944.

In Memoria della Rev. Madre Francesca Saverio Cabrini. Rome, 1938.